URBAN
TRAILS
SAN FRANCISCO

URBAN TRAILS

TRAILS

SAN FRANCISCO

Coastal Bluffs · The Presidio
Hilltop Parks & Stairways

ALEXANDRA KENIN

MOUNTAINEERS
BOOKS

To Adah Bakalinsky, whom I've never met, but who has inspired
people the world round (including me) to explore San Francisco

**MOUNTAINEERS
BOOKS**

Mountaineers Books is the publishing division of
The Mountaineers, an organization founded in 1906
and dedicated to the exploration, preservation, and
enjoyment of outdoor and wilderness areas.

1001 SW Klickitat Way, Suite 201, Seattle, WA 98134
800.553.4453, www.mountaineersbooks.org

Printed in China
Distributed in the United Kingdom by Cordee, www.cordee.co.uk
First edition: first printing 2016, second printing 2017

Copyeditor: Joeth Zucco
Design: Jen Grable
Layout: Jennifer Shontz, www.redshoedesign.com
Cartographer: Bart Wright, Lohnes + Wright

Cover photograph: *Batteries to Bluffs Trail*
Frontispiece: *The John Muir Sand Ladder on the Fort Funston Loop (Trail 4)*
All photos by author unless noted otherwise.

Library of Congress Cataloguing-in-Publication data is on file for this title
at https://lccn.loc.gov/2016011066.

ISBN (paperback): 978-1-68051-020-1
ISBN (ebook): 978-1-68051-021-8

CONTENTS

Trail Locator Map 8

Trails at a Glance 9

Acknowledgments 12

Introduction 14

    Map Legend 18

WATERFRONT WANDERS

1 Fort Funston to the Cliff House 24

2 Lands End Trail 29

3 Batteries to Bluffs 33

4 Fort Funston Loop 37

5 Lake Merced 41

6 A Stroll with Sutro 45

7 Candlestick Point State Recreation Area 50

8 India Basin to AT&T Park 54

9 AT&T Park to Pier 39 59

10 Pier 39 to the Golden Gate Bridge 63

CITY GREENWAYS

11 Stow Lake and Strawberry Hill 72

12 Land of Lakes 76

13 Interior Greenbelt and Mount Sutro 82

14 Creeks to Peaks 86
15 Mount Davidson and Edgehill Mountain 91
16 Pine Lake to the Panhandle 97
17 The Philosopher's Way 102
18 Visitacion Valley Greenway 107
19 Bayview Park 112

THE PRESIDIO

20 Park Trail 118
21 Mountain Lake Trail 122
22 Lobos Creek Valley Trail 128
23 Presidio Promenade 131
24 Goldsworthy Gallery Tour 136
25 Presidio Coastal Trail 142
26 Presidio Bay Area Ridge Trail 147
27 Presidio Anza Trail 152

ISLAND HOPPING

28 Angel Island 160
29 Wine Tasting on Treasure Island 165
30 Alcatraz Agave Trail 170

TALES OF THE CITY

31 Old Mission Road 176
32 Barbary Coast Trail 181
33 Bay to Breakers 188
34 Castro to Twin Peaks Loop 193
35 The 500 Club 198
36 Stairways to Heaven 204
37 Walk on the Wild Side 210
38 Beauty of Bernal 216

39 Peaks of Potrero 220
40 Sunset Stairway Stroll 225

SOUTH OF THE BORDER

41 San Bruno Mountain North Loop 232
42 Eucalyptus Loop Trail 236
43 Summit Loop Trail 239
44 Sign Hill 243

MOUNTAINS OF MARIN

45 Slacker Hill 250
46 Hill 88 254
47 From Pirates to Zen 258
48 Muir Woods from Mountain Home Inn 262
49 Matt Davis and Steep Ravine Loop 267
50 Mount Tam East Peak 270

Appendix: Trails by Type 275
Appendix: Land Managers 280
Index 283

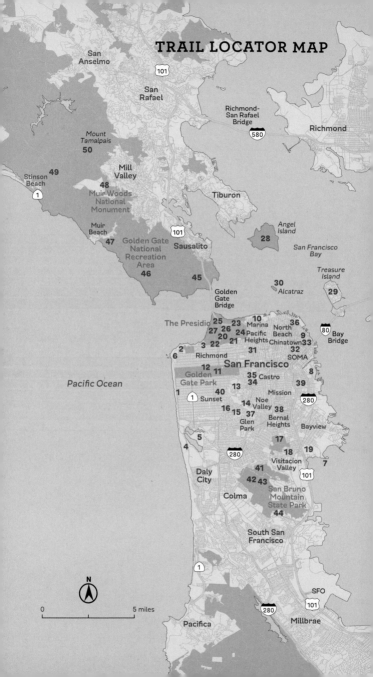

TRAILS AT A GLANCE

NOTE: Half circles indicate that part of the trail is suitable for a given use; see the trail description for details.

Trail and/or Park	Distance	Walk	Hike	Run	Kids	Dogs
WATERFRONT WANDERS						
1. Fort Funston to the Cliff House	5 miles one way	●	●		◐	●
2. Lands End Trail	3.3 miles	●	●	●	◐	●
3. Batteries to Bluffs	1.2 miles		●			
4. Fort Funston Loop	1.7 miles	●	●		●	●
5. Lake Merced	4.5 miles	●	●	●	●	●
6. A Stroll with Sutro	2 miles	●	●		●	●
7. Candlestick Point State Recreation Area	2.9 miles	●	●	●	●	●
8. India Basin to AT&T Park	5 miles one way	●	●	●	●	●
9. AT&T Park to Pier 39	2.9 miles	●	●	●	●	●
10. Pier 39 to the Golden Gate Bridge	4.6 miles	●	●	●	●	●
CITY GREENWAYS						
11. Stow Lake and Strawberry Hill	1.9 miles	●	●		●	●
12. Land of Lakes	5.6 miles	●	●	●	◐	●
13. Interior Greenbelt and Mount Sutro	2.3 miles	●	●	●	◐	●
14. Creeks to Peaks	4 miles		●		◐	●
15. Mount Davidson and Edgehill Mountain	3.4 miles		●		◐	●
16. Pine Lake to the Panhandle	5.6 miles one way		●		◐	●
17. The Philosopher's Way	2.7 miles	●	●	●	●	●

Trail and/or Park	Distance	Walk	Hike	Run	Kids	Dogs
18. Visitacion Valley Greenway	0.8 mile	•	•		•	•
19. Bayview Park	1.2 miles	•	•	•	›	•
THE PRESIDIO						
20. Park Trail	3.3 miles	•	•	•	•	•
21. Mountain Lake Trail	5.2 miles	•	•	•	›	•
22. Lobos Creek Valley Trail	1 mile	•	•		•	
23. Presidio Promenade	4.2 miles	•	•	•	•	•
24. Goldsworthy Gallery Tour	4 miles	•	•	•	›	•
25. Presidio Coastal Trail	3.1 miles	•	•	•	•	•
26. Presidio Bay Area Ridge Trail	5.2 miles	•	•	•	›	•
27. Presidio Anza Trail	5.3 miles	•	•	•	›	•
ISLAND HOPPING						
28. Angel Island	5.1 miles	•	•		›	
29. Wine Tasting on Treasure Island	3 miles	•	•	•	•	•
30. Alcatraz Agave Trail	0.4 mile	•	•		•	
TALES OF THE CITY						
31. Old Mission Road	4 miles one way	•	•	•	›	•
32. Barbary Coast Trail	4.4 miles one way	•	•		•	•
33. Bay to Breakers	7.5 miles one way	•	•	•		•
34. Castro to Twin Peaks Loop	4.8 miles		•		›	•
35. The 500 Club	3.1 miles		•		›	•
36. Stairways to Heaven	4 miles		•		›	•

Trail and/or Park	Distance	Walk	Hike	Run	Kids	Dogs
37. Walk on the Wild Side	4.1 miles		●		▸	●
38. Beauty of Bernal	2.9 miles		●		▸	●
39. Peaks of Potrero	2.3 miles	●	●		▸	●
40. Sunset Stairway Stroll	2.7 miles	●	●		▸	●
SOUTH OF THE BORDER						
41. San Bruno Mountain North Loop	2.9 miles	●	●	●	●	
42. Eucalyptus Loop Trail	1 mile	●	●	●	●	
43. Summit Loop Trail	3.3 miles		●		▸	
44. Sign Hill	1.1 miles		●		▸	●
MOUNTAINS OF MARIN						
45. Slacker Hill	3.3 miles		●		▸	
46. Hill 88	5.2 miles		●		▸	●
47. From Pirates to Zen	9.0 miles		●		▸	
48. Muir Woods from Mountain Home Inn	4.3 miles		●		▸	
49. Matt Davis and Steep Ravine Loop	6.5 miles		●		▸	
50. Mount Tam East Peak	6.1 miles		●		▸	

ACKNOWLEDGMENTS

WHEN I SET OFF TO WRITE THIS BOOK, I could not have envisioned all the support I'd need—or receive—from my community. Though my helpers were countless, there are some people I'd like to call out for going above and beyond the call of duty.

First, my family: thank you to my parents, Maxine and David, and my brother, Josh Kenin. You have been the biggest cheerleaders I have had in this life. Thank you to other dear family members, including Krystal Chang, Mary Herne, Justine Kenin, Jean and Bruce Lider, Lindsay Morris, and Carol Shurr for your steadfast support.

Thanks to Brett Lider, my partner in life and love, who enthusiastically did six hikes with me in one day (and so many more besides those) to help me meet my deadlines. Thank you for being my perma-adventure buddy and exploring everything with me—from the natural beauty of the Golden Gate National Recreation Area to the industrial landscapes of India Basin, Candlestick Point State Recreation Area, and Treasure Island!

Thank you to my friends, guides, and other supporters (in alphabetical order by last name):

Laura Bergheim, my amazing manager at Wordsmithie (and an accomplished author herself), for letting me keep my day job while I wrote, and for coaching me through the publishing process.

Alexandra Friedman for being my de facto business coach throughout this process and for cheering, "You've got this!"

Ksenya Gusak for being my morning hiking buddy on numerous 7:00 AM city hikes and for helping me solidify my Marin hiking routes, doing all those routes with me, and reviewing those write-ups. Without your guidance and input, this book would not exist.

Debbie Leight for being an enthusiastic and thorough field tester. I wish you could have tested all of my hikes!

Ken MacInnis, who tested no fewer than six routes for this book. I thank you for your time and fantastic feedback.

Debra Schwartz and Katrina Sostek for proofreading my galleys with me.

Robert and Christina Wallace, my fantastic contacts at the Presidio Trust. Robert read and gave input on every Presidio hike featured in this book.

My Urban Hiker SF guides, including Faris Ghani, Greer Goings, Dawn Paulinski, and Max Van Engers, who tirelessly tested routes for the book.

Other fantastic field testers, including Stephanie Brown, Sean Chu, Edwin d'Haens, Blake Engel and Jessica Taylor, Lillian Fleer and Zoe Polk, Shruti Gandhi and her parents, Andre Glaus, Susy Guerrero, Haresh Kumar and Jia Li (plus baby Annika), Walter Lee and Anna Peterson, Gilles Lorand, Paul Mansfield, Jackson Meredith, Mina Radhakrishnan, Tyler Sterkel, Lauren Usui, and Danielle Zhu and Robin Gandhi (plus baby Corabel).

Thanks to Oliver for taking me on my first urban hike and to Kate for joining on that adventure.

Thank you to Rebecca Buonadies, Kristen Caldwell, Katie Neligan, and Heather Walton for a lifetime of support and friendship.

Finally, thank you to the San Francisco Recreation and Park Department and San Francisco Public Works for fielding all my questions.

INTRODUCTION

IF YOU HAD ASKED ME a decade ago what my favorite out-door activity was, I would have said "brunch outside on the sidewalk." I was living in New York City at the time and didn't get much exposure to nature or the outdoors.

After I decided to move to San Francisco in 2007, my father bought me a copy of Adah Bakalinsky's *Stairway Walks in San Francisco*. I flipped through the book with excitement. I wanted to discover all the hidden wonders the city had to offer. As soon as I moved to the Bay Area, I found myself hiking in Point Reyes and the Marin Headlands and biking over the Golden Gate Bridge with new friends.

One day, my friend Oliver took me on an urban hike to the Embarcadero from Russian Hill. We walked on the Vallejo Stairs, through Ina Coolbrith Park, and down the Filbert Street Steps. From that moment, I wanted to see more. Whenever my partner, Brett, and I didn't have something specific to do on the weekend, we'd take off for the hills and parks, always discovering something new. For a while, we'd go on monthly 15-plus-mile hikes with a group of friends.

San Francisco is a world-class city with easy access to nature. In our compact, seven-by-seven-mile square, we have upward of 220 parks. There are more than forty hills to climb, and by my estimation, we have 70-plus miles of hiking trails. The variety of our natural areas is striking too. We have 10 miles of Pacific coastline, the Presidio's 24 miles of hiking trails, multiple lush eucalyptus forests, 1017-acre Golden Gate Park with its ten lakes, and the industrial bay shore of the south-eastern waterfront. Trails are paved or not, flat or steep. Some feel very urban and others make you forget you're in a city.

The book is organized into seven sections: Waterfront Wanders, City Greenways, The Presidio, Island Hopping, Tales of the City, South of the Border, and Mountains of Marin. And in each hike, you'll learn the history behind the area and the sights along the route. Researching this book has deepened my understanding of San Francisco and enhanced my appreciation of the city and the surrounding areas.

Waterfront Wanders describes hikes on or near the coastline from Fort Funston to the Golden Gate Bridge to Candlestick Point State Recreation Area. The hikes feature everything from breathtaking coastal bluffs to tourist hubs to industrial landscapes. Next City Greenways takes you through city parks, including Golden Gate Park and McLaren Park. You'll also summit San Francisco's highest hill and walk through miles of eucalyptus forest. Then the Presidio, with 24 miles of trails, is the city's single best hiking neighborhood. The trails vary widely, but one similarity connects many of these hikes—a stop at the Golden Gate Bridge. Island Hopping takes you on the nature-filled trails of Angel Island, a wine tasting adventure on Treasure Island, and a short but sweet walk on Alcatraz. Tales of the City combines city streets and trails through smaller parks. These routes may have less nature than other hikes, but they are often centrally located, include interesting architecture and views, and are filled with history.

South of the Border includes hikes just south of the city. On these trails, you'll find eucalyptus trees, dirt trails lined with coastal scrub, and incredible San Francisco views. And Mountains of Marin ventures across the Golden Gate Bridge to visit larger natural areas including the Marin Headlands, Muir Woods, and Mount Tamalpais. These hikes challenge you with more mileage and reward you with amazing views.

The hikes in this book range from 0.4 mile to 9 miles, so hikers of any level can pick and choose which ones work for them. If you see a shorter route in the book, but want to go farther, chances are there's a nearby trail you can do in tandem. For example, I did all three San Bruno Mountain hikes in one day for a total of 7.2 miles. I also did the entire Coastal Trail route (Fort Funston to the Cliff House, Lands End Trail, and Presidio Coastal Trail) in a day for a 10-mile hike.

In many cases and in many places, hiking requires a car to get to the trailhead. I love hiking in San Francisco as every trail in our city can be reached by public transportation, on foot, by bike, or with a ridesharing service. It's been incredibly freeing to know I can get out into nature without venturing far from home. While public transportation options aren't great for some of the hikes north and south of the city, I've managed to do all of them without owning a car.

There is something for everyone in this book. Enjoy, and I hope you fall for my adopted home city the way I have.

HOW TO USE THIS GUIDE

Welcome to *Urban Trails: San Francisco*. Each hike described in this book includes information—at times a bit subjective—to help you decide if the route is right for you and your hiking companions.

Distance: This is the length of the hike in miles. Unless otherwise noted, all distances listed are roundtrip. I used a GPS watch to measure all distances for these hikes.

Elevation Gain: Most routes include both ascents and descents, but this statistic gives you an overall picture of how much you'll be climbing. I used a GPS watch to measure the elevation gain for these hikes.

High Point: This is the highest elevation on a given hike.

Difficulty: Hikes in this book are rated **easy**, **moderate**, or **challenging**. The ratings are based on trail surfaces and conditions, distance, and total elevation gain.

Time: This is how long it took me to hike a given route. My estimated times are for continuous hiking and do not include breaks at overlooks or picnic areas. Though I hike a lot, I am not a particularly fast hiker; however, you may want to allocate additional time for snacks, views, and other stops.

Fitness: Each description mentions whether walkers, hikers, or runners might like the route. This admittedly is a little subjective, but I've based my rationale on the assumption that walkers would probably like all the routes rated easy plus some of the longer ones on well-maintained trails. I assumed runners wouldn't like the steep trails, and I assumed hikers would like all of the trails!

Family Friendly: I note optional stopping points such as parks and scenic overlooks along the way, and I suggest early turnaround points or alternate start points or end points for families with small children. While I offer ideas and suggestions for some hikes, parents are the best judges of whether their child is capable of completing a given route.

Dog Friendly: This information is based on the regulations for each trail and natural area. If dogs are allowed, I have listed whether they need to be on leash. If an area allows dogs off-leash, be sure to keep your dog under voice command, and be sure to clean up after your pup.

Amenities: These include restrooms, benches, picnic areas, and playgrounds.

Contact: This is the organization (or organizations) that manages the land the trail passes through. See the appendix for contact information.

GPS: GPS coordinates for the trailhead (in degrees, minutes, and seconds) are provided for each hike.

Map to: Since many people use a map app on their phone to get to the trailhead, I list the address you should enter in your preferred map app to get there. I have verified that all of these addresses work for Google Maps; however, they may not work with *all* map apps.

A detailed map also shows the trailhead, the route, points of interest, and amenities. "Getting There" provides public transportation routes when available and parking options. A route summary is included to help you decide whether you want to do the hike. "Get Moving" provides the directions to follow (along with the map) and the sites you will see on your route. And "Go Farther" includes information for extending your hike or places you may want to visit after the hike. If you can't decide where to start, see the appendix, Hikes by Type, to choose hikes by distance, types of views, elevation gain, and difficulty.

POISON OAK

San Francisco is home to a variety of flora, including eucalyptus trees, cypress trees, fennel, blackberry, and, unfortunately, poison oak. Poison oak contains urushiol, an oil that can cause a skin rash or blisters. Remembering the old adage—"leaves of three, let it be"—can help you avoid it.

LEGEND

🛡5	Interstate Highway	〰️	View/Overlook
101	US Highway	▲	Summit
4	State Highway	▪	Building/Landmark
▬▬▬	Surface Road	——	River/Stream
----------	Hiking Route	🏞️	Lake
ⅢⅢⅢⅢⅢ	Stairs	☲	Wetland/Marsh
- - - - - -	Other Trail	▬▬	Park/Open Space
S	Start	][	Bridge
P	Parking	] [	Tunnel
🚻	Restrooms	**T**	Transit Stop
🅰	Picnic Area	——▭——	Bay Area Rapid Transit (BART)
▲	Campground	——**J**——	SF MUNI Metro
❶	Information	·············	Cable Car

To distinguish poison oak from other plants with clusters of three leaves, remember that poison oak leaves have smooth edges, rather than jagged ones, and can be green or red depending on the season. In winter, when there might not be leaves to help you identify poison oak, stay away from smooth branches; if the plant you're looking at has thorns, it may be blackberry. On official trails, you are unlikely to come into direct contact with poison oak. If you think you or your pet has been exposed, wash your clothes and your pet; the oil can linger on both. Products like Tecnu can remove poison oak oil from your skin in case of exposure.

ADOLPH SUTRO

Adolph Heinrich Joseph Sutro was a prominent player in San Francisco's history. Born in Aachen, Prussia, on April 29, 1830, he arrived in New York with his mother and ten siblings in October 1850. Hoping to leverage a mining engineering background in the gold rush, he took off for San Francisco. When he finally arrived on November 21, 1851, it was after the gold rush's peak. But Sutro would have another shot at riches: in 1859 the Comstock Lode silver mines in Nevada made headlines. Sutro traveled to East Dayton and then to Virginia City, where he decided to execute his big idea—the Sutro Tunnel. The 4-mile-long tunnel would drain and ventilate the mines and make them suitable for silver extraction. The tunnel was completed in October 1878, silver was found, and Sutro returned to San Francisco an extremely wealthy man. Upon his return, he bought up one-twelfth of the city's land area. Others in Virginia City did not fare as well; shortly after Sutro sold his shares in the tunnel in 1879, the mines dried up.

Sutro planted eucalyptus trees on Yerba Buena Island and in many areas of the city, including Mount Parnassus (now Mount Sutro), Glen Canyon Park, and Mount Davidson, among others. Many of these trees are still thriving and you'll walk through them on your hikes. He was elected mayor in 1894, an office he filled for two years. He died in San Francisco on August 8, 1898, but his memory lives on in the many places throughout the city that bear his name.

WILDLIFE

San Francisco is a thriving habitat for animals. On my hikes, I have seen a variety of birds—from hummingbirds to hawks—plus gophers, squirrels, and occasionally coyotes. I have spotted coyotes in the Presidio, at Lands End, in Glen Canyon Park, in McLaren Park, and even on Twin Peaks! There is no way to know how many coyotes live in San Francisco, but it is estimated that there may be around a hundred.

Coyotes are generally nocturnal, but can be active in the early morning and at sunset. You are less likely to see a coyote in the middle of the day, but if you do see one, it does not mean it's sick. Do not feed it (or any wildlife), do not let your dog off its leash, and do not turn your back on it or run. Coyote attacks on people are very rare, so there is no need to be afraid. But if one approaches you, shout at it or throw small rocks in its direction (not at it!).

In Marin, it's rare, but you may encounter mountain lions or bobcats. If you do see either of these animals, stay calm and don't run. Hold your ground or back away slowly. If it starts to become aggressive, make yourself as large as possible: stand tall, wave your arms, grab a stick and wave it. If you are attacked, fight back.

A NOTE ABOUT SAFETY

Safety is an important concern in all outdoor activities. No guidebook can alert you to every hazard or anticipate the limitations of every reader. Therefore, the descriptions of roads, trails, routes, and natural features in this book are not representations that a particular place or excursion will be safe for your party. When you follow any of the routes described in this book, you assume responsibility for your own safety. Under normal conditions, such excursions require the usual attention to traffic, road and trail conditions, weather, terrain, the capabilities of your party, and other factors. Keeping informed on current conditions and exercising common sense are the keys to a safe, enjoyable outing.

—*Mountaineers Books*

In Marin, seeing a rattlesnake is also rare but still possible. You will probably hear the telltale rattle before you see the snake. If you encounter a rattlesnake, keep your distance, and if you can't go around it, turn around and walk the other way. Stay on marked trails and avoid brush where they may be hiding during the day. If you are bitten, stay calm and seek medical attention as quickly as possible.

Do a full-body tick check after each hike. If you find a tick on yourself, remove it with tweezers (be sure you get the head) and put it in a jar or plastic bag that you can keep in the freezer for later identification if necessary. Wash the area with warm water and soap. While mosquito- and tick-borne illnesses are rare in the Bay Area, monitor bites for any suspicious changes in appearance.

TEN ESSENTIALS: A SYSTEMS APPROACH

No matter the length of your urban hike, it's always good to have the Ten Essentials, developed by The Mountaineers, along in case of an emergency.

- **Navigation** (map and compass)
- **Sun protection** (sunglasses and sunscreen)
- **Insulation** (extra clothing)
- **Illumination** (headlamp or flashlight)
- **First-aid supplies**
- **Fire** (firestarter and matches/lighter)
- **Repair kit and tools** (including a knife)
- **Nutrition** (extra food)
- **Hydration** (extra water)
- **Emergency shelter**

With so many trails to choose from, you're bound to discover even more reasons to love the San Francisco Bay Area, whether you are visiting or live here. See you out on the trail.

Next page: A sandy stairway leads down to the beach at Fort Funston

WATERFRONT WANDERS

San Francisco is surrounded by water on three sides. You can only go so far without reaching the ocean or the bay. In this section, you'll hike the 20 miles of coastline from Fort Funston in the west to the Golden Gate Bridge in the north to Candlestick Point State Recreation Area in the east. Along the way, you'll hike part of the California Coastal Trail, or CCT, which will one day connect 1200 miles of oceanside trails from the Oregon border down to the Mexico border. You'll also spend time on the Bay Trail, which will span more than 500 miles of bayside trails when complete. The trails in this section range from dune landscapes to coastal bluffs to paved lakeside trails.

01 Fort Funston to the Cliff House

DISTANCE:	5 miles one way
ELEVATION GAIN:	80 feet
HIGH POINT:	175 feet
DIFFICULTY:	Easy
TIME:	1 hour 45 minutes
FITNESS:	Walkers, hikers
FAMILY FRIENDLY:	Flat hike with many places to cut out early. Families may want to take a taxi or ridesharing service back to the start.
DOG FRIENDLY:	On leash; off-leash walking permitted at Fort Funston only
AMENITIES:	Porta potties and restrooms along the way; benches along the seawalls
CONTACT:	Golden Gate National Recreation Area; California Coastal Trail
GPS:	37° 42' 52.5024'' N 122° 30' 9.3636'' W
MAP TO:	206 Fort Funston Rd., San Francisco

GETTING THERE

Public Transit: MUNI bus 57 to John Muir Dr. and Skyline Blvd.
Parking: Free parking is available in the lot at Fort Funston off State Route 35 (Skyline Blvd.).

For me, Fort Funston means two things: dogs and dunes. This sandy spot, situated in San Francisco's southwest corner, is well loved by canines and their humans alike. If you're not a fan of our four-legged friends, you may want to skip this hike. It is a veritable puppy paradise—full of sights, smells, and space unparalleled elsewhere in the city. What's more, the absence of leash laws here means that your dog can roam free and unfettered along the trails.

Other remarkable features of this area include strong, steady winds and 200-foot sandstone cliffs that overlook the Pacific. Both factors combine to create an air current called

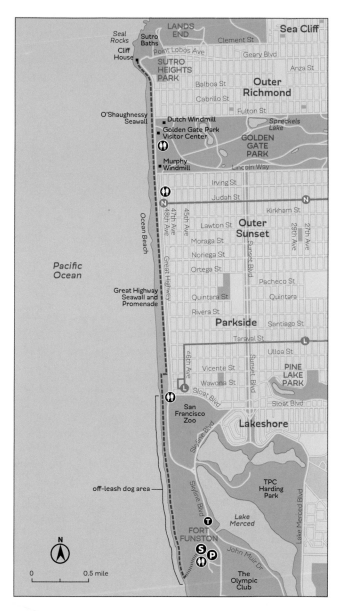

A camera obscura sits behind the Cliff House.

the Funston Shear, which makes the area a choice spot for hang gliders.

Next up, you reach Ocean Beach, a flat 3.5-mile-long beach popular with surfers and sunbathers. Pay attention to the tide tables, as a few segments leading to Ocean Beach are impassable at high tide. You should be in good shape if you're hiking during low tide all the way up to the halfway point of low and high tide. If you forget to reference the tide tables, you won't be completely stuck. The impassable parts are obvious from far away.

You may want to wear water shoes or sandals. If you get tired of walking on sand, take the paved multiuse trail that runs between the two sides of Great Highway between Sloat Boulevard and Lincoln Way and then east of Great Highway between Lincoln Way and Fulton Street. The hike ends at the Cliff House, a restaurant and San Francisco institution since the mid-1800s.

GET MOVING
From the Fort Funston parking lot, locate the Funston Beach Trail to the left of the observation deck with the wind sock. Take the sand-covered stairway down to the beach below.

Once you reach the beach, turn right to head north. At 0.4 mile, pass graffiti-covered battery ruins adorned with a dog goddess (you'll know what I mean when you see it), and at 1 mile, you come across a half-buried circular gun mount that has fallen from the cliffs above. Continue for another mile to reach Ocean Beach at the intersection of Great Highway and Sloat Boulevard. Here, you find a parking lot and restrooms to your right. (At this point, dogs will need to be leashed.)

FORT FUNSTON'S MILITARY PAST

In 1900 the US government acquired this land to establish the Lake Merced Military Reservation. It was renamed in 1917 for Maj. Gen. Frederick Funston. During the 1906 earthquake, Funston took over local law enforcement, dynamited buildings to create firebreaks, and led relief efforts. He was seen as a national hero and the media called him "the man who saved San Francisco."

After World War II, the area where the parking lot you started in stands today was a Nike missile launch site. The fort was decommissioned in 1963 and later turned over to the National Park Service to become part of the Golden Gate National Recreation Area.

After the intersection with Sloat, continue on the beach to reach a graffiti-covered sewage and storm water structure, marking Great Highway's intersection with Vicente Street. From here, I suggest changing scenery. Turn right to walk toward Great Highway, but just before you get there, turn left on a sandy pathway parallel to the road. After 0.4 mile, at Great Highway's intersection with Santiago Street, bear left on a paved path (which may be partially covered in sand drifts) to reach the Great Highway Seawall and Promenade, a concrete walkway that you'll stay on for the next 0.6 mile. This promenade was created between 1987 and 1993 to prevent damage to the sewage and storm water system that runs

THE ICON ON THE CLIFF

Sen. John Buckley and C. C. Butler built the first Cliff House in 1863 as a resort for the wealthy. Butler leased the building to Capt. Junius Foster, and under Foster's management, three presidents as well as the Hearst, Stanford, and Crocker families dined here.

Mining and real estate millionaire Adolph Sutro bought the Cliff House in 1883 and turned it into a popular San Francisco attraction, but a chimney fire burned it down on Christmas Day 1894. Sutro spent $75,000 to rebuild the Cliff House, which reopened in February 1896. This second Cliff House was eight stories high and featured four spires and an observation tower. Thanks to a railroad line that Adolph's cousin Gustav Sutro helped develop, everyday San Franciscans could now reach western San Francisco and dine here. The building endured the 1906 earthquake only to burn down on September 7, 1907. The Cliff House was once again rebuilt—this time with $75,000 from Adolph Sutro's estate (Sutro died in 1898)—and reopened on July 1, 1909.

The Cliff House was shut down during most of Prohibition, and brothers George and Leo Whitney, owners of nearby Playland amusement park, bought it in 1937. They reopened it a year later. The National Park Service (NPS) acquired the Cliff House and surrounding properties in 1977, and Dan and Mary Hountalas have been running the restaurants in the building since 1973. Between 2002 and 2004, the Hountalas family worked with the NPS to carry out renovations to restore the building to its 1909 neoclassical style.

below Great Highway. At the end of the promenade at 3.1 miles (at the intersection with Noriega Street), parallel Great Highway again and pick up another sandy path for 0.7 mile. Parts of it are packed down and easy to walk on, and other parts will have you climbing over dunes. (You can always walk on Great Highway's median if you get tired of walking on sand!)

At Lincoln Way, a windmill marks the entrance to Golden Gate Park. And just north of here along Great Highway, you'll encounter the O'Shaughnessy Seawall. Built between 1916 and 1929, the seawall is named for Michael Maurice O'Shaughnessy, an Irish immigrant and city engineer who worked on San Francisco's largest infrastructure projects, such as the Hetch Hetchy Reservoir, San Francisco Municipal Transportation Agency (MUNI), the Twin Peaks Reservoir, and the Stockton Street Tunnel, among others. The seawall takes you the remaining 1.1 miles to the Cliff House.

Retrace your steps for a 10-mile roundtrip. If you want to return by public transit, the closest MUNI stop is at 48th and Point Lobos avenues.

GO FARTHER
Explore the Cliff House, its gift shop, and the camera obscura behind the restaurant, or, keep hiking! From here, it's easy to visit the Sutro Baths (see Hike 6, A Stroll with Sutro) or take the Lands End Trail (see Hike 2).

02 Lands End Trail

DISTANCE:	3.3 miles (includes labyrinth)
ELEVATION GAIN:	480 feet
HIGH POINT:	200 feet
DIFFICULTY:	Moderate
TIME:	1 hour 20 minutes
FITNESS:	Walkers, hikers, runners
FAMILY FRIENDLY:	Stairs to the labyrinth and at the end of the trail may be challenging for young children.
DOG FRIENDLY:	On leash
AMENITIES:	Restrooms at Lands End Visitor Center; benches along the trail
CONTACT:	Golden Gate National Recreation Area; California Coastal Trail
GPS:	37° 46' 50.3688" N 122° 30' 42.2316" W
MAP TO:	Merrie Way, San Francisco

GETTING THERE
Public Transit: MUNI bus 38 to 48th Ave. and Point Lobos Ave. (Check with your driver regarding your bus's terminus; some 38 buses end at the VA Hospital.) **Parking:** Free parking is

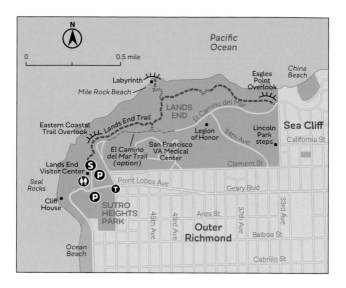

available at the Lands End Visitor Center at 680 Point Lobos Ave. Find additional parking across Point Lobos Ave. slightly southwest of the main parking lot entrance.

During the gold rush era, Lands End was a getaway for San Franciscans intrepid enough to endure a buggy ride over miles of sand dunes. Then, in the 1880s, mining magnate Adolph Sutro and others invested in a railway line—built by his cousin Gustav—that extended out to the ocean. In 1887 the Sutros sold the line to the Powell Street Railroad, and in 1888 the Ferries and Cliff House Railway opened. The railroad's east-west route used a cable car and a steam train to transport people to Lands End. The one-way, five-cent fare included the transfer between the lines. The Lands End portion of the route ran along the cliffs, at points dropping away almost vertically to the ocean below. Over the years, electric streetcars replaced the steam train; all services to Lands End stopped in 1949 when the depot at the end of the line burned down.

Although the tracks are gone, you can still trace the original steam train route with a hike along the Lands End Trail.

This is perhaps the city's premier hike with long, uninterrupted views of San Francisco Bay, the Golden Gate Bridge, and the Marin Headlands. A notable detour to Mile Rock Beach takes you to an elaborate stone labyrinth designed by local artist Eduardo Aguilera. This trail reminds residents why they live in San Francisco and may inspire visitors to turn their day trip or vacation into a permanent move.

GET MOVING

The Lands End trailhead is in the parking lot next to the Lands End Visitor Center. Look for a large, semicircular concrete plaza with a few steps leading up to a dirt trail. After 0.2 mile on the trail, you arrive at the Eastern Coastal Trail Overlook for your first views of the Golden Gate Bridge. From here, you can spot Mile Rock and its lighthouse. Mile Rock is part of a rock formation that has caused at least a dozen shipwrecks since the 1850s, including the 1901 sinking of the *City of Rio de Janeiro*, which killed 128 people.

Look for a junction with a large signpost on your right at 0.6 mile. Stay on the trail here and continue another 175 feet to a stairway on your left heading down to Mile Rock Beach. (An emergency call box is just behind the stairway.)

THE LABYRINTH

The Lands End labyrinth is worth the 0.3-mile roundtrip detour, but there are a lot of stairs to climb, which may make some decide this detour is not for them. To visit the labyrinth, take the stairs almost all the way down to Mile Rock Beach and then take a well-worn path to your right (ignore the first path on your right at a landing). Walk along the edge of a steep slope to a small piece of land that juts into the ocean. Here you find the stone labyrinth. Retrace your steps to return to the Lands End Trail where you turn left.

Hikers make their way around the Lands End labyrinth.

After the labyrinth detour, continue 0.2 mile, where a dirt and wooden stairway presents your last significant elevation gain. Descend another set of stairs lined with eucalyptus trees, and continue straight for another 0.3 mile on the mostly flat path. The trail ends at 1.8 miles just after the Eagles Point Overlook. Before returning to the start, you may want to take a quick two-block detour to the Lincoln Park mosaic steps, located at the western end of California Street (closest intersection is 32nd Avenue). Return to the start the way you came.

Option: To change up your roundtrip route with no change in overall distance, return to the Lands End Visitor Center on El Camino del Mar Trail. From the Eagles Point Overlook, follow the Lands End Trail back the way you came. At 0.7 mile, you'll pass the stairway for the labyrinth on your right. Continue 0.1 mile farther to reach a stairway on your left with a sign for the El Camino del Mar Trail. Climb the stairs and turn right on the El Camino del Mar Trail. In 0.3 mile, reach the parking lot above the Eastern Coastal Trail Overlook. From here, visit the USS *San Francisco* Memorial or take a paved trail for West Fort Miley to visit a picnic area and Battery Chester. Or, descend the stairway from the parking lot and turn left to return to the Lands End Trail and your start.

GO FARTHER
You can easily combine this hike with a visit to the Cliff House (Hike 1) and Sutro Baths (Hike 6), or a hike on the Presidio Coastal Trail (Hike 25) or the Batteries to Bluffs Trail (Hike 3).

03 Batteries to Bluffs

DISTANCE:	1.2 miles
ELEVATION GAIN:	450 feet
HIGH POINT:	245 feet
DIFFICULTY:	Challenging
TIME:	1 hour
FITNESS:	Hikers
FAMILY FRIENDLY:	Elevation gain may be too much for younger children
DOG FRIENDLY:	No
AMENITIES:	Bench along trail
CONTACT:	Golden Gate National Recreation Area; Presidio Trust
GPS:	37° 47' 48.4296'' N 122° 28' 45.8220'' W
MAP TO:	Sand Ladder, San Francisco

GETTING THERE
Public Transit: For the south trailhead, take MUNI bus 29 to its terminus at Bowley St. and Lincoln Blvd. (not to be confused with the Lincoln Blvd. and Bowley St. stop two stops away). For the north trailhead, take MUNI bus 28 to Golden Gate Bridge Tunnel/Merchant Rd. **Parking:** Limited parking on the west side of Lincoln Blvd. near the north trailhead and a few parking spots above the south trailhead below Immigrant Point.

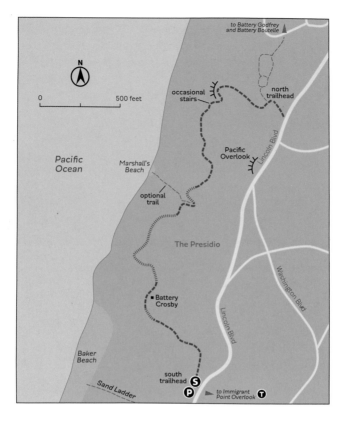

While this gorgeous bayside trail is short, it manages to pack a major punch due to the 470 or so steps along its way. But don't worry too much about the stairs—there is plenty to distract you. When you're not enjoying breathtaking views of the San Francisco Bay, the Golden Gate Bridge, or the Marin Headlands, you can learn about the historic gun batteries you'll encounter on the cliffs.

The trail was completed in October 2007, and construction wasn't easy. At times, materials were delivered by helicopter to protect the sensitive habitat. In 2008 San Francisco

Beautiful, a nonprofit organization with a mission "to create and protect the unique beauty and livability of San Francisco," awarded the trail a beautification award. When you do this hike, you'll understand why.

GET MOVING

You can start from either the north or south trailhead; both are accessible from Lincoln Boulevard. This description starts at the south trailhead, which is just north of the Baker Beach Sand Ladder. Make sure your trail is marked "Batteries to Bluffs" as there is a trail for the Sand Ladder and Baker Beach just south of this trailhead.

From the trailhead, take the wide, sandy downhill path for 0.1 mile until you reach your first flight of stairs and Battery Crosby. This is just one of many batteries lining the Pacific coast of San Francisco.

Flowers line a stairway on the Batteries to Bluffs Trail.

COASTAL GUN BATTERIES

As a direct result of the gold rush, San Francisco's population swelled from 50 in 1844 to more than 20,000 in 1850. With this massive influx of people (there's gold in them thar hills) and San Francisco on the figurative map, a joint army-navy board called for a plan to defend the San Francisco Bay and Pacific Coast. The first forts were constructed in the 1860s and '70s on either side of the Golden Gate (the strait, not the bridge)—at Fort Point in San Francisco and at Fort Lime in Marin.

In 1885 President Grover Cleveland established the Endicott Board (named for Secretary of War William Endicott) to modernize forts at twenty-two seaports across the United States. Construction of San Francisco's first Endicott-era battery, Battery Marcus Miller, was started in 1891. The battery was armed in 1897, and the 10-inch guns had a range of 7 miles. The guns were removed in 1920.

Battery Godfrey was built in 1895. Its guns met or exceeded the range of battleship guns at the time, which was up to 10 miles. The battery was declared obsolete in 1943.

Battery Crosby and Battery Boutelle were both completed around 1900. While the guns of Battery Boutelle were removed in 1917 for use in World War I, Battery Crosby remained in operation until 1943.

Climb the stairs to reach the top of the battery, where you have a great panoramic view of Lands End to the south and the Golden Gate Bridge to the north. Walk to the far side of the battery and descend more than 150 stairs. The stairs are flanked with thick vegetation. From here, look along the trail for a greenish-colored rock, serpentine, which is California's state rock.

After the stairs end, you'll see a sign pointing you in the direction of the Marshall's Beach turnoff 320 feet down the trail, an option that adds 0.1 mile to your hike. This gives you gorgeous view of the Golden Gate Bridge and Marshall's ...h, which is covered with large black stones. If you take ...our, return to the trail and turn left to start your climb ...n Boulevard. The ascent starts with fifty stairs and then alternates between dirt trail and stairs. After 0.1 mile, you'll reach a lookout on your left with a bench and fantastic view of the bridge and bay. And after another 0.1 mile, you'll climb the last stair on the trail at the north trailhead, just west of Fort Scott. Turn around here to return to your start.

GO FARTHER
For an extra half mile, continue to the Golden Gate Bridge and visit Battery Godfrey, Boutelle, Marcus Miller, and Cranston (see Hike 25, Presidio Coastal Trail).

04	**Fort Funston Loop**

DISTANCE:	1.7 miles
ELEVATION GAIN:	110 feet
HIGH POINT:	200 feet
DIFFICULTY:	Easy
TIME:	50 minutes
FITNESS:	Walkers, hikers
FAMILY FRIENDLY:	Yes
DOG FRIENDLY:	Off-leash walking permitted
AMENITIES:	Porta potties in Fort Funston lot; benches in park
CONTACT:	Golden Gate National Recreation Area; California Coastal Trail
GPS:	37° 42' 52.5024" N 122° 30' 9.3636" W
MAP TO:	206 Fort Funston Rd., San Francisco

GETTING THERE
Public Transit: MUNI bus 57 to John Muir Dr. and Skyline Blvd.
Parking: Free parking available in the lot at Fort Funston off State Route 35 (Skyline Blvd.).

Fort Funston is often foggy and breezy, but no matter what the weather, you can enjoy the clean ocean air and the sandy landscape alternately covered in ice plants, eucalyptus, and Monterey cypress. If you happen upon this cliff-side

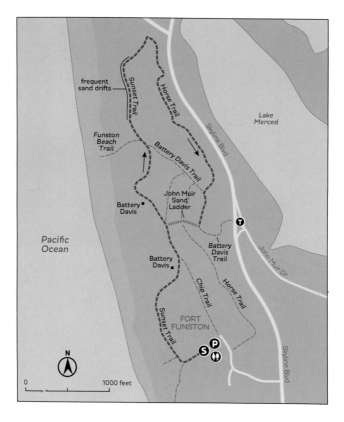

destination on a sunny day, you'll also be treated to views of Sutro Tower, the Cliff House, the Golden Gate Bridge, and the Pacific Ocean. The challenge on this route is not the distance (short), the cumulative elevation gain (minimal), or the sand ladder (you can do it!); it's literally just finding and keeping track of the Sunset Trail. Fort Funston is an ever-changing labyrinth of dunes, so the hike looks different every day. While some days the Sunset Trail is clearly visible, on other days, you'll be hunting it down. On those days, use your map to stay on track and your sense of adventure to enjoy the journey.

You may want to skip this hike if you don't like dogs. There can be literally hundreds of pups at Fort Funston at any time. Also, as a lot of this hike is on sand, you may want to wear sandals.

GET MOVING

Start your hike on the Sunset Trail, a flat paved path that departs from the back of the Fort Funston parking lot. On either side of the trail, the sandy landscape is covered with an abundance of ice plants. The trail parallels the ocean and then curves to the right. At 0.2 mile, reach Battery Davis, built in 1938 and named for Richmond Pearson Davis, a major general in the army who fought in World War I. Neither of its two sixteen-inch guns was ever used in combat, and both were removed in 1948.

About 0.1 mile later, your path forks. Stay left at the fork to continue on the Sunset Trail, and you soon come across a second part of Battery Davis. The trail then heads downhill for 0.1 mile. If it's sunny, look for the Cliff House in the distance. As the trail flattens, the Battery Davis Trail (unsigned) meets up with your trail from the right. Shortly after that, pass a turnoff for the Funston Beach Trail on your left, but stay right.

The next 0.2 mile of the trail can be partially or completely obscured by sand. If this is the case for you, look for traces of the fence that parallel the trail. The fence is made of wooden posts strung together with coated wire, and sometimes just one or two inches of the posts surface from the sand. When in doubt, continue straight and not toward the cliffs on your left. The Sunset Trail heads slightly inland as the paved path reemerges (if it hasn't already) and the dunes are sudden' covered with coastal scrub. At 0.8 mile, the Sunset Trail de ends, and you take a sharp right behind a fence to pick v Horse Trail. A trail marker on the fence confirms you'r right place.

Hundreds of dogs visit Fort Funston's dunes every day.

To complete your loop, follow the Horse Trail for 0.1 mile as it passes above Skyline Boulevard. You will hear the buzz of cars below and see Lake Merced on your left. Continue 0.2 mile more through groves of eucalyptus and cypress trees and then find yourself on an exposed trail. After another 0.1 mile, you'll reach a fork in your path with major trails on your left and right and a minor trail in the middle. Stay left here. After about 175 feet, you'll find yourself at a T with a paved path. Stay left to pick up the Battery Davis Trail (unsigned) and follow it for another 0.1 mile until you find yourself at the bottom of the John Muir Sand Ladder, a sand and wooden stairway. Take the stairway all the way to the top, ignoring the break between the two flights of stairs (which is an intersection with the Horse Trail). At the top of the stairs, walk to the paved path and turn left to meet up with the Sunset Trail. Stay ɔ this trail past Battery Davis and back to the parking lot.

ＡRTHER

ɔ easily combine this short hike with the Lake Merced ᵉ 5) or Fort Funston to the Cliff House hike (Hike 1).

05 Lake Merced

DISTANCE:	4.5 miles
ELEVATION GAIN:	70 feet
HIGH POINT:	100 feet
DIFFICULTY:	Easy
TIME:	1 hour 40 minutes
FITNESS:	Walkers, hikers, runners
FAMILY FRIENDLY:	Yes, as long as children can walk 4–5 miles
DOG FRIENDLY:	On leash
AMENITIES:	Porta potties at start point; porta potties and picnic area across from The Olympic Club; benches along the trail; picnic area in Broderick-Terry Park
CONTACT:	San Francisco Recreation and Park Department
GPS:	37° 43' 41.7288'' N 122° 29' 37.0356'' W
MAP TO:	Sunset Blvd. and Lake Merced Blvd., San Francisco

GETTING THERE

Public Transit: MUNI bus 29 to Sunset and Lake Merced boulevards. **Parking:** Free parking available in numerous lots around the lake. The lot closest to the start of the hike is at the intersection of Sunset and Lake Merced boulevards.

Located in the Lakeshore neighborhood in southwestern San Francisco, Lake Merced is part of 614-acre Lake Merced Park, a favorite spot for walkers, runners, boaters, and anglers. The lake is the largest in San Francisco, and is one of just a few remaining natural lakes in the city. Four lakes actually form Lake Merced: North, East, South, and Impound.

This is not the most peaceful hike in the city. Busy roads flank much of the route, so expect to hear cars whizzing by. Bikes are also common on the path, so keep your eyes and ears open. At times, tall trees, thick bushes, long fences, and a golf course obscure the lake from sight. But at other times, you'll get clear views of the water and of the birds and people enjoying it. There are many aspects of this hike to like. Fire you get a sense of accomplishment for encircling an entire lake. Second, the route is flat—a rarity in San Francisco. A third positive is the lake's distance: the 4.5-mile loop will get you close to your recommended 10,000 steps a day.

GET MOVING

Start your walk at the Juan Bautista de Anza statue in the parking lot at the intersection of Lake Merced and Sunset boulevards. (Read more about Juan Bautista de Anza and his expedition in Hike 27, Presidio Anza Trail.) Take the paved

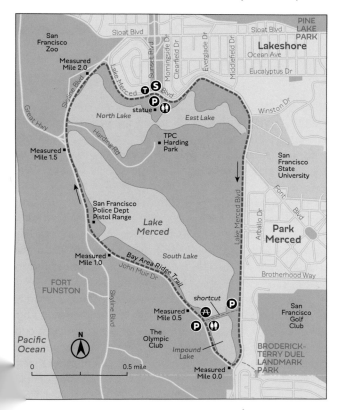

A peaceful view of Lake Merced

path (which, for most of the route, will also have a dirt path alongside it) east to walk clockwise around the lake. At 0.6 mile, you'll pass Winston Drive, where San Francisco State University is on your left and TPC Harding Park golf club is on your right. For the length of the golf course, you'll see more green than blue, but views of South Lake appear as soon as you reach the end of the course. Continue on the trail past Brotherhood Way at 1.6 miles and then to a parking lot.

MID-HIKE DETOUR: BRODERICK-TERRY DUEL LANDMARK PARK

Lake Merced was the backdrop for a famous 1859 duel between David C. Broderick and David S. Terry (see Lake Merced History, next page). To visit the duel site (a side trip that adds 0.6 mile roundtrip), cross to the far side of Lake Merced Boulevard at the southern tip of Impound Lake and head left on a dirt path. Take your first right after 0.1 mile onto a driveway for Lake Merced Hill. Walk through a parking lot to reach the entrance of Broderick-Terry Duel Landmark Park. You are now in Daly City! When you make a left to enter the park, pass some picnic benches and a stone pillar labeled "Duel Site Broderick & Terry." Continue down the path to reach two additional stone pillars that mark where Broderick and Terry stood for their duel.

Shortcut: From the parking lot after Brotherhood Way, if you want to decrease your total distance by 0.3 mile, take a trail on your right to reach a bridge that takes you to another parking lot across the lake.

When you reach the southern tip of the lake at 2 miles, look for a mile marker that says "0.0 mi." This is part of the Bay Area Ridge Trail and the start of the Lake Merced Measured Mile, which marks half-mile increments for 2 miles along the west side of the lake. Continuing around the lake, another golf club, The Olympic Club, is on your left. You are now walking along John Muir Drive. After 0.3 mile, you arrive at the parking lot where the shortcut let out. There is a small picnic and seating area here if you need a rest or a snack.

For the next 0.8-mile stretch, the lake views go in and out as you pass trees, bushes, fences, businesses, and a San Francisco

LAKE MERCED HISTORY

For thousands of years, Lake Merced periodically connected to the Pacific Ocean, but in the 1880s, a permanent sandbar formed. In 1775 the Anza expedition (read more about Juan Bautista de Anza and his expedition in Hike 27, Presidio Anza Trail) named the lake La Laguna de Nuestra Señora de la Merced, or "The Lake of Our Lady of Mercy." The name Lake Merced has been used since the 1850s.

In September 1859, a duel took place near here between US senator David C. Broderick and chief justice of the Supreme Court of California David S. Terry. Terry wanted to bring slavery to California, but Broderick was a staunch abolitionist. Terry blamed Broderick for his failed reelection campaign. A fight escalated and Terry challenged Broderick to a duel.

The first duel attempt had too many spectators and was shut down by the police. On the second attempt, Broderick's first shot discharged early, leaving him open to Terry's attack. Terry hit Broderick in the chest, and he died a few days later. Thousands attended Broderick's funeral and the city of San Francisco named a street in his honor. Today you can visit the duel site at Terry-Broderick Landmark Park.

Police Department Pistol Range with its own tall, green fence. In another 0.6 mile, you pass Harding Road, the main entrance for TPC Harding Park golf club. Continue for another 0.4 mile until your path heads east to reach Lake Merced Boulevard and the parking lot where you started your hike.

GO FARTHER
From here it's a short jaunt to Fort Funston, where you can hike to the Cliff House (Hike 1) or the Fort Funston Loop (Hike 4).

06   A Stroll with Sutro

DISTANCE:	2 miles
ELEVATION GAIN:	290 feet
HIGH POINT:	195 feet
DIFFICULTY:	Moderate
TIME:	50 minutes
FITNESS:	Walkers, hikers
FAMILY FRIENDLY:	Yes, aside from a steep hill and stairway at the Sutro Baths, and a climb at the end of the hike
DOG FRIENDLY:	On leash
AMENITIES:	Restrooms at Lands End Visitor Center; benches in Sutro Heights Park and Sutro Dunes
CONTACT:	Golden Gate National Recreation Area; San Francisco Recreation and Park Department
GPS:	37° 46' 50.3688" N 122° 30' 42.2316" W
MAP TO:	Merrie Way, San Francisco

GETTING THERE
Public Transit: MUNI bus 38 to 48th Ave. and Point Lobos Ave. (Check with your driver regarding your bus's terminus; some 38 buses end at the VA Hospital.) **Parking:** Free parking is available at the Lands End Visitor Center at 680 Point Lobos Ave. Find additional parking across Point Lobos Ave. slightly southwest of the main parking lot entrance.

The stone parapet in Sutro Heights Park offers great ocean views.

This route is a tribute to Adolph Sutro and visits three attractions named after him: the Sutro Baths, Sutro Heights Park, and Sutro Dunes—plus a fourth attraction formerly *owned* by him, the Cliff House. The ruins of Sutro Baths are all that remain of the grand bathhouse that opened in 1896 and once welcomed up to 25,000 people a day. Sutro Heights Park is the site where Adolph Sutro's estate stood from 1881 to 1939. And Sutro Dunes is a sandy park that re-creates western San Francisco's natural dune habitat.

On the way back to your start, you'll pass by the Cliff House, where you can stop for a snack or cliff-side beverage (read more about the Cliff House in Hike 1, Fort Funston to the Cliff House). Throughout much of the hike, you will enjoy close-up views of the ocean and Ocean Beach. And, hopefully, you'll return to your start more knowledgeable about the San Francisco of the past.

GET MOVING

The Lands End trailhead is located in the parking lot of the Lands End Visitor Center. Look for a large, semicircular concrete plaza with a few steps leading up to the dirt trail, and walk just under 0.1 mile before you take a left and head down a stairway toward the Sutro Baths. You'll reach a rocky and sandy landing with an aerial view of the baths. Continue down to a concrete landing at Point Lobos, where you can take in more views of the baths and ocean below. Head left and follow the path to get closer to the ruins. At a trail junction after 0.1

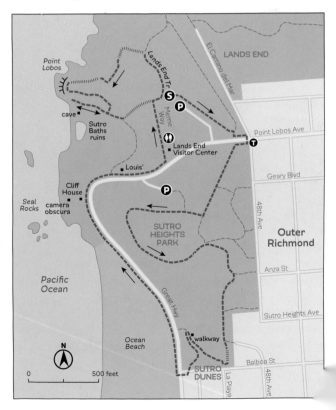

mile, take a right and head downhill to get even closer to the ruins. If you follow the path to its end, you can visit a cave on your right. Check out the ruins up close if you like and then walk the steep uphill path toward the long stairway on your left. Climb the stairway to return to the Lands End parking lot at 0.5 mile.

A RESORT IN RUINS

Adolph Sutro opened the Sutro Baths on March 14, 1896 as an affordable getaway for the masses. The baths' seven pools (one freshwater and six saltwater) could accommodate 10,000 bathers at once, and up to 25,000 per day. The baths had more than 500 dressing rooms, 40,000 towels for rent, and 20,000 bathing suits for rent. Sutro wanted the baths to be educational, so there was a museum filled with souvenirs from his travels, including Egyptian mummies, Aztec pottery, and Chinese and Japanese swords.

A number of factors contributed to the baths' eventual decline: the Great Depression, the reduction of public transit services after the Sutro railroad depot burned down in 1949, and the introduction of modern health codes. In 1964 real estate developers bought the Sutro Baths and began their demolition. A fire destroyed the baths completely in 1966, and plans to develop the area with apartments were scrapped.

To continue to Sutro Heights Park, pass by the Lands End trailhead and walk slightly uphill along the north and east edge of the parking lot. When your path meets up with a sidewalk and road on your right, make a left to continue to the intersection of Point Lobos Avenue and El Camino del Mar (48th Avenue). Cross Point Lobos Avenue, turn right, and take a quick left to enter Sutro Heights Park on a pathway flanked by two lion statues.

A GRAND ESTATE NO MORE

In 1881 Adolph Sutro bought this land, which was the estate of Samuel Tetlow, owner of the Bella Union Music Hall. Sutro built an addition onto Tetlow's cottage that included a conservatory and an observatory. He also created gardens and placed more than 200 European-style statues throughout his property. Sutro opened his estate to the public in 1885. When he died in 1898, his daughter Emma took over the grounds, but as she got older, they fell into disrepair. In 1939 the Works Progress Administration demolished what was left of the once grand estate.

Follow the path from the entrance for 0.1 mile and take your first right to explore the outer grounds of the park. The first structure you'll see is a gazebo, actually a "well house" that used to contain drinking fountains. As you reach the western edge of the park, take in views of the Pacific and Ocean Beach at 0.9 mile. Continue on the path to pass the stone parapet (which you can climb for higher-up ocean and beach views), and then reach a junction with a path that takes you left back to your start. But instead of heading left on that path, stay right and take your next possible right onto a slightly downhill, wood-chip-covered path. After a short stretch on dirt, the path bears right, turns to sand, and leads to a stairway along a fence. Descend the stairway, turn right and then right again at the La Playa street sign to enter Sutro Dunes at 1.3 miles. This 3.3-acre park was the site of the seaside amusement park Playland at the Beach from the 1920s through 1972.

Follow the path to the right and to the end of the walkway. Turn around and take a spur path to the right to exit the park. Cross Balboa Street, cross Great Highway, and then turn right (north) to pick up the paved sidewalk along Ocean Beach for 0.3 mile to reach the Cliff House. To head back to the start, continue on the sidewalk along Point Lobos Avenue until you reach the Lands End parking lot.

GO FARTHER
Check out the Cliff House, its gift shop, and the camera obscura behind the restaurant, or take the Lands End Trail (see Hike 2).

07 Candlestick Point State Recreation Area

DISTANCE:	2.9 miles
ELEVATION GAIN:	None
HIGH POINT:	40 feet
DIFFICULTY:	Easy
TIME:	1 hour
FITNESS:	Walkers, hikers, runners
FAMILY FRIENDLY:	Yes
DOG FRIENDLY:	On leash
AMENITIES:	Multiple picnic areas and restrooms
CONTACT:	San Francisco Bay Trail; California Department of Parks and Recreation
GPS:	37° 42' 45.9684" N 122° 22' 52.9104" W
MAP TO:	Candlestick Point State Recreation Area or Donner Avenue and Hunters Point Expy.

GETTING THERE
Public Transit: MUNI bus 29 to Fitzgerald Ave. and Keith St.; if the driver is heading inbound, stay onboard until Gilman Ave. and Bill Walsh Way. **Parking:** Parking is free. To access the best parking lot for this hike, drive through the main entrance at the intersection of Donner Ave. and Hunters Point Expy., and turn right. Park in the closest free spot to the entrance.

A quiet path in flat, sunny Candlestick Point State Recreation Area

In 1978 Candlestick Point became California's first urban state park. In addition to hiking, the park is popular for picnicking, fishing, and windsurfing. For a state park, the area is still a little rough around the edges, but Candlestick Point's bay-front location is full of potential. Anyone who visits can appreciate the pleasantly flat terrain and views of the bay, the East Bay, and San Bruno Mountain. This hike follows part of the San Francisco Bay Trail. On this short route, you'll take waterfront trails to visit scenic Sunrise Point, a quiet cove, and a large-scale artwork built right into a sidewalk. This hike is best in spring when there is green grass around the trail.

GET MOVING

At the park's main entrance, look for a yellow gate, and turn right on a gravel path just behind it. When your path splits, turn left onto a paved path. And when the path becomes a sidewalk in 250 feet, turn right and walk to the water. When you reach the water, turn right on a paved path. When you reach a T, stay left. Follow this bayside path for 0.2 mile toward Sunrise Point, passing picnic areas and restrooms.

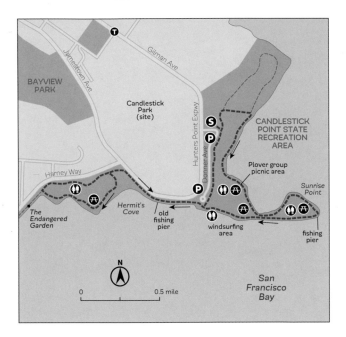

When the path forks after the Plover group picnic area, turn left to follow the dirt path, which meets up with a paved path as you reach the Sunrise Point peninsula at 0.6 mile. Continue left along the dirt path to the tip of Sunrise Point, where you'll find another set of picnic tables and restrooms. Look for the fishing pier and walk to the end and back if you like (more than 0.1 mile).

Behind the restrooms, pick up a dirt path and follow it along the water on the south side of this peninsula. After 0.1 mile, the dirt path merges with a paved path on your right; stay on this paved path along the bay until you reach the southern end of the parking lot and another set of restrooms. If you're ready to end your hike (and take 1.4 miles off the total distance), turn right on a paved path to return to the start in 0.2 mile.

FROM SHIPYARD TO STATE PARK

During World War II, Candlestick Point was created out of a landfill to house a US Navy shipyard that was never built. The area sat unused for decades, and many neighbors used it as their own personal dump. The state of California bought Candlestick Point for $10 million in 1973, and in 1977, the California legislature voted to develop the park as the state's first urban park. The park opened one year later.

The origin of Candlestick Point's name is unknown. Some say it comes from the curlew, a shorebird sometimes called the "candlestick bird." Others say it comes from a long-gone rocky outcropping in the bay that was shaped like a candlestick. Still others say it's from a nineteenth-century custom of burning abandoned ships in the bay—the flames from the ships' masts looking like candlesticks.

Most San Francisco residents can't think of this area without thinking of Candlestick Park. The stadium was torn down in 2014 and now a 500,000-square-foot shopping center and apartment complex are planned for the space.

To continue exploring, pass the lot, keeping the water on your left. A thin strip of land runs along a wooden fence between the road and the bay. (At one point, due to erosion, you may have to walk along the road.) Pass the old fishing pier and walk along the fence until it ends. When the path forks, bear left and continue to walk along the bay. Continue for 0.3 mile until the path reaches a purple squiggly artwork and a red, black, and yellow sidewalk. From here, take your next right on the path that parallels Harney Way.

Option: Or take a quick 0.3-mile out-and-back detour; turn left along the colorful sidewalk, an artwork by Patricia Johanson called *The Endangered Garden*. The sidewalk, the cover for a storage sewer, is designed to look like a garter snake. Turn back when you reach its head (a bumpy area in the sidewalk).

Continue on the path that parallels Harney Way. You will pass a housing development on your left and a restroom on your right. Stay on this path toward a pedestrian overpass, but do not go over it. Take the narrow dirt path to the right that winds back to the path along the wooden fence. Now the water should be on your right. Pass the old fishing pier and head back to the parking lot. Just past the lot and to the right of the bathroom, pick up a paved path. Turn left to return to your start in 0.2 mile.

GO FARTHER

Head to nearby Bayview Park for a quick 1.2-mile loop (see Hike 19) or go north to India Basin to hike to AT&T Park (Hike 8).

08 India Basin to AT&T Park

DISTANCE:	5 miles one way
ELEVATION GAIN:	40 feet
HIGH POINT:	40 feet
DIFFICULTY:	Easy
TIME:	2 hours
FITNESS:	Walkers, hikers, runners
FAMILY FRIENDLY:	Shorten the route to 2.4 miles by turning back after Heron's Head Park
DOG FRIENDLY:	On leash
AMENITIES:	Picnic area and benches in most parks along the way; restrooms in Heron's Head Park
CONTACT:	San Francisco Bay Trail; Port of San Francisco; San Francisco Recreation and Park Department
GPS:	37° 44' 3.7608" N 122° 22' 34.7988" W
MAP TO:	India Basin Shoreline Park, San Francisco

GETTING THERE

Public Transit: MUNI bus 19 to Innes Ave. and Hunters Point Blvd.; MUNI bus 44 to Middle Point Rd. and Hare St.; MUNI bus 54 to Northridge Rd. and Harbor Rd. **Parking:** Free parking at India Basin Shoreline Park on Hawes St. at its intersection with Hunters Point Blvd.

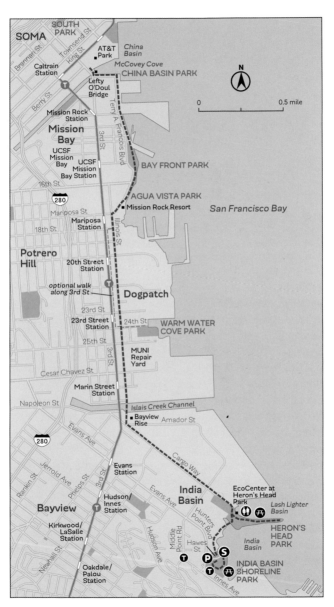

Heron's Head Park attracts more than 100 species of birds.

In some ways, this section of the San Francisco Bay Trail feels like it's on its way, but it's not quite there yet. The trail is often well marked, but it would benefit from a few more nature breaks. Still, while not all of this hike is traditionally scenic, it gives you a more nuanced view of the city.

Two early highlights of this route include India Basin Shoreline Park and Heron's Head Park, significant wetland habitats for approximately one hundred bird species. The middle section of the hike continues on industrial Illinois Street or one block west on 3rd Street in the heart of the rapidly developing Dogpatch neighborhood. The end of the hike passes by waterfront restaurants where you can stop for a bite or drink before taking in baseball history in China Basin Park and at AT&T Park.

GET MOVING

Start your hike in the India Basin Shoreline Park parking lot on Hawes Street. Find the path marked with two metal poles closest to the intersection with Hunters Point Boulevard and follow it as it curves left near a basketball court. As you continue, pass a jungle gym on your right where you take the stairs (or a slide!) to a path below you. Turn left and walk to a lower part of the parking lot, where you'll look across Hawes Street and find another path marked with two metal poles (or feel free to explore the other paths in the park to your right). Follow the path along the shoreline for 0.3 mile and then cross a bridge. Take a left after the bridge and then cross a narrow strip of land to Heron's Head Park at 0.6 mile. At 0.7 mile, take a right on the main path through the park and walk 0.5 mile to the eastern end of Heron's Head Park at 1.2 miles. Here, you can enjoy peaceful views of the bay. Head back, stopping at the EcoCenter (an educational community center) if you like, and continue to the parking lot and park exit.

A BIRD LOVER'S PARADISE

Owned by the Port of San Francisco, Heron's Head Park is a twenty-two-acre wetland habitat that attracts more than 100 bird species a year. It is named for its resemblance (when viewed from above) to the great blue heron, a frequent park visitor. Heron's Head opened to the public in 1999, but its history is decades old. In the 1970s, the Port of San Francisco wanted to construct a shipping terminal on this site (then Pier 98). The terminal was never built, and the land sat empty for two decades while a bird-friendly salt marsh emerged. In the late '90s, the port began renovating the pier.

In 2010 the nonprofit Literacy for Environmental Justice constructed the EcoCenter at Heron's Head Park for recreation and education and to highlight green building technology. It was the first LEED Platinum Zero Net Energy building certified in San Francisco. It runs 100 percent on solar power, has a living roof, boasts on-site water and rainwater harvesting, and more.

Exit the park onto Cargo Way, and stay on this long industrial block for 0.6 mile. Take a wide right onto Illinois Street, and then cross the Islais Creek Channel at 2.5 miles. Starting on Cargo Way and just before you cross the channel, you see *Bayview Rise*, a vibrant mural painted on two old grain elevators. Continue on Illinois Street until you reach 24th Street, passing a MUNI repair yard on your way. At 24th Street you can turn right to visit Warm Water Cove Park.

A TOXIC BEACH, RENEWED

Once called "Tire Beach" or "Toxic Beach" for the trash that littered its shores, Warm Water Cove has been landscaped and paved with trails. At times, there are more homeless residents than park visitors, but I hope this park, with its prime bay-front real estate, will soon see better days. This side trip will add about a half mile to your hike.

Past 24th Street, the Bay Trail continues on Illinois Street, but I think 3rd Street (one block west) is a more interesting route. While busier with cars, this 0.7-mile stretch takes you through the heart of the Dogpatch neighborhood with restaurants, breweries, and the Museum of Craft and Design. If you're walking on 3rd Street, return to Illinois at 18th Street. One block later, at Mariposa Street, turn right on Terry A. Francois Boulevard. Just past Mission Rock Resort (a restaurant), enter Agua Vista Park at 4.3 miles on the dedicated bayside trail to your right. This quickly becomes Bay Front Park. In both of these parks, you have clear, unobstructed views of the water and the East Bay. After 0.2 mile Bay Front Park drops you back on Terry A. Francois Boulevard.

When Terry A. Francois Boulevard turns left after 0.4 mile, head straight into China Basin Park and then walk left to parallel the road. When your path lets out onto the road, head right to cross the Lefty O'Doul (3rd Street) Bridge. Once across the bridge, you've reached AT&T Park and the end of the hike.

CHINA BASIN PARK

This small spot has been transformed into a popular pre- and post-game gathering spot for Giants fans. It features a statue of former Giants great Willie McCovey, who hit 521 home runs during his career. It also features a 570-foot-long history walk with a list of rosters and achievements for every Giants team from 1958 through 1999.

To return to the start via public transit, pick up the MUNI KT line at 2nd and Townsend streets.

GO FARTHER

From here, you can return the way you came for an epic 10-mile hike or continue north on the Bay Trail (see Hike 9).

09 | AT&T Park to Pier 39

DISTANCE:	2.9 miles
ELEVATION GAIN:	None
HIGH POINT:	10 feet
DIFFICULTY:	Easy
TIME:	1 hour
FITNESS:	Walkers, hikers, runners
FAMILY FRIENDLY:	The Exploratorium, a children's science museum, is 1.9 miles into the route
DOG FRIENDLY:	On leash
AMENITIES:	Restrooms in the Ferry Building and at Pier 39; benches along the trail
CONTACT:	San Francisco Bay Trail; Port of San Francisco
GPS:	37° 46' 37.9272" N 122° 23' 25.0512" W
MAP TO:	Juan Marichal Statue, San Francisco

GETTING THERE

Public Transit: MUNI trains N and KT to 4th and King streets; MUNI buses 10, 30, 45, 47, and 82X to 4th and Townsend

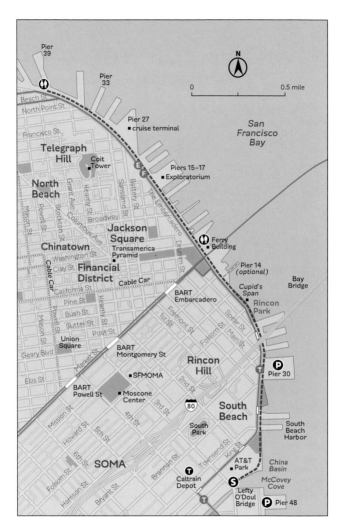

streets. **Parking:** Street parking in this neighborhood can be tough—especially when the Giants are playing. There are paid parking lots at Piers 30 and 48.

This segment of the San Francisco Bay Trail is an easy stroll along the bay. After AT&T Park, you'll walk along a single road, the Embarcadero, all the way to Pier 39. For this reason, instead of giving you turn-by-turn directions, I'll focus more on the sights you'll see along the way. As you hike, remember it wasn't so long ago that part of this route—between Folsom Street and Broadway—was once the Embarcadero Freeway. Built in 1958, it cut off the city from the water and enraged citizens so much that the Board of Supervisors voted to ban future city freeways north of Market Street. While many residents hated the freeway, voters actually rejected a ballot measure to tear it down in 1986—perhaps for fear of the unknown.

The 1989 Loma Prieta Earthquake was a turning point. The freeway was damaged in the quake, and within three weeks, plans were drawn for demolition, which began in February 1991. It was another six years until the city solid-ified the Waterfront Land Use Plan, which aimed to ensure thoughtful planning for the city's eastern shoreline. The plan is looked at as a success for revitalizing the waterfront with bike lanes, retail stores, restaurants, and a renovated Ferry Building.

GET MOVING

Start your walk at the north end of the Lefty O'Doul (3rd Street) Bridge. Take the Bay Trail behind AT&T Park and then along South Beach Harbor. The Giants moved from Candle-stick Park to AT&T Park in 2000. The stadium seats 41,503 people (not including standing-room-only spots), and the right field wall backs up to the bay so that home runs drop into the water. The stadium has been extensively tested to resist earthquake damage.

At the end of the harbor, the Bay Trail joins the Embar-cadero, where you'll bear right. Pass various piers that house everything from cafés to San Francisco's cruise ship terminal to the Exploratorium, and more. The piers' numbers start at

The stunning view from Pier 14

the Ferry Building. To the north are the odd-numbered piers, and to the south, the even-numbered piers.

After 0.9 mile, walk under the Bay Bridge, and after another two blocks, reach Folsom Street and Rincon Park. This is where the old Embarcadero Freeway began. Here, you'll also see the large-scale artwork *Cupid's Span*, a half-buried bow and arrow that was created by Claes Oldenburg and his wife, Coosje van Bruggen, in 2002. The arrow stands sixty feet tall.

At 1.3 miles, take an optional detour and walk out on Pier 14 for unobstructed views of the bay and Bay Bridge. At 1.5 miles, reach the Ferry Building (at Market Street). Construction began in 1896, and ferries began departing from the building in 1898. The building's signature clock tower is 245 feet tall and is modeled after the bell tower in the twelfth-century Seville Cathedral. At one time, 50,000 people a day commuted by ferry; however, ferry travel waned when the Bay Bridge and Golden Gate Bridge were completed in 1936 and 1937, respectively.

At Broadway, pass the end of the former Embarcadero Freeway. One block later, at 1.9 miles, you'll reach the

Exploratorium, which moved from the Palace of Fine Arts to Piers 15–17 in April 2013. The children's science museum was opened by Frank Oppenheimer, a physicist and the brother of J. Robert Oppenheimer, who is often referred to as the father of the atomic bomb.

Reach the Pier 27 cruise ship terminal at 2.3 miles. This served as the home base for the 2013 America's Cup. Next up is Pier 33, where you pick up ferries for Alcatraz. At 2.9 miles, reach Pier 39. This tourist hub, opened in October 1978, includes an aquarium, shops, restaurants, and sea lions, which began arriving in January 1990. While at first there were somewhere between 10 and 50, their population grew rapidly to 300 and can now reach 900 each winter. In the summer, a majority of the sea lions migrate to the Channel Islands in Southern California.

To return to the start, there are several MUNI stops near Pier 39.

GO FARTHER

From here, return the way you came for a 5.8-mile roundtrip hike or continue on the Bay Trail to the Golden Gate Bridge (see Hike 10).

10	**Pier 39 to the Golden Gate Bridge**

DISTANCE:	4.6 miles
ELEVATION GAIN:	300 feet
HIGH POINT:	225 feet
DIFFICULTY:	Easy
TIME:	1 hour 40 minutes
FITNESS:	Walkers, hikers, runners
FAMILY FRIENDLY:	Many places to stop along the way
DOG FRIENDLY:	On leash; off-leash walking is permitted on some parts of Crissy Field

AMENITIES:	Restrooms at Pier 39, near the Yacht Road parking lot, near the Warming Hut, and at the Golden Gate Bridge Welcome Center; benches and picnic tables along the trail
CONTACT:	San Francisco Bay Trail; Golden Gate National Recreation Area; Port of San Francisco
GPS:	37° 48' 31.2228" N 122° 24' 35.3556" W
MAP TO:	Pier 39, San Francisco

GETTING THERE

Public Transit: MUNI E and F train to the Embarcadero and Stockton St.; MUNI bus 47 to the intersection of Powell and Beach streets. MUNI buses 8, 8X, and 39 to Powell and Bay streets. **Parking:** Parking can be difficult. Paid lot at Pier 39 (2350 Stockton St.).

This section of the Bay Trail (also known as the Golden Gate Promenade between Fort Mason and the Golden Gate Bridge) is a great way to explore the city's north waterfront including Fisherman's Wharf, San Francisco Maritime National Historical Park, Fort Mason, the Marina Green, and Crissy Field. If you like Golden Gate Bridge views, this is a great hike for you.

In the not-too-distant past, Fort Mason and Crissy Field belonged to the US Army. However, in the 1950s and 1960s, these areas, plus a number of other areas in Marin, were declared surplus. Real estate developers wanted to build housing, but local residents fought to block development. A local activist group, People for a Golden Gate National Recreation Area, plus the San Francisco Planning and Urban Renewal Agency, the San Francisco Recreation and Park Department, and Congressman Phillip Burton, teamed up to turn the area around the Golden Gate Bridge into a national park. During Richard Nixon's 1972 reelection campaign, the president was encouraged to visit this area. After his trip, Nixon signed An Act to Establish the Golden Gate National Recreation Area (GGNRA) on October 27, 1972, and since then, GGNRA land has been parkland for all to enjoy.

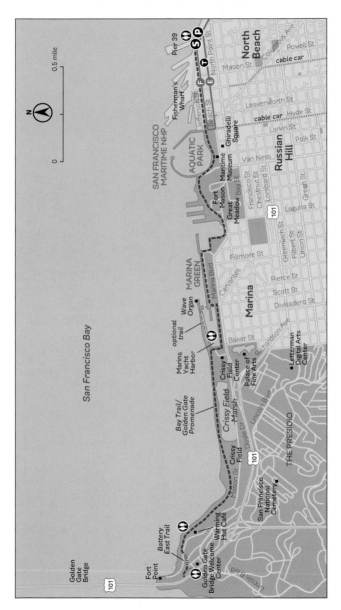

GET MOVING

From Pier 39, walk west on the Embarcadero, and after 0.2 mile, the Embarcadero runs into Jefferson Street. You are now in the heart of Fisherman's Wharf and surrounded by souvenir shops and restaurants. Continue on Jefferson past Hyde Street, where Jefferson Street peters out into a sidewalk at 0.6 mile and leads into Aquatic Park Cove, a part of San Francisco Maritime National Historical Park. Continue through the park, and when the path dead-ends on Van Ness Avenue, turn right. When Van Ness ends at a pier, turn left to head uphill on a paved multiuse path. Follow the path as it leads through trees and onto a grassy lawn, the Fort Mason Great Meadow.

FORT MASON, THEN AND NOW

In 1850 the US Army established Point San Jose military reservation. For years, the army did nothing with the land, and five civilian homes were even built here. But during the Civil War, priorities shifted. The army evicted the civilians and built a full military post with a headquarters, a hospital, barracks, and mess halls around a central parade ground.

In 1882 the fort was renamed Fort Mason after Col. Richard Barnes Mason, the second military governor and commander of California. The fort later served as a temporary city hall and a refugee camp for thousands of San Franciscans after the great earthquake and fire of 1906. The Department of Defense deemed Fort Mason surplus in the 1960s, and after the GGNRA was established, the area was transformed into a park.

Exit the Great Meadow on Laguna Street, then take a right, and follow Laguna as it curves and becomes Marina Boulevard. At the next crosswalk (the intersection with Buchanan Street), turn right and walk through a parking lot to a paved

The sunset lights up Fort Mason and the Golden Gate Bridge.

path along the water. Turn left and stay on this path, which borders the Marina Green Triangle and Marina Green for 0.6 mile. At the end of the Marina Green, turn left on Scott Street and then right to keep following the Bay Trail along Marina Boulevard, this time passing the Marina Yacht Harbor. At the end of the harbor (Marina Boulevard and Baker Street), turn right to continue on the Bay Trail.

When a dirt path branches off to the left, take it to a parking lot. You are now in the Presidio at 2.5 miles. From the parking lot, cross Yacht Road (unsigned) to continue on the Bay Trail along the water.

Option: For an extra mile, visit the *Wave Organ*, an acoustic sculpture made of PVC and concrete pipes that make music when waves crash against them. Turn right at the Marina Yacht Harbor parking lot and walk to the end of the jetty.

Turn left and walk 2.1 miles along Crissy Field Marsh and then Crissy Field to reach the Warming Hut Café and bookstore. From the Warming Hut, you can walk 0.3 mile (not included in total mileage listed for trip) to Fort Point or 0.5 mile (included in total trip mileage) to the Golden Gate Bridge. To reach the bridge, walk past the Warming Hut and look for a wood and dirt stairway on your left, which is a trailhead for the Battery East Trail. Climb the stairway and when you reach a landing after 0.2 mile, follow the signs for the Golden Gate Bridge.

To get back to your start, head to the MUNI stop at the Golden Gate Bridge parking lot.

GO FARTHER

Cross the Golden Gate Bridge. If you're returning the way you came, you can visit Fort Point or the Warming Hut Café.

FROM AIRFIELD TO RECREATION FIELD

Named for Maj. Dana Crissy, who died near Salt Lake City during a cross-country army test flight on October 8, 1919, Crissy Field became part of San Francisco's coastal defense system in 1921. In 1924 the field was the landing spot for the first dawn-to-dusk transcontinental flight, which started in New York.

The airfield was moved to Hamilton Field in Marin County in 1936 because of San Francisco's foggy, windy weather and the construction of the Golden Gate Bridge. Crissy Field became part of the GGNRA in 1972. Though it took time, the former airfield was completely remade. By 2001, seventy acres of asphalt and concrete had been removed and repurposed, 87,000 tons of hazardous materials had been removed, and more than 100,000 plants had been planted. Birds have returned to the area and nearly one hundred species have been spotted here.

HISTORY UNDER THE BRIDGE

Fort Point was built between 1853 and 1861, and while it never saw battle, it was used as part of the coastal defense system through World War II. It was supposed to be torn down for the construction of the Golden Gate Bridge, but Chief Engineer Joseph Strauss was able to build the bridge above the fort without damaging it.

Next page: Boardwalk on the Glen Canyon Park segment of the Creeks to Peaks Trail

CITY GREENWAYS

San Francisco has more than 220 parks and open spaces, and this section celebrates these areas, large and small. At 1017 acres, Golden Gate Park is the city's largest park. Here, you'll explore the park's highest point and 9 of its 10 lakes. You'll also head to San Francisco's second-largest park, named for John McLaren and home to the Philosopher's Way, a meditative journey with grassy hillsides, panoramic views, and a redwood grove.

Just downhill from here is the Visitacion Valley Greenway, a collection of six pint-sized parks making a large impact on their neighborhood. Both the Interior Greenbelt and Mount Sutro hike and the Mount Davidson and Edgehill Mountain route take you through lush eucalyptus forests. Mount Davidson is the city's tallest hill, and on its summit is a 103-foot cross, plus hard-to-beat panoramic views.

Completed in 2015, the new Creeks to Peaks Trail takes you from Glen Canyon Park and Islais Creek to the top of Twin Peaks. Pine Lake to the Panhandle, part of the Bay Area Ridge Trail, strings together numerous parks and hilltops, including Stern Grove, Twin Peaks, Mount Olympus, and Buena Vista Park. And lastly, there's Bayview Park, a hike that mixes up eucalyptus forest with amazing views. Because it's still relatively secluded, you may have the trails to yourself.

11 Stow Lake and Strawberry Hill

DISTANCE:	1.9 miles
ELEVATION GAIN:	140 feet
HIGH POINT:	425 feet
DIFFICULTY:	Easy
TIME:	55 minutes
FITNESS:	Walkers, hikers, runners
FAMILY FRIENDLY:	Yes
DOG FRIENDLY:	On leash
AMENITIES:	Snack bar at and restrooms near boathouse; benches around lake; picnic area at summit
CONTACT:	San Francisco Recreation and Park Department
GPS:	37° 46' 14.8548" N 122° 28' 36.8400" W
MAP TO:	Stow Lake Boathouse, San Francisco

GETTING THERE

Public Transit: Many bus lines serve Golden Gate Park. Some of the most convenient lines include MUNI buses 5, 5R, 28, and 28R to Fulton St. and Park Presidio Blvd.; and MUNI buses 7, 7R, 7X, and 29 to Lincoln Way and 19th Ave. **Parking:** Free parking at the Stow Lake Boathouse (50 Stow Lake Dr.). The parking lot at the boathouse is small, but there are other parking spots on Stow Lake Dr. East and Stow Lake Dr.

This short and easy loop takes you around Stow Lake and Strawberry Hill. Stow Lake is one of the best-loved lakes in Golden Gate Park. It's a great place for a picnic or a paddle-boat rental and has a paved trail around its periphery that makes it ideal for walkers too.

The manmade lake, initially created as a reservoir to provide water for the rest of the park, was completed in 1893. Its name comes from gold rush–era lawyer William Walter Stow, a lobbyist for the Southern Pacific Railroad. On the topic of the railroad, the waterfall on this route is named for Collis P.

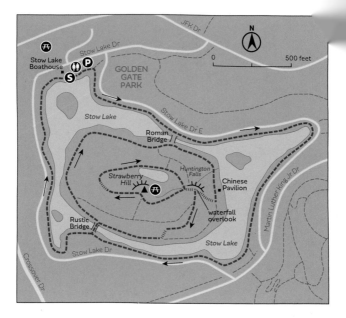

Huntington—one of the Big Four railroad barons. Huntington donated $25,000 to construct the falls, which were the idea of Golden Gate Park superintendent John McLaren. McLaren was inspired to include waterfalls in the park during a hike in the Sierra with naturalist John Muir. Strawberry Hill, the largest island in the lake, and the highest point in Golden Gate Park at 430 feet, gets its name from the fruit that once grew along the island's shore.

GET MOVING

With the Stow Lake Boathouse on your right and the lake in front of you, turn left to start walking on the paved path that surrounds the lake. At 0.1 mile, pass a yellow gate and the Roman Bridge, one of two bridges constructed in 1893 that connect the perimeter path to the island. Don't cross this bridge, but continue walking around the lake. You will see ount Sutro and Sutro Tower in the distance and eventually the Chinese Pavilion on your right. At 0.3 mile you've reached the far east side of the lake. Reach the start of the lake's south shore 0.2 mile later, where you can see the pavilion from a different angle.

At 0.7 mile, you come to Rustic Bridge, which you cross to reach Strawberry Hill. Turn left to start walking on the cypress-lined path. Stay on the path closest to the water for 0.2 mile. The Roman Bridge will be on your left and a set of stairs on your right. Continue on this path and you soon see 110-foot-tall Huntington Falls on your right. Continue to the Chinese Pavilion, a gift from the city of Taipei built to commemorate California's early Chinese settlers. Walk through the pavilion and across the small white bridge. After the bridge, take a quick right and then a quick left on a dirt path to find a flight of log steps. Climb two flights of steps, and make a right at the top of the second flight. When a green railing is on the right side of your path and a small flight of stairs is on your left, walk straight ahead to reach a short brown bridge that overlooks Huntington Falls. Take in the view and then head back a few paces to climb the stairs you just passed (which are now on your right).

At the top of the stairs, turn right. When you reach a gated reservoir, head left to climb a wide path. At the top, reach a clearing on your right with picnic benches. Walk a little farther to Strawberry Hill's summit at 1.2 mile. Continue walking north and west looking north for views of the Golden Gate Bridge between the trees. At the far west end of the summit, take a dirt path that leads down to a wood and stone stairway. Descend the stairs, turn right, and soon you'll arrive back at the reservoir.

After the reservoir, pass a few large rocks at the top of the waterfall on your left. Just after the rocks, descend the stair-way with the green railing on your left (the same stairs you climbed before) and head right. Stay on this path, ignoring

The Chinese Pavillion commemorates California's early Chinese settlers.

any paths on the left, and turn right at a junction. Continue a little farther and then descend a few stairs and turn right on the lake-level path to continue to Rustic Bridge. Cross Rustic Bridge to leave the island, and then turn right to follow the paved path 0.3 mile back to the boathouse.

THE GHOST OF STOW LAKE

Some say there's a ghost that haunts Stow Lake. The legend dates back to the early 1900s. As the story goes, a mother was walking her baby in a stroller around the lake when she decided to rest on a bench with the stroller beside her. While seated there, a woman joined her and the two ended up chatting. While they talked, the stroller rolled into the lake and the baby drowned. It was only after the two women finished their conversation that the mother noticed her baby was missing. She spent all day and night walking around Stow Lake asking others if they had seen her baby. She then went into the lake to look for her child and never resurfaced.

When people claim to see her ghost, they say she has long hair, is soaking wet, and is wearing a dirty white dress. She is most often spotted wandering the lake's edge looking into the water.

GO FARTHER

Rent a boat from the boathouse or get a snack at the nearby Japanese Tea Garden.

12 Land of Lakes

DISTANCE:	5.6 miles
ELEVATION GAIN:	280 feet
HIGH POINT:	290 feet
DIFFICULTY:	Moderate
TIME:	2 hours
FITNESS:	Walkers, hikers, runners
FAMILY FRIENDLY:	Plenty of places to stop and rest along the way; may be too long for young children
DOG FRIENDLY:	On leash
AMENITIES:	Restrooms in Mother's Meadow, at entrance to Polo Field, on JFK Dr., on 36th Ave. south of Spreckels Lake, in lot behind boathouse, and in Hellman Hollow Meadow; picnic area near Stow Lake
CONTACT:	San Francisco Recreation and Park Department
GPS:	37° 46' 10.6176" N 122° 28' 10.8192" W
MAP TO:	Japanese Tea Garden, San Francisco

GETTING THERE

Public Transit: Many bus lines serve the park. Some of the most convenient lines include MUNI buses 5, 5R, and 28 to Fulton St. and Park Presidio Blvd.; MUNI buses 7, 7R, and 7X to Lincoln Way and 9th Ave.; MUNI bus 44 to Concourse Dr. and the Academy of Sciences (inbound) and 9th Ave. and Lincoln Way (outbound); and MUNI N train to Irving St. and 9th Ave.

Parking: Free parking on JFK Dr. and MLK Dr., but spots may be hard to find on weekends. There is also pay-per-hour parking underneath the de Young Museum.

While three-quarters of Golden Gate Park's land area was sand dunes until the 1870s, these "outside lands" were never

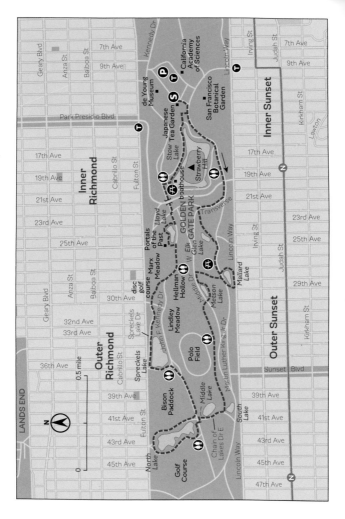

completely dry. Scattered throughout the dunes were four-teen marshy lakes. Today, five of the original lakes remain, though they have been landscaped and altered from their original state. They're known as the Chain of Lakes: North

Lake, Middle Lake, and South Lake. The park's other lakes are manmade, but you wouldn't be able to tell by the diversity and quantity of animals that have made their homes in and around them.

This route takes you on a grand tour of nine of Golden Gate Park's 10 lakes in less than 6 miles. While you may know Stow Lake, Lloyd Lake, and Spreckels Lake, you will explore Mallard Lake, Metson Lake, and more. In addition to the lakes, you'll visit the park's herd of bison and zigzag through the disc golf course. This route takes you on paved roads and on the park's maze of trails, many of which are dirt paths. In order to stay on the route and not get lost, pay careful attention to the directions and map. On some of the more hidden trails, you may feel like you have the entire park to yourself.

GET MOVING

Start your hike at the Japanese Tea Garden on Hagiwara Tea Garden Drive. With the building on your right, head south to Martin Luther King Jr. Drive.

Lake 1: Elk Glen Lake. Turn right onto a sidewalk along MLK Drive and follow the road for 0.6 mile. Take a right on Transverse Drive, the first street after busy Crossover Drive (19th Avenue). Turn left onto a dirt path after 0.2 mile where Transverse and Middle Drive West split at stop sign (ignore any dirt trails you see before this). There are two dirt paths here; take the one farther down the road that heads downhill. When the path splits again as you reach the lake, head left on the dirt path closer to the lake and walk the full length of the south shore of the lake. As you pass the end of the lake, turn left onto a gravel path to return to MLK Drive and turn right.

Lake 2: Mallard Lake. After 0.1 mile on MLK Drive, Mallard Lake is on your left. When you reach the lake, cross the street carefully (no crosswalk), and explore the path that hugs the lake. When you arrive back at MLK Drive, cross carefully again, turn right, and take your first left onto a gravel path

Lillies in bloom at Metson Lake

with a map of Golden Gate Park on one side and a streetlight on the other.

Lake 3: Metson Lake. Stay on the gravel path until you reach a paved road, Middle Drive West. Turn left on the sidewalk, and continue 0.2 mile, during which time your path turns to a dirt singletrack and veers to the left to reach Metson Lake. Walk on the path beside the lake and return to Middle Drive West when the dirt path veers left on the west side of the lake at 1.7 miles.

Lake 4: South Lake. Cross to the north side of Middle Drive West and pick up a dirt path to the left of the light post. Stay left when the path splits almost immediately, and stay on this path as other paths join yours from the right and left. Continue toward a small building that houses restrooms. After you pass the restrooms, reach a paved path and turn left (the restrooms are on your left and an entrance to the Golden Gate Park Polo Fields is on your right). Continue past the end of the Polo Fields and through a parking lot, and look for a continuation of the paved path on the west side of the lot. Follow the paved path 0.3 mile and reach South Lake on your left just before you meet Chain of Lakes Drive East.

Lake 5: Middle Lake. From South Lake, turn right on Chain of Lakes Drive East. Middle Lake is on your right after 0.2 mile, but it's obscured by tall marsh-loving plants. *Option (+0.1 mile):* Take a narrow out-and-back path on the north side of the lake for a close-up view.

Lake 6: North Lake. Continue walking north on Chain of Lakes Drive East until you reach JFK Drive. Cross Chain of Lakes Drive East at the crosswalk and then cross JFK Drive (no crosswalk) to reach the northwest corner of the intersection. Descend the stairway to your left and turn left to follow a path clockwise around the lake for 0.6 mile. You arrive back at JFK Drive at 3.1 miles.

Lake 7: Spreckels Lake. Continue east on JFK Drive for 0.3 mile as it passes by the Bison Paddock. When the path reaches 36th Avenue, cross both sides of the street (it's split in two here) to reach Spreckels Lake, where you'll take a left on a paved path that circles the lake. Follow the path along the north shore of the lake, and when the lake path starts to curve back toward JFK Drive, turn left through a dirt area to meet up with Spreckels Lake Drive. Take an almost immediate right onto a paved path blocked with wooden barriers and one yellow metal pole. Walk 0.2 mile to 30th Avenue, cross the street, and continue on a dirt path marked with a single yellow pole. You are now entering the disc golf course (near hole 7). Head right and onto the pathways lined with logs. At times, the logs will disappear, so keep walking until you see the next pathway.

Look out for holes 8 and 9. Hole 9 leads you out of the course and into Marx Meadow. *Note:* You may feel a little lost here, but you will find your way! If all else fails, walk to Marx Meadow using JFK Drive and continue east from there.

Lake 8: Lloyd Lake. From Marx Meadow, turn right to reach JFK Drive, turn left on JFK Drive, and follow it for 0.2 mile to Lloyd Lake. Walk on the dirt path along the outer periphery of the lake past the Portals of the Past (ruins of Alban Nelson Towne's Nob Hill home from the 1906 earthquake) and the waterfall at the east end of the lake.

Lake 9: Stow Lake. Turn left to return to JFK Drive. When you reach Transverse Drive after 0.1 mile, cross JFK Drive and then turn left to cross Transverse Drive. Continue on a sidewalk on JFK Drive toward an overpass at Crossover Drive. After crossing under the overpass, head uphill on the dirt path with wooden stairs on your right. Reach a clearing and turn left at the boulders and a cluster of cross sections of tree stumps on your left. Walk along a fence on top of more tree cross sections. When the tree cross sections end, turn right and walk through a picnic area and turn left when you reach Stow Lake Drive East. You soon reach the boathouse parking lot. Walk to the far side of the boathouse, then climb a small ramp on your right to reach a paved path that circles the lake. (To explore an option that adds about 1.9 miles, visit Stow Lake and Strawberry Hill, Hike 11).

Turn left on the path and continue for 0.3 mile until you reach two crosswalks. Take either across the street to descend a stairway. Stay right when the path splits around a tree and continue right to MLK Drive. Turn left on MLK Drive and left on Hagiwara Tea Garden Drive to complete the hike.

GO FARTHER

Visit the park's tenth lake, Alvord Lake, off Kezar Drive. The easiest way to locate the lake is to head toward the park entrance at Stanyan and Haight streets. If you've had your fill of lakes, get a snack or beverage at the nearby Japanese Tea Garden or visit the de Young Museum or California Academy of Sciences.

13   Interior Greenbelt and Mount Sutro

DISTANCE:	2.3 miles
ELEVATION GAIN:	650 feet
HIGH POINT:	908 feet
DIFFICULTY:	Challenging
TIME:	50 minutes
FITNESS:	Walkers, hikers, runners
FAMILY FRIENDLY:	The 1.3-mile ascent of Mount Sutro is challenging, but children will love running around in the forest
DOG FRIENDLY:	On leash
AMENITIES:	None
CONTACT:	San Francisco Recreation and Park Department; University of California, San Francisco Campus Planning
GPS:	37° 45' 41.0292" N 122° 27' 7.2684" W
MAP TO:	17th St. and Stanyan St., San Francisco

GETTING THERE
Public Transit: MUNI bus 33 to Clayton and Carmel streets; MUNI bus 37 to 17th and Cole streets; MUNI bus 43 to Parnassus Ave. and Stanyan St. **Parking:** Free street parking on Stanyan and 17th streets and other streets near the hike start.

The twenty-one-acre Interior Greenbelt and sixty-one-acre Mount Sutro Open Space Reserve are nestled between the northwest end of Twin Peaks and the southeast end of Golden Gate Park. A single road, Medical Center Way, winds its way through the parks. Together, they form a vast eucalyptus forest, the result of a mass planting by Adolph Sutro in the

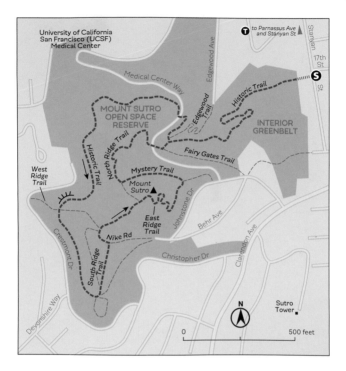

late 1800s. The shady, cool, and peaceful parks are untapped wonders and have clearly marked and well-maintained trails that make them easy to visit.

This hike takes you on a roundtrip journey to and from the 908-foot summit of Mount Sutro, one of San Francisco's seven major hills. It is a perfect escape for those who want a little wilderness inside the city. At many points during this hike, you'll be completely cut off from any trace of the surrounding urban landscape. While on the trails, be aware of mountain bikers who often speed by (though you have the right-of-way). This trail can be wet after a winter rain and condensation from fog can drip from the trees in summer. Wear layers, especially ones that will keep you dry.

Nasturtium, ferns, and eucalyptus line the Mount Sutro reserve trails.

GET MOVING

Start your hike at the wooden stairway just uphill from the intersection of 17th and Stanyan streets. Climb the stairway to enter the Interior Greenbelt and pick up the Historic Trail. You will be struck by the almost immediate transition from neighborhood to forest. As you enter the forest, look up to see a large expanse of eucalyptus trees. At your feet are ivy, ferns, nasturtium, miner's lettuce, blackberry, and, unfortunately, some poison oak too. The first part of the hike is a steady climb with a few long switchbacks. At 0.4 mile, you reach a trail marker. Take the upper right trail to continue on the Historic Trail (the lower right trail is the Edgewood Trail). At this turn, you have crossed the invisible border into the Mount Sutro Open Space Reserve.

When you reach Medical Center Way, locate the trail marker for the Historic Trail across the street, hop the guardrail, and cross. Be careful while crossing as there is no crosswalk, and cars are not expecting pedestrians in the woods. After you pass a large rock formation on your left, look right to see if you can catch a glimpse of the Golden Gate Bridge. At 0.9 mile, reach a trail marker for the West Ridge Trail on your left, but stay on the Historic Trail. At the trail marker, turn around for views of Golden Gate Park, the Golden Gate Bridge, and the ocean.

A LUSH URBAN FOREST

In the mid-1800s most of today's Mount Sutro was part of 4443-acre Rancho San Miguel, land granted by Mexico to José de Jesús Noé in 1845. Noé was the last Mexican *alcalde* (mayor) of Yerba Buena, now San Francisco. The original grant spanned from present-day Parnassus Avenue to Ocean Avenue.

After making a fortune in Nevada's silver-mining boom, Adolph Sutro bought 1200 acres of the former rancho in 1880 and called it Mount Parnassus. While this land was once covered in native grasses and shrubs, Sutro planted eucalyptus, Monterey cypress, and Monterey pine in 1886 in celebration of Arbor Day. The nonnative and invasive eucalyptus thrived in its new environment and became the main tree species on the hill. From 1895 to 1954, donations by the Sutro estate and purchases by the University of California San Francisco, private owners, and the city of San Francisco chipped away at the original 1200 acres and transformed the area into what it is today. In 2006 the Sutro Stewards was formed to improve Mount Sutro's trail network and bring native plants back to the park. In 2011 the San Francisco Recreation and Park Department cleared trails for the Interior Greenbelt and opened them to visitors.

The Historic Trail ends 0.1 mile later when you reach a five-way intersection. Take the immediate left onto the South Ridge Trail toward the summit. Soon after starting on this trail, ignore a dirt path to the left. After another 0.1 mile the South Ridge Trail ends and you take a left on an unsigned paved road (Nike Road). Stay on Nike Road until it becomes a dirt trail, and after 0.1 mile you will see informational signage at the Mount Sutro summit at 1.3 miles.

Past the signs, bear slightly right to pick up the East Ridge Trail, which leads into a clearing where you will look slightly left for another trail marker for the East Ridge Trail and Aldea housing. Enter the woods and head downhill on a number of switchbacks. Reach an intersection after 0.1 mile and go left on the Mystery Trail. Follow this trail until you reach a trail marker and the junction with the North Ridge Trail. Turn right and take the North Ridge Trail 0.1 mile to Medical Center Way. Cross the street and pick up the Fairy Gates Trail. You soon come to a T, turn left, and almost immediately reach a trail marker. Stay right toward the Edgewood and Historic trails, and at the next trail marker, turn right toward the Historic Trail and Stanyan Street to return to your start.

GO FARTHER

Head to Golden Gate Park or Tank Hill. Or if you're up for a bite, choose from the many restaurants near Cole and Carl streets.

14   Creeks to Peaks

DISTANCE:	4 miles
ELEVATION GAIN:	800 feet
HIGH POINT:	922 feet
DIFFICULTY:	Challenging
TIME:	2 hours
FITNESS:	Hikers

Glen Canyon Park's trails may make you forget you're in a city.

FAMILY FRIENDLY:	May be too strenuous for young children, but families can enjoy a walk around Glen Canyon Park
DOG FRIENDLY:	On leash
AMENITIES:	Restrooms near overlook on Twin Peaks and in recreation center; picnic area behind nursery school
GPS:	37° 44' 10.0464" N 122° 26' 23.2692" W
MAP TO:	Chenery St. and Elk St., San Francisco

GETTING THERE

Public Transit: Glen Park BART is at the corner of Diamond and Bosworth streets; MUNI bus 44 to Bosworth and Elk streets. **Parking:** Free street parking near the Glen Canyon Park entrance.

Created in 2015, the Creeks to Peaks Trail takes you from Glen Canyon Park's Islais Creek to the top of Twin Peaks—an ascent of some 800 feet. Already gorgeous Glen Canyon Park just got a major makeover with new stairways and signed

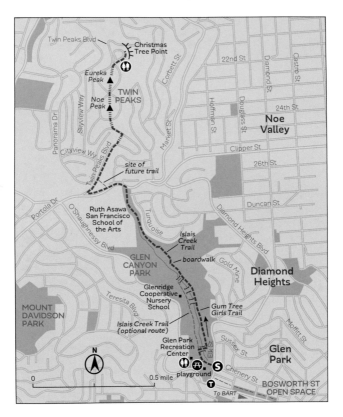

trails. As you traverse the area from south to north, you'll climb gradually out of the park. After exiting Glen Canyon Park, arrive at the base of Twin Peaks. Using trails and stairs, you'll climb toward views that get better with every step. Once you summit both peaks, head down to their famous overlook, Christmas Tree Point. As you look around at the tourists and tour buses, pat yourself on the back for reaching this high point by foot. Hike Twin Peaks on sunny days for the best views, and avoid Glen Canyon Park when its trails are muddy.

GET MOVING

If you're starting from the Glen Park BART Station at the corner of Bosworth and Diamond streets, walk one block north on Diamond Street (toward downtown Glen Park), and take your first left on Kern Street. Cross Brompton Avenue to pick up a dirt path slightly to your left. Continue on this path through Bosworth Street Open Space for three blocks until you reach Burnside Avenue. Go right on Burnside and left on Paradise Avenue. After one block, turn right on Elk Street to reach the entrance to Glen Canyon Park, just north of Chenery Street.

If you're starting at Glen Canyon Park, walk through a plaza and follow the sidewalk past a playground and to the park's recreation center. Then continue past the center on a paved path, and at 0.1 mile, take a right when your path forks. You are now on the Gum Tree Girls Trail, which follows Islais Creek. Continue on this flat, wide trail for 0.4 mile. After you pass Glenridge Cooperative Nursery School across the trail, the trail forks and you stay right to continue on the Gum Tree Girls Trail.

Over the next 0.1 mile, you'll walk on two sections of the Islais Creek boardwalk. After the boardwalks, stay left at the trail marker to head toward Portola Drive. Continue past the next trail marker (with stairs on either side of the trail) at 0.5 mile to continue toward Portola Drive. You are now on the Islais Creek Trail. After 0.1 mile, the Islais Creek Trail makes a sharp switchback to the right. When you quickly arrive at the next intersection, turn left. On the right of your path are a number of houses on stilts. At the next trail marker at 0.7 mile, stay left toward Portola Drive.

After 0.15 mile, pass a fenced-in area with a number of basketball hoops. Then, take a trail and stairs up the hill until you reach another fence and the perimeter of the Ruth Asawa San Francisco School of the Arts. From here, turn around to take in views of the canyon below. Walk to the end of the fence

THE DYNAMITE PAST
OF GLEN CANYON PARK

Glen Canyon Park covers sixty acres and was once a hunting ground for the Ohlone people. Under Spanish rule, the land was used for cattle and sheep grazing. Then in 1845, this land became part of José de Jesús Noé's 4443-acre Rancho San Miguel.

In 1868, Glen Canyon was the home to the first dynamite manufacturing plant in the United States, licensed by Swedish scientist Alfred Nobel, of Nobel Prize fame. Just a year later, an explosion destroyed the plant, killing two and injuring nine.

In 1880 Adolph Sutro bought the land, naming it Gum Tree Ranch after the blue gum eucalyptus he planted here. Sutro sold the park to the Crocker Real Estate Company in 1889.

With the goal of attracting homebuyers, the company opened a small amusement park, zoo, and bowling alley. There were also hot-air balloon rides and a tightrope walker who walked across the canyon. After neighbors complained about rowdy behavior in the park, the city bought it in 1922.

and take a left. You are done with the "creeks" part of the trail when you reach Portola Drive at 1 mile.

A new trail (see map) is planned for the north side of Portola Drive to Twin Peaks Boulevard. If the trail is open by the time you're reading this, follow the trail and go right on Twin Peaks Boulevard. If the trail is not complete, cross Portola, turn left, and after 0.1 mile take a right onto Twin Peaks Boulevard. Follow a dirt trail to the right of the guardrail for 0.3 mile, continuing uphill until you reach a break in the guardrail at a crosswalk. Cross Twin Peaks Boulevard here and take the dirt path with stairs uphill until you reach Twin Peaks Boulevard again. Turn left, walking along the guardrail until you see a break in the guardrail at a crosswalk. Cross the street and take the stairs to reach Twin Peaks Boulevard yet again at 1.5 miles.

From here, cross Twin Peaks Boulevard one last time to take the stairs up and down Noe and then Eureka peaks (the two peaks have names!). At the bottom of Eureka Peak, turn right onto Christmas Tree Point Road, a loop road (to the right of two cell towers) that leads to Christmas Tree Point (a.k.a. Twin Peaks Scenic Overlook) at 2 miles. Turn around to return to the start.

THE BREASTS OF THE MAIDEN

Called "Los Pechos de la Choca" (Breasts of the Maiden) by early Spanish settlers, Twin Peaks covers twenty-nine acres and comprises Eureka (or North) Peak and Noe (or South) Peak. Eureka Peak is 904 feet high; Noe Peak is slightly taller at 922 feet and is the second tallest hill in the city after 938-foot-tall Mount Davidson.

GO FARTHER
For a different roundtrip, head back the way you came. When back in Glen Canyon Park, take the Islais Creek Trail back to your start. The end of the trail has great views of the park's rock formations. Or, continue heading north from Twin Peaks to meet up with the Bay Area Ridge Trail (see Hike 16, Pine Lake to the Panhandle).

15 Mount Davidson and Edgehill Mountain

DISTANCE:	3.4 miles
ELEVATION GAIN:	860 feet
HIGH POINT:	938 feet
DIFFICULTY:	Challenging
TIME:	1 hour 30 minutes
FITNESS:	Hikers

FAMILY FRIENDLY:	Suitable for older children
DOG FRIENDLY:	On leash
AMENITIES:	Benches on top of Mount Davidson and in Edgehill Mountain Open Space; no restrooms
CONTACT:	San Francisco Recreation and Park Department
GPS:	37° 44' 21.0948'' N 122° 27' 28.4292'' W
MAP TO:	Mount Davidson Hiking Path Entrance, San Francisco

GETTING THERE

Public Transit: MUNI bus 43 to Miraloma Dr. and Marne Ave. or Miraloma Dr. and Juanita Way; MUNI bus 48 to Portola Dr. and Rex Ave. **Parking:** Free street parking is available near the hike start.

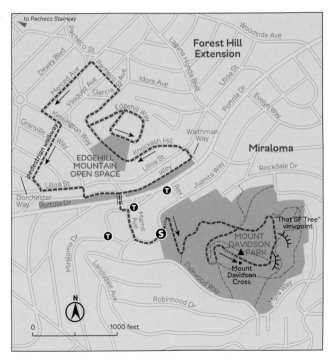

The 103-foot-tall cross on Mount Davidson

Tucked into San Francisco's Miraloma neighborhood is forty-acre Mount Davidson Park, home to the city's tallest peak at 938 feet. The west side of the park is covered with a dense eucalyptus forest, and the east side has grassy expanses and panoramic views of downtown San Francisco. Perhaps the best-known feature of Mount Davidson is the 103-foot cross that adorns its summit. After summiting, you'll head to a hidden park, Edgehill Mountain Open Space. You'll catch views of the Pacheco Stairway, perhaps San Francisco's most elegant stairs; walk a rare dirt road in the city; and stroll down a peaceful three-block-long pedestrian-only path.

GET MOVING

Start your hike on the Juanita Way stairs between Marne Avenue and Rex Way. Pick up the forested trail and turn left at a T at 0.1 mile (ignoring spur paths along the way). At 0.25 mile, turn right when your path splits. (There will be a turnoff to the

A DEBATE ON CHURCH AND STATE

The 103-foot Mount Davidson cross started as something smaller. The first cross was 40 feet tall, made of wood, and built for Easter services in 1923. A concrete cross replaced the wooden cross in 1934. For the present cross's inauguration in 1937, President Franklin D. Roosevelt flipped a switch in Washington, DC, to remotely light it for a crowd of 50,000 spectators.

In the 1980s a debate arose over the separation of church and state: some were upset about a religious symbol standing on public land. To resolve the situation, the Council of Armenian-American Organizations of Northern California purchased a small area around and including the cross. It now serves as a memorial to the 1.5 million Armenian lives lost during the Armenian Genocide in the Turkish Ottoman Empire between 1915 and 1923. You can still head to the cross each year for sunrise Easter services.

left just before this.) Continue until you reach a fire road and stairway. Climb two flights of stairs and take a right. Climb the next stairway and emerge behind the Mount Davidson cross at 0.6 mile. Walk around to the front and look up!

With the cross at your back, take the wide path to a viewpoint where you see San Bruno Mountain to your right, downtown San Francisco in front of you, and Sutro Tower to your left. Toward the end of this viewpoint, descend a stairway on your left and walk to another scenic viewpoint. Here, you'll see an iconic dead tree known as "That SF Tree." After the second viewpoint, backtrack about 90 feet and take a narrow path down to your right—a short downhill stretch littered with loose rocks. When you reach a T with a wider dirt path, turn left to reenter the woods. After about 450 feet, stay right when the path splits (ignoring the right turn just after this). After another 0.25 mile, turn right (ignoring spur paths on your way).

At 1.3 miles descend the stairs you climbed at the start, head left on Juanita Way, and take your first right onto Marne Avenue. Turn left at the end of the block and use the overpass to cross Portola Drive. Cross Kensington Way and turn right onto a narrow unsigned alley lined with a wooden fence. Follow this alley for one long block. Turn left at Waithman Way, and at the end of Waithman, walk to the left side of the gate across the street and head uphill, following a sign for Knockash Hill. At the end of the block (0.1 mile), reach the entrance to Edgehill Mountain Open Space. Walk through the park on the 400-foot-long eucalyptus-lined path.

Exit the park on Edgehill Way. When you reach a steel bear sculpture at a fork in the road, turn right. When you reach another fork, stay right to loop around the hill and get a great view of Mount Davidson. When you close the loop, continue down the hill to return to the fork and turn right at the bear. Option: If you want to skip this loop entirely and shave 0.3 mile off the total distance, bear left at the bear when you first come upon it.

MOUNT DAVIDSON HISTORY

Part of José de Jesús Noé's Mexican rancho in the mid nineteenth century, Mount Davidson was bought and sold a number of times before Adolph Sutro acquired it in the 1880s. As he did with many of his other land holdings, Sutro planted the hill with eucalyptus trees. After Sutro's death, the hill was sold to A. S. Baldwin, the appraiser of Sutro's estate. Baldwin was responsible for the creation of public trails on Mount Davidson. The hill's name was changed from Blue Mountain to Mount Davidson in 1911 after George Davidson, the surveyor for the US Coast and Geodetic Survey.

A HIDDEN HILL

Adolph Sutro once owned 734-foot Edgehill Mountain. After his death, part of the hill was used as a rock quarry, but the quarrying made the hill unstable. During a rainstorm in the winter of 1952–53, a home slid down the hill. Another landslide occurred in 1997, so the hill is now closed to new development.

From the bottom of Edgehill Way, bear right onto Garcia Avenue. After 100 feet, take a small concrete stairway on your left and cross to the lower half of Garcia Avenue. Continue right on Garcia, then turn left onto an open patch of land between two houses (60 and 70 Garcia)—this is the dirt section of Pacheco Street. Continue on Pacheco past Vasquez Avenue and then to Merced Avenue. At Merced Avenue, you'll see the elegant Pacheco Stairway to the northwest a couple blocks away.

Turn left onto Merced Avenue and continue to Kensington Way. Take a wide left onto the lower part of the street (which is split in two here), and after 250 feet turn right onto the unsigned pedestrian walkway on your right. Continue on the walkway for three blocks to Dorchester Way (unsigned), and turn left. After one block turn left on Ulloa Street and take your first right onto Granville Way. When Granville dead-ends at an unsigned alley, turn left and go one block to Kensington Way. Cross Portola Drive at the same overpass as before and then head left as you cross the street to take Marne Avenue. Take a left when you reach Juanita Way to get back to the start of the hike.

GO FARTHER

Visit the shops and restaurants of the quaint West Portal neighborhood on West Portal Avenue between Ulloa Street and 15th Avenue.

Pine Lake to the Panhandle

DISTANCE:	5.6 miles one way
ELEVATION GAIN:	950 feet
HIGH POINT:	922 feet
DIFFICULTY:	Moderate
TIME:	2 hours 30 minutes
FITNESS:	Hikers
FAMILY FRIENDLY:	Families with young children may shorten to a 2-mile roundtrip that includes Pine Lake and Stern Grove
DOG FRIENDLY:	On leash
AMENITIES:	Restrooms and benches in Pine Lake Park and Twin Peaks, benches in Stern Grove, Buena Vista Park, and the Panhandle
CONTACT:	Bay Area Ridge Trail; San Francisco Recreation and Park Department
GPS:	37° 44' 14.5608" N 122° 29' 28.2696" W
MAP TO:	Wawona St. and Crestlake Dr., San Francisco

GETTING THERE:

Public Transit: MUNI bus 23 to Sloat Blvd. and Clearfield Dr.; MUNI bus 29 to Sunset Blvd. and Wawona St.; MUNI bus 66 to Vicente St. and 30th Ave (inbound) or 30th Ave. and Ulloa St. (outbound); MUNI L train to 32nd Ave. or 35th Ave. and Taraval St. **Parking:** Free street parking near the start.

This hike takes you on a long stretch of the Bay Area Ridge Trail. When complete, the Ridge Trail will be a 550-mile continuous loop above the San Francisco Bay. On this hike, you'll walk through the center of the city, climbing Twin Peaks, Tank Hill, Mount Olympus, and Buena Vista Park. While the official Ridge Trail route runs alongside most of these hills, this route takes you over them. But it's not all hills on this hike: you start with a stroll through Pine Lake Park and Stern Grove and then head just moderately uphill through the West Portal

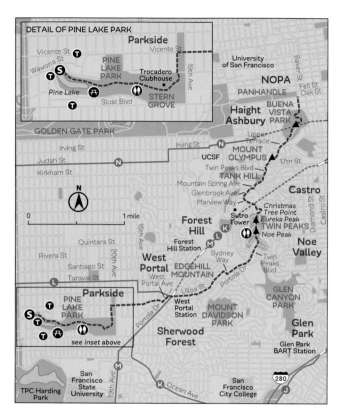

and Forest Hill Extension neighborhoods. After climbing Twin Peaks, your route is mostly downhill to the Panhandle.

GET MOVING

Enter Pine Lake Park at the intersection of Wawona Street and Crestlake Drive. A paved path leads downhill to Pine Lake. Once called Laguna Puerca (Pig Lake), Pine Lake is one of the few remaining natural lakes in the city, and it's also a stop for migratory birds on the Pacific Flyway between Patagonia and Alaska. At the end of the lake, stay left. Restrooms and benches appear in a clearing. Continue through the park and to the left side of a parking lot at 0.5 mile. Stay left past the lot and then pick up a railing-lined path to your left. Walk through the stone seating area for Stern Grove amphitheater at 0.7 mile.

When the seating area ends, pick up another railing-lined path, descend a few stairs, and stay left to check out the Trocadero Clubhouse. From the clubhouse, walk to the left of a pond and redwood grove, and then take a paved path to your left that zigzags up the hill and into a grassy field. Take the paved path to the right, and stay left when the path splits. When the path splits again, take the path to the left behind a building and exit on 20th Avenue.

THE GIFT THAT KEEPS ON GIVING

The Trocadero Clubhouse was built in 1892 as a roadhouse with dancing and gambling. In 1931 Rosalie Stern, head of the Recreation Commission, bought the land the clubhouse was on and named it Sigmund Stern Grove after her late husband. She donated the property to the city with the goal of making this a place for people to enjoy admission-free music, dance, and theater performances. Two weeks after the park's dedication in 1932, the San Francisco Symphony played its first concert in the park. In 1938, she founded the nonprofit Stern Grove Festival Association to oversee what is now the longest-running free outdoor music festival in the United States.

Head north on 20th Avenue one block to Vicente Street. Turn right and continue for 0.6 mile. Take a left on West Portal Avenue, and after a block, turn right on Ulloa Street. Stay on Ulloa for 0.7 mile. On the stretch between Kensington Way and Knockash Hill, you'll have Edgehill Mountain on your left and Mount Davidson on your right (see Hike 15, Mount Davidson and Edgehill Mountain). After you cross Laguna Honda Boulevard, take your next right on Sydney Way. Take your next left on Portola Drive, and in 0.2 mile make a left on Twin Peaks Boulevard.

Follow a dirt trail to the right of the guardrail for 0.3 mile, continuing uphill until you reach a break in the guardrail at a crosswalk. Cross Twin Peaks Boulevard here and take the dirt path with stairs uphill until you reach Twin Peaks Boulevard again. Turn left, walking along the guardrail until you see a break in the guardrail at a crosswalk. Cross the street and take the stairs to reach Twin Peaks Boulevard yet again. At the top, at 3.5 miles, cross Twin Peaks Boulevard to take the stairs up and down Noe and then Eureka peaks (the two peaks have names!). Learn more about Twin Peaks in Hike 14, Creeks to Peaks.

At the bottom of Eureka Peak, turn right onto Christmas Tree Point Road, a loop road (to the right of two cell towers) that leads to Christmas Tree Point (a.k.a. Twin Peaks Scenic Overlook) at 3.8 miles. Enjoy the views and then follow Christmas Tree Point Road to Twin Peaks Boulevard, cross the street and turn right (no sidewalk). Continue on Twin Peaks Boulevard to reach a reservoir. Jump the guardrail at the reservoir and take the paved trail (that turns to dirt) to Marview Way, where you turn right.

Take a left onto Palo Alto Avenue and a right on Glenbrook Avenue. At the end of Glenbrook, go right onto Mountain Spring Avenue and left on Twin Peaks Boulevard. When you reach a T with Clarendon Avenue, cross and turn right to stay on Twin Peaks Boulevard (sign will say Clarendon Avenue). After passing a few houses, look for a wooden stairway on your left if you want to visit Tank Hill for its stunning northern and downtown views.

After enjoying the view from Tank Hill, descend the stairway and continue downhill on Twin Peaks Boulevard. At the bottom of the hill, pass Carmel Street on your left and continue to 17th Street, where you cross and turn right. Almost immediately look for a concrete stairway on your left signed

A redwood grove and pond near the Trocadero Clubhouse

for the Bay Area Ridge Trail. Take the stairs to reach Upper Terrace, go left, and continue 0.1 mile to reach Mount Olympus; you'll know you're here when you reach a statueless pedestal. (Learn about Mount Olympus in Hike 35, The 500 Club.) When you're done visiting this hilltop, look for a stairway on your left between 455 and 480 Upper Terrace, descend the stairs, and make a left. Walk four blocks northeast to Buena Vista Avenue West. As you pass Masonic, look for a distinctive brick house on your right. The house was built with so-called clinker bricks, which were the result of charring during the 1906 earthquake.

Note: The Buena Vista Park section can be hard to follow as none of the paths are named or signed. It's no problem at all if you lose your way; explore the park, making sure you end up at Haight and Baker streets.

From Buena Vista West cross the street to turn right on the sidewalk that runs along the eastern edge of Buena Vista Park. Stay left immediately when the path splits and take a walkway with a wooden railing. When you reach an intersection with a number of paths after 0.2 mile, take the paved path straight ahead of you (second from the right). This paved walkway becomes a dirt path. Pass a stairway on your right and continue until the path becomes a stairway with a great view leading all the way down to a paved path. (Stay right when the stairway forks.) At the bottom of the stairway, turn left. Then, ignore a path that joins yours from the right, and when your path splits into three, stay right. At the next junction, stay left on the lower of the two paths (to the left of a building and a small flight of stairs). A path joins yours from the right. When your path splits again, stay right to parallel a stone wall to the top of a double stairway. Descend the stairs to Haight Street. Cross Haight, and take Baker Street two blocks to Oak Street and the Golden Gate Park Panhandle.

The closest MUNI stop for returning to your start is at Divisadero and Oak streets.

GO FARTHER

From the Panhandle, continue to Golden Gate Park. Or before you reach the end of the hike, turn left on Haight Street to explore the area's shops and restaurants.

17 The Philosopher's Way

DISTANCE:	2.7 miles
ELEVATION GAIN:	420 feet
HIGH POINT:	505 feet
DIFFICULTY:	Moderate
TIME:	50 minutes
FITNESS:	Walkers, hikers, runners
FAMILY FRIENDLY:	Bring small children on the short route (1.3 miles) and older children on the full route.
DOG FRIENDLY:	On leash; off-leash sections in the park

AMENITIES:	Restrooms at Jerry Garcia Amphitheater and tennis courts to the north of Mansell St. between John F. Shelley Dr. and University St.; benches throughout the park; two picnic areas
CONTACT:	San Francisco Recreation and Park Department
GPS:	37° 43' 5.2500" N 122° 24' 44.1900" W
MAP TO:	Mansell St. and Visitacion Ave., San Francisco

GETTING THERE

Public Transit: MUNI bus 29 to Mansell St. and John F. Shelley Dr. **Parking:** Free parking is available in the overlook parking lot on Mansell St. and Visitacion Ave.

John McLaren Park, the second-largest park in San Francisco, opened in 1934. The park is named for John Hays McLaren, a Scottish immigrant who was superintendent of Golden Gate Park for more than fifty years. In the park's 312 acres, you'll find 7 miles of trails, a golf course, water tower, reservoir, lake, and the Jerry Garcia Amphitheater (Garcia grew up in the area). The park is surrounded by neighborhoods such as Portola, Excelsior, Crocker Amazon, and Visitacion Valley, whose reputations range from family friendly to crime ridden. In recent years, the park has become a safer place, but you should still use caution and common sense when you visit.

In 2007, artists and community members met to discuss plans for a public art project for the park, and in February 2008, local artists Susan Schwartzenberg and Peter Richards presented their idea: the Philosopher's Way, a self-guided outdoor experience inspired by similar walks in Heidelberg, Kyoto, and Toronto. According to the artists, philosophers' walks are "places where poets, philosophers, and intellectuals strolled through in conversation, considering the ideas of their times." The trail was completed in 2012.

The hike features a series of stone pillars etched with arrows to guide you down the long or short route. In addition, a number of "musing stations"—plaques with quotations, park history, photographs, and more—add to your experience.

One of many stone pillars guiding hikers on the Philosopher's Way

While the trail is well marked, you can lose your way. If you don't see an arrow or musing station for a while, retrace your steps to the last marker to find your way again. Also don't get thrown off if you see an arrow on more than one side of the stone pillars as the route can be done in different directions from different start points.

GET MOVING

This description is for the long route, which isn't that long after all (if you're doing the 1.3-mile short route, it starts in the same place). From the overlook parking lot at Mansell Street and Visitacion Avenue, take in views of the bay, San Bruno Mountain, and the Cow Palace. From the west end of the parking lot, locate the paved path lined with stone benches. Almost immediately, you'll see a stone pillar with an introduction to the Philosopher's Way and your first musing station. Count out the first seven arrows. At 0.6 mile, reach arrow 8, where you make a sharp right uphill.

Arrow 9 is one of two pillars on the route that has two arrows on it. Go left to continue climbing to Mansell Street, or go right for the 1.3-mile short route. For the long route, the next arrow is on a paved path across Mansell Street (no crosswalk). Follow the next few arrows until you come to an open, grassy meadow. Sutro Tower and Mount Davidson loom in the distance. Leave the meadow and head in and out of a small cypress grove until you reach an intersection with a paved path. Follow the next arrow right onto the paved path. Almost immediately, you'll see a bench behind a path to your left. Don't turn here, but stay straight and continue on the paved path you're on until you see the next arrow, which takes you left and up to La Grande Tank, the eighty-foot-tall blue water tower at 1.3 miles.

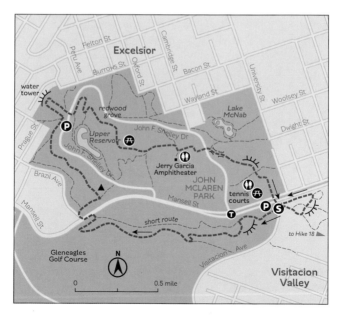

Take the paved path around the water tower to enjoy 270-degree views of the city, including Mount Davidson, Twin Peaks, and downtown San Francisco. Look for your next arrow to the northeast of the tower (with the view ahead and the tower at your back, turn right). This path leads to John F. Shelley Drive, where you'll cross the street (no crosswalk). The parking lot here is an alternate start point for the Philosopher's Way. In 0.3 mile, enter a gorgeous redwood grove that leads into a picnic area. Your next arrow appears shortly after the picnic area. At the fourth arrow after the picnic area (near a fire hydrant), remain on the path (or turn right for a 0.15-mile roundtrip detour to the Jerry Garcia Amphitheater).

Reach John F. Shelley Drive (no crosswalk) again at 2.1 miles. Cross a wooden bridge and head right across another bridge. Climb a paved path interspersed with steps. After 0.1 mile, arrive at a lookout point over San Francisco. Next, cross a paved path that takes you into an area with picnic tables, tennis courts, and a restroom. Shortly after that, cross Mansell Street (no crosswalk), but instead of returning to your start, follow the arrow left. Continue on the path to two stone pillars at a viewpoint with two musing stations. (If you're extending your hike to the Visitacion Valley Greenway, see Go Farther from this point.)

To return to the start, stay left here and follow the arrows back to Mansell Street. Turn left on Mansell Street, cross Visitacion Avenue, and a final arrow leads you back to the parking lot where you started.

GO FARTHER

For two more miles of walking, head to the Visitacion Valley Greenway (see Hike 18). From the viewpoint with the two musing stations, take a stairway and path to the left to the intersection of Ervine Street and Wilde Avenue. Take Wilde Avenue one block east to reach Delta Street. Make a right and then follow Delta Street south for seven blocks to reach

Leland Avenue. (Delta Street between Tioga and Tucker avenues is not well maintained. Walk with caution!) Turn left on Leland and reach the start of the greenway on Leland at its intersection with Peabody Street (just after Rutland Street).

18 Visitacion Valley Greenway

DISTANCE:	0.8 mile
ELEVATION GAIN:	140 feet
HIGH POINT:	210 feet
DIFFICULTY:	Easy
TIME:	30 minutes
FITNESS:	Walkers, hikers
FAMILY FRIENDLY:	Yes
DOG FRIENDLY:	On leash
AMENITIES:	Benches; picnic area in the herb garden; small playground in Children's Play Garden
CONTACT:	San Francisco Recreation and Park Department; Visitacion Valley Greenway Project
GPS:	37° 42' 44.2260" N 122° 24' 23.5260" W
MAP TO:	Leland Ave. and Peabody St., San Francisco

GETTING THERE

Public Transit: MUNI bus 8 or 8BX to Visitacion Ave. and Rutland St.; MUNI bus 8AX, 9, or 9R to San Bruno Ave. and Arleta Ave.; MUNI train KT to Bayshore Blvd. and Sunnydale Ave. **Parking:** Metered and unmetered parking spots on Leland Ave. Plentiful, unmetered parking on other streets near the greenway.

In 1995 Fran Martin and Anne Seeman had a vision to transform Visitacion Valley. They wanted to develop six adjacent plots of empty, weed-filled lots and a dilapidated mini park. Their plan was to create an outdoor classroom to revitalize the neighborhood; educate visitors about natural sciences,

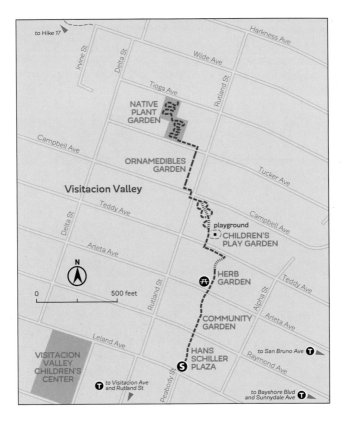

nutrition, and plants; create space for recreational activities; and make the area more pedestrian friendly.

First, however, they needed permission. The land was owned by the San Francisco Public Utilities Commission, which wanted to sell it to private developers. But the Trust for Public Land and the San Francisco Recreation and Park Department, in partnership with the community, were able to negotiate an agreement for its use. In 2000, with a generous grant from the Trust for Public Land and the Columbia

Foundation, construction began on the Visitacion Valley Greenway Project. It was officially completed in June 2014. The greenway includes Hans Schiller Plaza, a community garden, an herb garden, a children's "play garden," an "orna-medibles" (ornamental edibles) garden (formerly called the agriculture garden), and a native plant garden.

You will notice common themes in the parks: decorative gates, terra-cotta-colored walkways, and mosaic art. Additionally, the parks were designed with accessibility in mind, so wheelchair users can enjoy at least some part of each park in the greenway. Lastly, there aren't always crosswalks here, so cross with caution.

Blooming artichokes in Visitacion Valley Greenway's Community Garden

GET MOVING

Hans Schiller Plaza. Find the start of the greenway on Leland Avenue and Peabody Street, where you see whimsical mosaic columns and a low mosaic wall. A colonnade topped with lush green plants welcomes you into this first section of the greenway. Follow the walkway to Raymond Avenue.

Community Garden. Look for the familiar gates and cross Raymond Avenue to enter the community garden. The walkway hugs the left side of the park while the garden occupies most of the land. The garden features more than thirty plots and two greenhouses.

Herb Garden. Cross Arleta Avenue to enter the herb garden. This garden features picnic tables and lavender-lined pathways. Toward the back of the park, climb a flight of stairs before exiting. Make sure to turn around to take in the view of San Bruno Mountain to the south.

Children's Play Garden. Exit the herb garden, walk left (west), and cross Teddy Avenue to reach the entrance to the children's play garden. This park features a playfully decorated front gate and a small playground. After your kids (or you) have had some fun, climb one full flight of stairs and two smaller flights to reach Campbell Avenue.

Ornamedibles Garden. At Campbell Avenue, take a left, cross Rutland Street, and then cross Campbell to enter the ornamedibles garden, which features seasonal crops and fruit trees—an ever-changing laboratory showcasing plants that thrive in the local climate. Plant propagation workshops are held weekly, and seeds, cuttings, and produce are shared with the community. On nonworkshop days, this part of the greenway may be closed.

Native Plant Garden. From the exit of the ornamedibles garden, cross Tucker Avenue and turn left to reach the native plant garden. Here, the walkway zigzags left and right for 200 feet, reaching an incline of 40 feet. The garden is a habitat for bees, butterflies, insects, and birds. Exit the native

VISITACION VALLEY: THEN AND NOW

Visitacion Valley's modern history began on July 2, 1777, when a group of Spanish soldiers and Franciscan friars lost their way to the Presidio in the fog. They camped for the night and awoke in this beautiful valley, which they named after the Catholic Feast of the Visitation.

Mexico gained its independence from Spain in 1821, and in 1841, Visitacion Valley became part of Rancho Cañada de Guadalupe la Visitación y Rodeo Viejo. This land grant, given to Jacob P. Leese, included the southeastern section of the city all the way down to Brisbane, a total of more than 6400 acres. Leese was an Ohio trader and the second permanent settler in Yerba Buena (now San Francisco).

The Mexican-American war was fought between 1846 and 1848, and the United States came out victorious. The Treaty of Guadalupe Hidalgo was supposed to honor Mexican land grants, but most of the land ended up for sale. Two of the first European landowners in the area were Frenchman François Pioche and German Henry Schwerin. Pioche was a bon vivant who introduced fine dining to San Francisco. When he arrived, he brought forty Parisian chefs and a boatload of French wines. Schwerin raised dairy cows that grazed where the Cow Palace parking lot stands today.

From 1925 until 1999, the neighborhood was home to the Schlage lock factory. Today, plans are being discussed to redevelop the Schlage land to accommodate housing, retail stores, and green space.

plant garden and the greenway at Tioga Avenue. Return the way you came or take a side street back to your start.

GO FARTHER

To lengthen this short hike, add on the Philosopher's Way (see Hike 17). To get there, from the end of the greenway at Tioga Avenue, turn left to reach Delta Street. At Delta, turn right, and at Wilde Avenue, turn left. At the intersection of Wilde Avenue and Ervine Street, look for a path and stairway that leads you to John McLaren Park. Then walk to Mansell Street and Visitacion Avenue to locate the Wilde Overlook parking lot and the start of the Philosopher's Way.

19   Bayview Park

DISTANCE:	1.2 miles
ELEVATION GAIN:	230 feet
HIGH POINT:	425 feet
DIFFICULTY:	Easy to moderate
TIME:	35 minutes
FITNESS:	Walkers, hikers, runners
FAMILY FRIENDLY:	If children can make it up the first hill, they will enjoy the rest of the hike
DOG FRIENDLY:	On leash
AMENITIES:	None
CONTACT:	San Francisco Recreation and Park Department
GPS:	37° 43' 6.0780" N 122° 23' 40.3944" W
MAP TO:	972 Key Ave., San Francisco

GETTING THERE

Public Transit: MUNI KT (K-Ingleside/T-Third St.) train to Le Conte Ave. and 3rd St. **Parking:** Street parking available near the start of the hike.

Tucked into the southeastern corner of the city, forty-six-acre Bayview Park is a place to get away from it all. The park's wide, peaceful trails are often empty, and you'll feel like you have a little piece of San Francisco all to yourself. The start of the hike is challenging with a short but steep climb. This leads to an easy, flat loop trail that rewards your efforts with 360-degree views of downtown San Francisco, the East Bay, and the San Francisco Peninsula. At times, the trail is lined with trees—hundreds of eucalyptus were planted here between 1915 and 1938—and at times, you'll have unobstructed views for miles.

GET MOVING

Start your hike at the park entrance at Key Avenue on the wide asphalt road where you'll gain almost 200 feet in 0.2 mile.

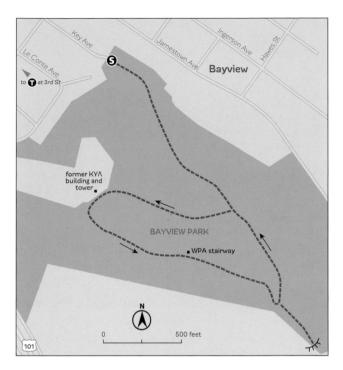

If you need a break as you head up the steep hill, look left for a novel view of the Bay Bridge, or turn around completely to see Sutro Tower and Twin Peaks. As you climb, eucalyptus trees greet you, and at the very top of the hill, head right. Walking along the north side of the hill, enjoy lovely downtown and bridge views between the trees. After 0.1 mile, you pass a low stone wall, a remnant of development by the Works Progress Administration (WPA) during the Great Depression. No improvements have been made to the park since.

After another 0.1 mile, the trees clear on your right as you reach a small building and tower. These were built in the thirties for KYA, a radio station owned by William Randolph Hearst. The art deco building was designed by Julia Morgan,

Bayview Park offers some of the best panoramic views of San Francisco.

who also designed Hearst Castle. The building and tower have been out of use since the forties. Shortly after this, you'll see a gate to the right that leads to a path with a lookout point with some rock outcroppings. (This is not an official path; please steer clear of it.) In another 0.2 mile, you reach a crumbling red stairway just to the left of the trail, another sign of former WPA work. You can check out the stairway, but it quickly becomes overgrown. As you walk along the southern end of the park, keep an eye out for Islais cherry trees. The leaves look like holly, and you may see fruit hanging off the branches (there were plenty when I visited in late August). The Ohlone used this fruit as a food source.

After 0.1 mile, the path hooks left to close out your loop, but instead of heading back to the start, stay right on a spur

A HILL SPARED FROM DEVELOPMENT

At the turn of the twentieth century, George Hearst (father of William Randolph) and the Bay View Land Company had plans to develop this area into an upscale neighborhood for the wealthy. Plans were scrapped after the location was deemed too remote and too far from downtown. In 1902 the city of San Francisco bought some of the land to build a "pest house" for people with communicable diseases. Not wanting such a building near his other properties, railroad magnate and landowner Charles Crocker donated his portion of the hill to the city if they agreed not to build the hospital. When the hill became a park in 1915, hundreds of eucalyptus trees were planted. Thousands more trees were planted between 1937 and 1938.

In the 1950s, privately owned areas of the hill were quarried to build Candlestick Park. And in 1997, the City and County of San Francisco acquired an additional sixteen acres of the upper northeast slope to be used as open space.

path to an open gate where you can walk out and enjoy a southern view. Return to the main trail, and it's just 0.1 mile to complete the loop. Emerge from the trees and head 0.2 mile down the steep hill to your start.

GO FARTHER
Head to nearby Candlestick Point State Recreation Area (see Hike 7).

Next page: Andy Goldsworthy's Wood Line
zigzags for 1200 feet in the Presidio.

THE PRESIDIO

With 24 miles of trails packed into just over 2 square miles, the Presidio is the city's most hikeable neighborhood. The 1200-plus-mile-long California Coastal Trail and Juan Bautista de Anza National Historic Trail pass through here as do the 500-plus-mile-long San Francisco Bay and Bay Area Ridge trails. The Presidio has also created its own network of trails highlighting the natural, artistic, and historic features of the area. You'll explore a natural lake, cross dunes to reach the ocean, and travel through peaceful cypress and redwood groves.

Founded in 1776, the Presidio was a Spanish (1776–1821), Mexican (1821–1846), and US (1846–1994) military base. When the Presidio became part of the National Park system, many of the military buildings were repurposed to become homes, schools, businesses, restaurants, and museums.

The Presidio also serves as a unique setting for art. Andy Goldsworthy has created four installations in the area—all within walking distance of the Presidio's Main Post.

Nature, history, art: the Presidio has it all.

20 | Park Trail

DISTANCE:	3.3 miles
ELEVATION GAIN:	440 feet
HIGH POINT:	305 feet
DIFFICULTY:	Moderate
TIME:	1 hour 30 minutes
FITNESS:	Walkers, hikers, runners
FAMILY FRIENDLY:	Children will enjoy the pet cemetery and Crissy Field
DOG FRIENDLY:	On leash
AMENITIES:	Snacks and restrooms in Presidio Golf Course's General Store
CONTACT:	Presidio Trust; Golden Gate National Recreation Area
GPS:	37° 47' 14.9856" N 122° 28' 24.0960" W
MAP TO:	Wedemeyer St. and 14th Ave., San Francisco

GETTING THERE

Public Transit: MUNI bus 1 or 28 to California St. and Park Presidio Blvd.; MUNI bus 2 to Clement St. and 14th Ave.; MUNI bus 44 to California St. and 12th Ave. **Parking:** Free street parking available at and near the trailhead on 14th Ave.

The Park Trail, the Presidio's main north-south hiking trail, unfurls slowly before you and grows more interesting along the way. It starts in the Presidio's Public Health Service District, where a former hospital, nurses' quarters, and other buildings have been renovated into apartments, houses, and offices. The path continues uphill through the Presidio Golf Course and reaches its peak elevation along Washington Boulevard. From there, it's all downhill as you pass the San Francisco National Cemetery, a cypress grove, the former cavalry stables, the Park Archives and Records Center, and the Presidio Pet Cemetery. The midpoint of the hike (or end if you're traveling one way) at Crissy Field features panoramic views of the Golden Gate Bridge and San Francisco Bay.

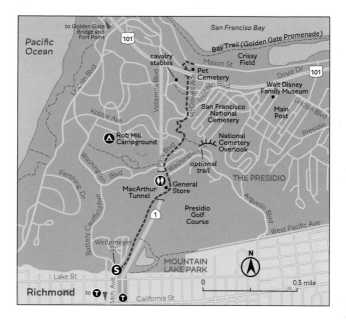

GET MOVING

Start your hike on a paved path in front of a small brick wall off 14th Avenue, just south of Wedemeyer Street. The brick building in front of you is the Public Health Service District's former nurses' quarters. Turn right to start on the path. You'll soon pass a loud patch on your right as you walk above busy Veterans Boulevard (Highway 1). On your left are military homes originally built for doctors and their families.

After 0.2 mile, your path forks. Bear left to continue on the Park Trail, and walk through a gate to enter the Presidio Golf Course. After 0.3 mile on this path, you reach the General Store, where you can stop for snacks and restrooms. Continue another 0.1 mile uphill on the concrete path to reach the course's exit.

Turn left to walk along Washington Boulevard (unsigned), and then take your first right at the crosswalk to pick up Park

A PRIVATE CLUB, NOW OPEN TO ALL

The Presidio Golf Course was built in 1895 and at first was restricted to military officers and members who joined the private Presidio Golf Club. In the aftermath of the 1906 earthquake and fire, the course played an important role, serving as a refugee camp for survivors. In the 1930s, thousands of trees were planted, giving the course the forested look it's known for today. Over the years, celebrities, including Bob Hope, Bing Crosby, Charles Schulz, and Joe DiMaggio, played the course, which became a national historic landmark in 1962. In 1995, one year after the Presidio became a national park, the course was opened to the public. A new public clubhouse was built, but a private Presidio Golf Club still exists and runs its own clubhouse just outside park boundaries.

Boulevard. Stay on this eucalyptus- and cypress-lined path for a quarter mile until you reach the turnoff on your right for the San Francisco National Cemetery Overlook. The cemetery is the final resting place for 30,000 American veterans. If you haven't been to the overlook, this 0.2-mile detour is worth a visit. If you're not visiting the overlook, continue on the Park Trail and stay right as your trail forks after 150 feet. A fence soon lines your path, creating a viewpoint for the cemetery. When your trail splits again, follow the Park Trail sign to stay on the trail and enter a large cypress grove, one of my favorite areas of the Presidio. Partway through the grove, stay right once again at the Park Trail sign to remain on the trail and reach Park Boulevard.

Bear right at the next Park Trail sign and cross the short crosswalk to continue along Park Boulevard. Continue one block to the intersection of Park Boulevard and Lincoln Boulevard. Cross Lincoln Boulevard and Park Boulevard (which is now McDowell Avenue). Turn right to pick up the trail and take a quick left to walk on a path through cypress

Fog shrouds the Golden Gate Bridge at Crissy Field.

trees. Return to the roadside path, which you'll follow past the Presidio Promenade Trail and a number of red brick buildings including the former cavalry stables and the Presidio's Park Archives and Records Center (last building on your right). Read more about these buildings in Hike 23, Presidio Promenade. As the trail goes under US Highway 101, look left to catch a glimpse of the Presidio Pet Cemetery. Here, McDowell Avenue becomes Crissy Field Avenue.

From Crissy Field Avenue, take your first right on Mason Street. At the end of the block, use the crosswalk to cross to the other side of the street and make a right onto the paved multiuse path. Turn left when you reach a dirt path that heads toward the bay. You have reached Crissy Field and the end of this route. Return the way you came.

REST IN PEACE, FIDO

No one knows the exact origins of the Presidio Pet Cemetery, but today it is the final resting place for 420 dogs, cats, birds, hamsters, lizards, goldfish, mice, and more who belonged to military families. The first headstones are from the early 1950s, but sadly you can't bury your pet here anymore: the cemetery closed to new interments in 1963.

GO FARTHER

Explore Crissy Field, an expansive lawn with great Golden Gate Bridge views, or Fort Point National Historic Site (see Hike 10, Pier 39 to the Golden Gate Bridge). You can also walk to the Golden Gate Bridge. To do this, take the dirt path you're on toward the water to reach the Golden Gate Promenade (Bay Trail). Head west on the trail, and just after you pass the Warming Hut, take a left onto the Battery East Trail, a stairway and trail that will lead you to the bridge.

21 | Mountain Lake Trail

DISTANCE:	5.2 miles
ELEVATION GAIN:	700 feet
HIGH POINT:	335 feet
DIFFICULTY:	Moderate
TIME:	2 hours
FITNESS:	Walkers, hikers, runners
FAMILY FRIENDLY:	Playgrounds at Julius Kahn and Mountain Lake parks; may be too long and have too much elevation gain for young children
DOG FRIENDLY:	On leash; off-leash on Baker Beach north of Lobos Creek
AMENITIES:	Restrooms and picnic areas in Julius Kahn Playground and Mountain Lake Park and at Baker Beach
CONTACT:	Presidio Trust; San Francisco Recreation and Park Department; Golden Gate National Recreation Area

GPS: 37° 47' 34.1124'' N 122° 26' 47.1696'' W
MAP TO: Lyon St. and Broadway, San Francisco

GETTING THERE

Public Transit: MUNI bus 3 to Jackson and Baker streets; MUNI bus 43 to Presidio Ave. and Jackson St. **Parking:** Free three-hour parking spots near the hike start.

This hike trends gently downhill as you head from the Presidio's Broadway Gate to Baker Beach. In a short distance, you encounter some interesting changes in scenery. For the first 0.8 mile, you find yourself within the nature of the Presidio but on the edge of ritzy Pacific Heights. On the way, you'll walk by Andy Goldsworthy's *Wood Line* plus Lovers' Lane, a centuries-old footpath. Next, you hike alongside the Presidio Golf Course to reach Mountain Lake, passing golfers, runners, and dog walkers. The last mile before the beach exposes you to the Presidio's natural dune environment as you'll be walking on or near sand all the way to Baker Beach. Partway through this section, you'll visit the Marine Cemetery Vista, a monument to a once-forgotten military cemetery.

GET MOVING

Start this hike at the intersection of Lyon Street and Broadway, at the Presidio's Broadway Gate, which was built around 1897. Enter the Presidio through this sandstone gate, taking in views of the bay off to your right, and following a paved path to Presidio Boulevard. Cross the street, turn right, and cross West Pacific Avenue. Turn left to follow West Pacific and start looking right to see Andy Goldsworthy's 1200-foot-long serpentine sculpture, *Wood Line*, unfolding in the eucalyptus grove below. Pass Lovers' Lane and continue to a small parking area on your right. (Learn more about Andy Goldsworthy and Lovers' Lane in Hike 24, Goldsworthy Gallery Tour.)

At the end of the parking area, turn right onto a sandy trail (sometimes covered in wood chips). After 0.2 mile the path is paved and you reach a baseball field, which marks the start of Julius Kahn Playground. Stay on this path for another 0.3 mile (it turns to dirt after you pass the park's tennis courts) and turn left at the crosswalk to cross West Pacific Avenue. Turn right to continue on West Pacific Avenue, and use the crosswalk at Arguello Boulevard, which has its own Presidio gate from around 1896. The paved path stays on West Pacific Avenue and passes the Presidio Golf Course on your right and the Presidio Golf Club on your left (read more about the Presidio Golf Course in Hike 20, Park Trail). At 0.2 mile after the Presidio Golf Club, stay straight on a pedestrian-only path lined by a stone wall on the left. After another 0.3 mile, the path bears right to Mountain Lake. After another 0.1 mile, you can bear left on a dirt path to relax on some lakeside benches.

MOUNTAIN LAKE: WHERE NATURE AND HISTORY MEET

Mountain Lake is one of the few remaining natural lakes in San Francisco. In 1775, Lieut. Col. Juan Bautista de Anza led an expedition of 240 people from New Spain (Mexico) to Alta California (a large area of land including present-day California). He arrived in San Francisco on March 27, 1776, and camped by Mountain Lake while choosing sites to build the Presidio and mission.

In more recent years, the lake became polluted. Building materials were dumped in the lake during construction of the MacArthur Tunnel, and fertilizer runoff from the Presidio Golf Course and lead (from the leaded gasoline era) from cars driving on nearby roads ended up in the lake. In addition, the lake became a dumping ground for unwanted aquatic pets. It was dredged in 2013 and invasive fish were removed in 2014.

Follow the path along the lake for 0.3 mile, pass under Veterans Boulevard (Highway 1), and reach a T in the trail marked with white poles. Bear left and after about 250 feet,

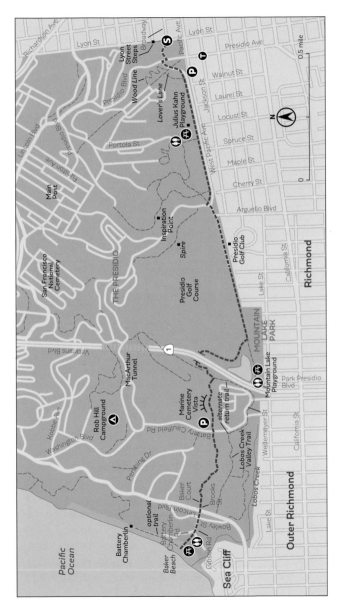

climb a stairway on your right and then a number of subsequent flights of stairs to stay on the trail. At the top of the stairs, you'll walk along a boardwalk raised slightly above the sand. In a little under 0.2 mile, you pass the Marine Cemetery Vista on your right.

FORGOTTEN SOLDIERS REMEMBERED

What looks like an expanse of sand is a merchant marine cemetery and the final resting place for 500 sailors. Men who died at the nearby US Marine Hospital (now the Presidio Landmark Apartments) between 1881 and 1912 were buried here when they had no family or money to transport their bodies home. The cemetery fell into disrepair, and by 1970 it was a parking lot. Rediscovered in 1989, the memorial was completed in 2011.

After another 0.1 mile, the trail arrives at a parking lot. Turn left and walk to Wedemeyer Street (Battery Caulfield Road), which you'll cross to pick up a sandy trail that leads into a cypress grove. At a junction with another sandy trail, turn right onto a wire-fence-lined path that leads out of the trees and into another grove. In this second grove of trees, stay on the main path and then bear left to stay in the trees when your path splits. Enter a clearing after 250 feet. Here, the path can be difficult to discern, but stay left and walk toward taupe-colored homes that are part of the Baker Beach Apartments.

Enter the apartment complex through a parking area that leads to Baker Court, which becomes Brooks Street after a block. Continue to Lincoln Boulevard, cross the street using the crosswalk, and pick up a dirt path that leads to Bowley Street (no crosswalk). Turn left here and make your first right onto Gibson Road (also no crosswalk). Pass Battery Chamberlin Road off to the right and walk through a parking lot to Baker Beach at 2.6 miles. The Burning Man Arts Festival

A boardwalk leads to the Marine Cemetery Vista.

started here in 1986, and the free-spirited flock to north Baker Beach where sunbathers take the "optional" in "clothing optional" very seriously. Return the way you came.

GO FARTHER

From Baker Beach, explore Battery Chamberlin, which is accessible from the main Baker Beach parking lot off Battery Chamberlin Road. For a different return trip that adds 0.3 mile to your distance (and if you're not hiking with a dog), take the Lobos Creek Valley Trail (see Hike 22) to Wedemeyer Street. Then pick up the Anza Trail (see Hike 27) to get back to Mountain Lake and the Mountain Lake Trail. If you still have energy at the end of the hike, explore the Lyon Street Steps, which run from Broadway down to a half block above Green Street. Or check out Billionaire's Row on Broadway between Lyon and Divisadero streets.

22 Lobos Creek Valley Trail

DISTANCE:	1 mile
ELEVATION GAIN:	110 feet
HIGH POINT:	180 feet
DIFFICULTY:	Easy
TIME:	25 minutes
FITNESS:	Walkers, hikers
FAMILY FRIENDLY:	Yes
DOG FRIENDLY:	No
AMENITIES:	Bench on boardwalk and at Lobos Valley Overlook
CONTACT:	Presidio Trust; Golden Gate National Recreation Area
GPS:	37° 47' 18.0780" N 122° 28' 55.4664" W
MAP TO:	El Camino del Mar and Bowley St., San Francisco

GETTING THERE

Public Transit: MUNI bus 29 to Lincoln Blvd. and Bowley St.; PresidiGo Shuttle's Presidio Hills route stops at the same intersection. **Parking:** The parking lot where you start your hike is located at the southern intersection of El Camino del Mar (Lincoln Blvd). and Bowley St. The lot is on the east side of El Camino del Mar (Lincoln Blvd).

At just 1 mile, this is one of the shorter hiking trails in the city. For someone who's looking for some serious exercise, this trail is best done as part of a longer route. However, if you want a small dose of nature in a less-explored area of the Presidio, this may be the hike for you. The hike features a wheelchair-accessible boardwalk, its own informational brochure, a sandy path lined with cypress trees, and an overlook where you can take in the Lobos Creek Valley. This area was a favorite for photographer and San Francisco native Ansel Adams. Adams's website mentions: "Nearly every day found him hiking the dunes or meandering along Lobos Creek, down to Baker Beach, or out to the very edge of the American continent."

GET MOVING

The trail starts near the entrance of the parking lot east of the intersection of El Camino del Mar (Lincoln Boulevard) and Bowley Street. Look for a kiosk labeled Lobos Creek at the entrance to the parking lot, and pick up a brochure that provides information on the area's flora and fauna. Find the boardwalk behind the kiosk, follow it to its end at 0.3 mile, and continue on the path to reach a sandy stairway. Climb the stairway and turn right to follow the trail through a cypress grove. When the trail veers right at 0.4 mile, head up toward a parking lot and the Presidio Landmark Apartments.

The US Marine Hospital, built in 1875, stood where the Presidio Landmark Apartments are today. A new hospital, the

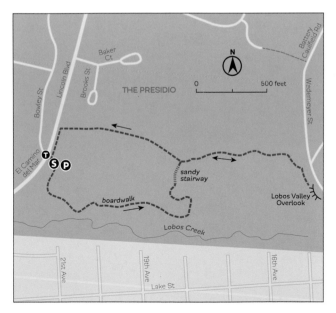

A RESTORED DUNE HABITAT

Lobos Creek originates in the southwest corner of the Presidio and flows into the Pacific Ocean at Baker Beach. It is the last free-flowing creek in San Francisco, while Yosemite, Islais, and Mission creeks have long been rerouted and in some cases diverted underground from their original paths. Lobos Creek used to provide water for Native inhabitants of the city and continues to be the Presidio's primary water source.

The Lobos Creek Valley was part of a system of sand dunes that once covered one-third of the city. The dunes around the creek were destroyed when the Presidio was an active military base. They were brought back to their natural state as part of a restoration project when the Presidio became a national park in 1994. The restoration was completed in 1995, and today the area is home to birds, butterflies, and more than 130 plant species.

Public Health Service Hospital, was built in 1932 and closed in 1981. The Military Language Institute used part of the building from 1982 to 1988. After that, it sat unused for decades before being renovated between 2006 and 2010.

Native plants line a sandy path on the Lobos Creek Valley Trail.

Stay right to pick up the paved path that runs along the parking lot. When you're about halfway along the lot (there will be a crosswalk on your left), take a right down the path to reach the Lobos Valley Overlook at 0.5 mile. Enjoy the valley below (and ocean views if it's sunny). To your far left in the distance, look for Mount Sutro, Sutro Tower, and Golden Gate Park.

To return to the start, retrace the cypress-lined trail, but when you reach the sandy stairs on your left, continue straight. Follow this path for another 0.1 mile until you reach Lincoln Boulevard. Take a left to walk on the sidewalk and continue to the parking lot where you started the hike.

23 Presidio Promenade

DISTANCE:	4.2 miles
ELEVATION GAIN:	220 feet
HIGH POINT:	180 feet
DIFFICULTY:	Easy
TIME:	1 hour 30 minutes
FITNESS:	Walkers, hikers, runners
FAMILY FRIENDLY:	Fairly flat and mostly paved
DOG FRIENDLY:	On leash
AMENITIES:	Restrooms in transit center at Lincoln Blvd. and Graham St., in the National Cemetery, and near Golden Gate Welcome Center
CONTACT:	Presidio Trust; Golden Gate National Recreation Area
GPS:	37° 47' 54.7008" N 122° 26' 50.6652" W
MAP TO:	Lombard Street and Lyon Street, San Francisco

GETTING THERE
Public Transit: MUNI bus 41 or 45 to Lyon and Greenwich streets; MUNI bus 43 to Lyon and Lombard streets; MUNI buses 28 and 28R to Richardson Ave. and Francisco St.; PresidiGo Shuttle's downtown route stops at Lombard Gate.
Parking: Free street parking is available outside the Lombard

View of Crissy Field from the overlook

Gate on Lyon St. and other nearby streets. Lombard St. offers metered spots.

This easy hike takes you from the Presidio's Lombard Gate to the Golden Gate Bridge—mostly on paved paths and sidewalks but with a little well-packed dirt at the end. This route definitely feels like an urban hike since you're walking near Lincoln Boulevard and US 101 for much of the time. You won't spend a lot of time in nature here, but you will see various historic areas of the Presidio, such as the Letterman District, the Main Post, San Francisco National Cemetery, and the former cavalry stables. You will also get views: The Crissy Field Overlook is a highlight, giving you views of Crissy Field, the bay, the Palace of Fine Arts, and the San Francisco skyline. And you'll have plenty of time to gaze at the Golden Gate Bridge too. You'll get some bridge views early on, and then the last 0.5 mile of the hike is bridge views all the way.

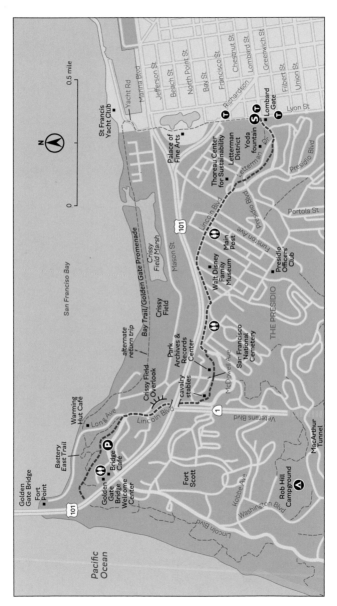

GET MOVING

Start your hike at the Presidio's Lombard Gate (at the intersection of Lyon and Lombard street). This sandstone gate dates back to around 1896, and the cannons outside the gate were cast in 1793, under the Presidio's Spanish rule. As you pass through the gate, you enter the Presidio's Letterman District.

LETTERMAN DISTRICT

This area of the Presidio was named after Maj. Jonathan Letterman, the father of modern battlefield medicine, who created the first ambulance corps during the Civil War. Before him, wounded soldiers were left on the battlefield, sometimes for days, without medical help.

The district was the site of the army's first permanent general hospital, which was built between 1899 and 1902. Between 1965 and 1976 some of the original buildings were demolished, but you can still see an original building on Torney Avenue where the Thoreau Center for Sustainability is located today.

More recently, the Presidio Trust worked with Lucasfilm to redevelop twenty-three acres, and in 2005 the Letterman Digital Arts Center was opened. The center includes Lucasfilm Ltd., Industrial Light and Magic, LucasArts, and the George Lucas Educational Foundation. While new, these buildings were designed to match the traditional Presidio style. Speaking of Lucasfilm, if you're a *Star Wars* fan, check out the Yoda Fountain near the start of the hike.

Walk on the sidewalk along Lombard Street for 0.1 mile. Cross Letterman Drive and walk on an asphalt path between Lombard and Letterman. The path lets out onto a sidewalk along Letterman Drive, and when it splits after about 200 feet, follow the asphalt path left to the intersection of Letterman Drive (Presidio Boulevard) and Lincoln Boulevard. Cross Letterman Drive and continue on Lincoln Boulevard.

Stay on the well-signed path along Lincoln for 0.3 mile, at which point you start to see the Presidio Main Post's iconic red brick buildings (built between 1893 and 1897) ahead and off to your left. The Walt Disney Family Museum, the Presidio Officers' Club, the Inn at the Presidio, and a few restaurants are some of the Main Post's attractions.

Continue walking on Lincoln Boulevard past the Main Post until you see a walkway blocked (to cars) by four white poles. Continue past the poles on the pedestrian path, and walk above the highway and behind the buildings of the Main Post. After 0.2 mile, reach the San Francisco National Cemetery. Founded in 1884, this was the first national military cemetery on the West Coast. Today, there are 30,000 soldiers buried here on nearly thirty acres. About 200 feet after you pass the last of the gravestones, take a turnoff to your right for the Presidio Promenade marked with one white pole. You'll stay on this tree-lined path (Patten Road) for 0.2 mile until you reach McDowell Avenue. As you cross the road, you'll pass the former cavalry stables.

STABLES AND STORAGE

The five brick buildings of the cavalry stables were built in 1914 and can house up to 102 horses each. After the Ninth Cavalry left the area, the buildings were used as a K-9 Corps facility and veterinary hospital. Today, one stable still houses US Park Police horses.

Another building in the complex contains the Park Archives and Records Center, a storehouse for nearly five million documents, photos, oral histories, and maps related to the history of the Golden Gate National Recreation Area from the Spanish period to today. The archives are open to the public Mondays and Thursdays.

After you pass the last of the stables, walk over a foot-bridge and under three overpasses (Veterans Boulevard and both directions of US 101). After about 250 feet, reach the Crissy Field Overlook, which gives you a great view of the field, the bay, and downtown San Francisco. Pass Long Avenue on your right in 0.2 mile, where you get your first clear shot of the bridge. Continue on the paved path, and after 0.2 mile, after passing a parking lot on your left, take the gravel hikers-only Battery East Trail through a low-clearance tunnel (get ready to duck!) to the Golden Gate Bridge. (Or, stay left to take the accessible path to the bridge.)

Walk across the bridge or turn around to return to the start. The nearest MUNI stop is at the Golden Gate Bridge parking lot.

GO FARTHER

For a different return trip (which adds about 0.2 mile), head back the way you came for 0.3 mile, and then turn left onto the Battery East Trail toward Crissy Field. The trail ends at the bottom of a long stairway, where you turn right to follow the Bay Trail (Golden Gate Promenade) to Crissy Field Marsh and Yacht Road (another 1.4 miles). Turn right onto Yacht Road to walk to the Palace of Fine Arts, and beyond that, pick up Lyon Street and continue to your start at Lombard Street. From the start, you're just a few blocks away from the Marina District's shopping and dining corridor on Chestnut Street.

24 Goldsworthy Gallery Tour

DISTANCE:	4 miles
ELEVATION GAIN:	620 feet
HIGH POINT:	350 feet
DIFFICULTY:	Moderate
TIME:	1 hour 45 minutes
FITNESS:	Walkers, hikers, runners
FAMILY FRIENDLY:	Children will love Goldsworthy's large-scale art; hike may have too much elevation gain for young children
DOG FRIENDLY:	On leash

AMENITIES: Restrooms in the Presidio Officers' Club, at the San
Francisco National Cemetery, at El Polín Spring, and
Julius Kahn Playground; benches at the National
Cemetery Overlook and Inspiration Point; picnic
area at El Polín Spring

CONTACT: Presidio Trust; Golden Gate National Recreation Area

GPS: 37° 47' 34.1124" N 122° 26' 47.1696" W

MAP TO: Lyon St. and Broadway, San Francisco

GETTING THERE

Public Transit: MUNI bus 3 to Jackson and Baker streets;
MUNI bus 43 to Presidio Ave. and Jackson St. **Parking:** Free
three-hour parking spots near the hike start.

This route is designed as a gallery tour for Andy Goldsworthy's
artwork in the Presidio. Goldsworthy crafts his varied works
out of natural materials, such as leaves, mud, trees, stone, and
even ice. Often his art is ephemeral: some works wash away

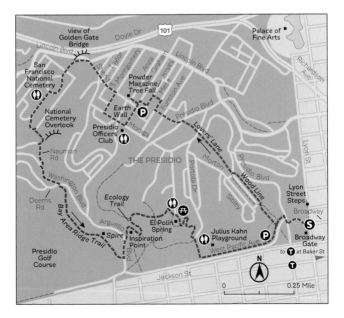

with the tide and others melt in the sun. Goldsworthy first visited the Presidio in 2006, and between 2008 and 2014, he created four works: *Spire*, *Wood Line*, *Tree Fall*, and *Earth Wall*.

If you want to visit all four, you'll need to time your hike accordingly. The Presidio Officers' Club and *Earth Wall* are closed on Mondays. *Tree Fall* is open Saturday and Sunday from 10:00 AM to 4:00 PM and by appointment Tuesday through Friday. Call (415) 561-5300 to make an appointment.

GET MOVING

Start this hike at the intersection of Lyon Street and Broadway at the Presidio's Broadway Gate, which was built around 1897. Enter the Presidio through this sandstone gate, taking in views of the bay off to your right, and following a paved path to Presidio Boulevard. Cross the street, turn right, and cross West Pacific Avenue. Turn left to follow West Pacific and start looking right to see Andy Goldsworthy's 1200-foot-long serpentine sculpture, *Wood Line*, unfolding in the eucalyptus grove below. Walk the length of the sculpture and then head left to meet up with Lovers' Lane, a streetlight-lined sidewalk. Turn right (downhill) onto Lovers' Lane. In the late 1700s this path was part of the Old Mission Road, a route that connected Misión San Francisco de Asís (Mission Dolores) with the Presidio (see Hike 31). The path earned its current name in the late 1800s, when US soldiers used it to head into town to visit their sweethearts.

When you reach the signpost for Liggett Avenue, look left: if you're a Goldsworthy expert, you may be able to discern *Spire* from the other cypress trees in the distance. Continue on Lovers' Lane 0.3 mile until it dead-ends at Presidio Boulevard. Cross Presidio Boulevard and follow the road left into the Presidio's Main Post. In two blocks Presidio Boulevard dead-ends at Mesa Street. Cross Mesa and turn right. Take your first left onto a sidewalk between buildings. Turn left onto Keyes Avenue (unsigned), and turn right at the crosswalk

The National Cemetery Overlook provides a sublime, but somber view.

next to a parking lot. Follow the sidewalk along the parking lot and cross Graham Street at another crosswalk. Walk across a small lawn to reach a white cubical building with a red-tile roof at 0.9 mile. This is the Powder Magazine, which held army ammunition from the Civil War until 1994, when the Presidio became a national park. *Tree Fall* is inside, so go in and look at the artwork. One interpretation of this work is that you are underground looking up at a tree's roots.

Exit the Powder Magazine and head back to Graham Street where you turn right. When the road dead-ends at Moraga Avenue, cross Moraga and head slightly left into the main entrance of the Presidio Officers' Club. Turn right to enter the Moraga Room. Walk diagonally across the room, turn left, and locate *Earth Wall* in an outdoor courtyard to your right. This work was created out of eucalyptus branches and soil from the grounds of the Presidio Officers' Club. After Goldsworthy constructed the sphere you see before you, he covered it and the rest of the wall in a layer of rammed earth. He then chiseled out the sphere by hand.

After visiting *Earth Wall*, return to Moraga Avenue and turn left. Take your second right onto Montgomery Street and then your second left onto Sheridan Avenue. Continue for 0.2 mile and then turn left into the San Francisco National Cemetery. (For your safety, use the crosswalk at Lincoln Boulevard.) Walk through the cemetery and exit through the gate at the back left corner. From the gate, walk to a landing with benches, the National Cemetery Overlook. Sit on the benches and enjoy a stunning view of the Golden Gate Bridge. When you're done with the views, walk to a paved path and turn left. Follow this path to reach Nauman Road (unsigned), a street with former military homes from the 1940s. At the end of the road, turn left onto Washington Boulevard. After 0.1 mile, cross Washington Boulevard at Deems Road and then turn left onto the Bay Area Ridge Trail. When a trail crosses both sides of your path after 0.1 mile, stay straight. After another 0.1 mile, follow a trail marker left to meet up with *Spire* at 2.6 miles. *Spire* is almost one hundred feet tall and is fifteen feet in diameter at its base. Made from thirty-seven Monterey cypress trees, the sculpture references the Transamerica Pyramid and church spires.

Return to the Bay Area Ridge Trail and follow it to Arguello Boulevard. Cross Arguello and turn left onto a sidewalk. You soon reach Inspiration Point on your right. Take in the views of the bay, the Palace of Fine Arts, and Alcatraz, and then look for a stairway in the parking lot that leads to the start of the Ecology Trail. At the bottom of the stairs, turn left to pick up the Ecology Trail. After 0.1 mile, when a trail intersects your path, follow the Ecology Trail right and into the woods at a sign for El Polín Spring. You are now in the Presidio's largest redwood grove. Stay on the Ecology Trail for 0.1 mile, cross another path, and stay straight to continue on the Ecology Trail to reach a stairway.

A closeup of Andy Goldsworthy's Earth Wall

Turn right at the bottom of the stairway to visit El Polín Spring at 3.2 miles. This source of fresh groundwater was used by generations of Ohlone people as well as by Spanish, Mexican, and US soldiers. Using either side of the path, walk to the back of the spring and toward a large weeping willow. Take the Connector Trail from the back of the spring to a parking lot. Follow the trail right to walk around the periphery of the lot. Then, head toward Julius Kahn Playground and walk through the playground. Just before West Pacific Avenue, turn left onto a paved path, which soon turns into dirt.

Walk 0.3 mile until you reach a small parking area at West Pacific Avenue. Turn left, pass Lovers' Lane and above *Wood Line*, then cross West Pacific Avenue and then Presidio Boulevard to return to the start.

GO FARTHER
Check out the epic Lyon Street Steps between Broadway and Green streets or visit Billionaire's Row on Broadway between Lyon and Divisadero streets.

25 Presidio Coastal Trail

DISTANCE:	3.1 miles
ELEVATION GAIN:	370 feet
HIGH POINT:	280 feet
DIFFICULTY:	Moderate
TIME:	1 hour 30 minutes
FITNESS:	Walkers, hikers, runners
FAMILY FRIENDLY:	Uphill for half the hike, but easy and downhill on the way back
DOG FRIENDLY:	On leash on the Coastal Trail; off-leash on Baker Beach north of Lobos Creek; prohibited on the Batteries to Bluffs Trail
AMENITIES:	Porta potties at Gibson Road lot; restroom in Battery Chamberlin lot and at Bridge Welcome Center
CONTACT:	Presidio Trust; California Coastal Trail; Golden Gate National Recreation Area
GPS:	37° 47' 32.4924" N 122° 28' 59.7648" W
MAP TO:	Baker Beach parking lot, San Francisco

GETTING THERE
Public Transit: MUNI bus 1 to California St. and 25th Ave.; MUNI bus 29 to Lincoln Blvd. and Bowley St. **Parking:** Free parking on 25th Ave.; two parking lots at Baker Beach on Gibson Rd. and at the end of Battery Chamberlin Rd.

This segment of the California Coastal Trail—which will one day cover 1200 miles of coastline trails—takes you from Baker Beach to the Golden Gate Bridge. On any given day on Baker Beach, you'll find walkers, dog owners and their pets, photographers, and anglers enjoying the ocean air and atmosphere.

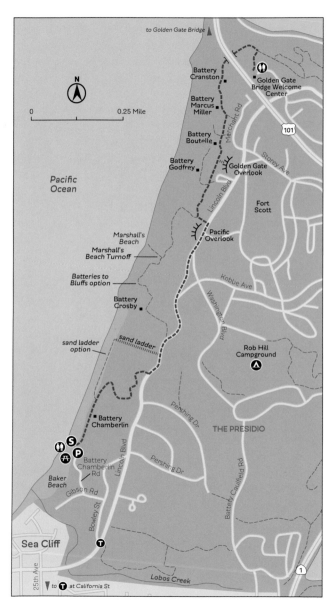

The Burning Man arts festival started here in 1986, and the area still expresses its free-spirited side on clothing-optional north Baker Beach. The beach has sensational views of the Golden Gate Bridge, Lands End, and the Marin Headlands.

Just inland from Baker Beach is Battery Chamberlin. This 1904 gun battery holds the last six-inch "disappearing gun" of its type on the West Coast. The gun doesn't actually disappear but instead swings down to be out of sight. There are monthly public demonstrations of the gun between 11:00 AM and 3:00 PM on the first Saturday and Sunday of the month.

Moving away from the beach and the battery, you walk along busy Lincoln Boulevard and visit four more batteries—Battery Godfrey, Battery Boutelle, Battery Marcus Miller, and Battery Cranston—before you reach the Golden Gate Bridge.

Baker Beach offers superb views of the Golden Gate Bridge.

GET MOVING

From the parking lot at the end of Battery Chamberlin Road, walk to the north end of the lot and through a gate with a sign for Battery Chamberlin. After you've visited the battery, there are two ways to reach Lincoln Boulevard: Go right and uphill on a sandy path for 0.3 mile, or go left to the beach, walk 0.2 mile, and take the sand ladder (a sandy stairway) on your right. While I've never counted, some say there are 200 to 300 stairs. Whichever path you choose, turn left when you reach Lincoln Boulevard.

Option: On Lincoln Boulevard, you will soon see a trailhead for the Batteries to Bluffs Trail (see Hike 3). This short, but stair-filled trail, an option that adds a little more than 0.2 mile, brings you closer to the ocean and provides great views of the Golden Gate Bridge. The end of this trail reconnects with the Presidio Coastal Trail.

Reach the Pacific Overlook at 0.9 mile (0.8 mile if you took the sand ladder). About 200 feet past the overlook, turn left at a sign for the Batteries to Bluffs Trail. Before you reach the Batteries to Bluffs steps on your left, turn right onto an unsigned trail after the fence on your right ends. Continue on this trail until you see Battery Godfrey, which was named in honor of Capt. George J. Godfrey of the Twenty-Second Infantry, who was killed in action in the Philippines in 1899. Completed in 1895, Battery Godfrey remained armed until 1943. (Learn more about coastal gun batteries in Hike 3.) As you walk past the battery, stairs on your right lead to a detour to the Golden Gate Overlook.

Follow the trail downhill to Battery Boutelle, named for Lt. Henry M. Boutelle, who was killed in battle in the Philippines in 1899. The battery was completed in 1900 and disarmed in 1917. Before you reach a metal footbridge above your current path, follow a sign for the Golden Gate Bridge (just 0.2 mile away) up a flight of stairs on a third battery, Battery Marcus Miller, constructed in 1891, closed in 1920, and named for

Baker Beach's Battery Chamberlin is one of many batteries on the Presidio Coastal Trail.

Brigadier General Marcus Miller, commanding officer of the Presidio in 1898. At the top of the battery, turn right for sweeping views of the Golden Gate Bridge. Pass one last battery, Battery Cranston, which was built in 1897 and closed in 1943. It was named for Lt. Arthur Cranston, Fourth Artillery, who had been stationed at the Presidio and was killed during the Modoc War in 1873.

As you near the bridge, the path narrows to make room for bike lanes on your right. Pass under the bridge and then take a crosswalk to turn right onto the pedestrian path that takes you to the bridge. Return the way you came.

GO FARTHER

From here, you can visit the Golden Gate Bridge. Or, to change up your return trip, take the Batteries to Bluffs Trail option (if you didn't before). And on your way back to Baker

Beach, return via the sand ladder or the dirt path to Battery Chamberlin, whichever you didn't take before. If you're interested in hiking the full California Coastal Trail in San Francisco, you can combine this hike with Fort Funston to the Cliff House (Hike 1) and the Lands End Trail (Hike 2).

26 Presidio Bay Area Ridge Trail

DISTANCE:	5.2 miles
ELEVATION GAIN:	390 feet
HIGH POINT:	385 feet
DIFFICULTY:	Moderate
TIME:	1 hour 40 minutes
FITNESS:	Walkers, hikers, runners
FAMILY FRIENDLY:	Families may want to do this as a one-way route and take a taxi or ridesharing service back to the start
DOG FRIENDLY:	On leash
AMENITIES:	Restrooms near Bridge Welcome Center; picnic area and restrooms at Rob Hill Campground
CONTACT:	Bay Area Ridge Trail; Presidio Trust; Golden Gate National Recreation Area
GPS:	37° 47' 22.7076" N 122° 27' 34.0956" W
MAP TO:	Jackson St. and Arguello Blvd., San Francisco

GETTING THERE

Public Transit: MUNI bus 1, 1BX, or 33 to Arguello Blvd. and California St. (you will have to climb five steep blocks to get to the hike start). **Parking:** Free street parking near the hike start.

On this hike, you're on a portion of the Bay Area Ridge Trail, which will one day trace a 550-mile loop along the ridgeline above the bay. My favorite aspects of the Presidio are history, art, and nature—and this route features all three. Get your dose of military history at the National Cemetery Overlook and Rob Hill Campground, a former army lookout station and the only overnight campground in San Francisco. Take in large-scale art at Andy Goldsworthy's *Spire*, a hundred-foot-tall sculpture made of cypress trees. And stroll through two stretches of eucalyptus and cypress forest—with almost no trace of the city around you.

GET MOVING

Start your hike at the Presidio's Arguello Gate, just north of the intersection of Arguello Boulevard and Jackson Street. As you pass the gate, look for a paved path on your right, and follow it to a crosswalk at West Pacific Avenue. Cross here and head left to pick up the Bay Area Ridge Trail. Then continue to a crosswalk on your left at Arguello Boulevard. Cross Arguello and pick up the dirt trail to the right of the Presidio Golf Course parking lot. After 0.1 mile, you reach Andy Goldsworthy's *Spire* on your right. (Read about *Spire* in Hike 24, Goldsworthy Gallery Tour.)

After checking out *Spire*, return to the Bay Area Ridge Trail, and at your next junction, turn right onto a beautiful stretch of trail with cypress trees on your right and eucalyptus trees (and the golf course) on your left. After 0.1 mile, ignore the path that branches off to your right, and start looking for views of Alcatraz and the Palace of Fine Arts to your right. At 0.5 mile total, reach Deems Road, take the crosswalk at Washington Boulevard, turn left, and walk alongside the road. Take your first right onto Nauman Road, a street with 1940s military homes.

Continue on a gravel path as it bears right into the woods. And when your path forks, head right to take a short 0.15-mile detour to the San Francisco National Cemetery Overlook. Besides the view of the Golden Gate Bridge and some of the cemetery's graves, the viewpoint also features a stone wall imprinted with stanzas of Archibald MacLeish's poem, "The Young Dead Soldiers."

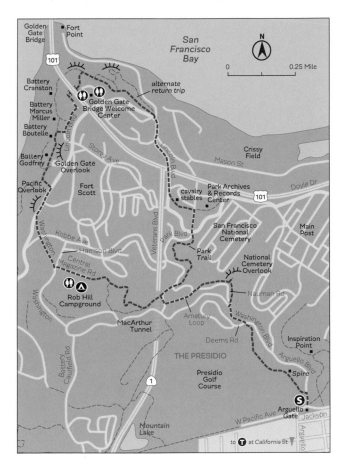

From the overlook, head back to where you just were and turn right, following a sign for Immigrant Point and the Golden Gate Bridge. After 0.2 mile, reach a road, Amatury Loop (unsigned), and turn left. At the end of Amatury, cross Park Boulevard to continue on the trail. After 0.1 mile head right on the pedestrian-only section of the trail. You are now

A misty morning hike on the Bay Area Ridge Trail

in a tall forest of eucalyptus and cypress trees; this is my favorite part of the hike. When the bike path merges with your path from the left, continue as the trail reaches Central Magazine Road (unsigned) at 1.5 miles. This is the parking area for Rob Hill Campground. Continue along the road and head left to explore the campground or stay straight to reach Washington Boulevard, where you'll take a wide right to remain on Washington (not your closest right onto Harrison Boulevard).

Continuing on Washington Boulevard, pass Kobbe Avenue and reach Lincoln Boulevard after 0.2 mile. Cross Lincoln Boulevard, turn right, and reach the Pacific Overlook at 1.9 miles. About 200 feet past the overlook, turn left at a sign for the Batteries to Bluffs Trail. Before you reach the Batteries to Bluffs steps on your left, turn right onto an unsigned trail after the fence on your right ends.

Continue on this trail until you see the first battery on this stretch, Battery Godfrey. As you walk past the battery, stairs on your right lead to a detour to the Golden Gate Overlook.

THE CITY'S ONLY
OVERNIGHT CAMPGROUND

At an elevation of 384 feet, Rob Hill Campground is perched atop the highest point in the Presidio. In 1852 US Army engineers planned a small fort on the hill, called a "redoubt." Instead of building the fort, they built a lookout station to watch incoming ships and called it "Telegraph Hill" (not to be confused with Coit Tower's Telegraph Hill). "Rob Hill" is an amalgam of these two names: "Redoubt" and "Telegraph Hill."

After World War II, when most of the Presidio was closed to civilians, the army turned Rob Hill into a Boy Scout camp. Today, the site is open to the public and is the only overnight campground in San Francisco.

Follow the trail downhill to Battery Boutelle. Before you reach a metal footbridge above your path, follow a sign for the Golden Gate Bridge (just 0.2 mile away) up a flight of stairs on a third battery, Battery Marcus Miller. At the top of the battery, turn right for sweeping views of the Golden Gate Bridge. Pass one last battery, Battery Cranston, on your route to the bridge. (Read more about coastal gun batteries in Hike 3, Batteries to Bluffs, and read more about Batteries Godfrey, Boutelle, Marcus Miller, and Cranston in Hike 25, Presidio Coastal Trail.)

As you near the bridge, the path narrows to make room for bike lanes on your right. Pass under the bridge and then take a crosswalk to turn right onto the pedestrian path that takes you to the bridge. Return the way you came.

GO FARTHER

To turn your hike into a loop, combine the Presidio Promenade (Hike 23) and the Park Trail (Hike 20). When you reach the intersection of Park Boulevard and Amatury Loop, connect to the Bay Area Ridge Trail to return to the start.

27 Presidio Anza Trail

DISTANCE:	5.3 miles
ELEVATION GAIN:	440 feet
HIGH POINT:	360 feet
DIFFICULTY:	Moderate
TIME:	1 hour 45 minutes
FITNESS:	Walkers, hikers, runners
FAMILY FRIENDLY:	Ample places to rest and a playground at Mountain Lake Park; may be too long for young children
DOG FRIENDLY:	On leash
AMENITIES:	Restrooms at Mountain Lake Park, Rob Hill Campground, and near Bridge Welcome Center
. CONTACT:	Juan Bautista de Anza National Historic Trail; Presidio Trust; Golden Gate National Recreation Area
GPS:	37° 47' 11.1696" N 122° 28' 20.4852" W
MAP TO:	Lake St. and Funston Ave., San Francisco

GETTING THERE

Public Transit: MUNI bus 44 to 12th and California streets; MUNI bus 1, 1AX, or 28 to California St. and Park Presidio Blvd.; MUNI bus 2 to Clement St. and 14th Ave.; MUNI buses 38, 38R, and 38BX to Geary and Park Presidio boulevards. **Parking:** Free two-hour street parking is available near the hike start.

Juan Bautista de Anza was born in 1736—most likely in Cuquiarachi, Sonora, New Spain (now Mexico), but possibly in the presidio of Fronteras. He joined the army in 1751, and in 1773, he asked the viceroy for permission to explore Alta California, a vast area that included present-day California, Arizona, Nevada, Utah, New Mexico, western Colorado, and southwestern Wyoming. One year later, he led a small expedition to Mission San Gabriel (near Los Angeles), with a side trip to the Presidio of Monte Rey (now Monterey). Based on the success of that journey, the viceroy asked him to help establish a colony in what is now San Francisco. He took off in

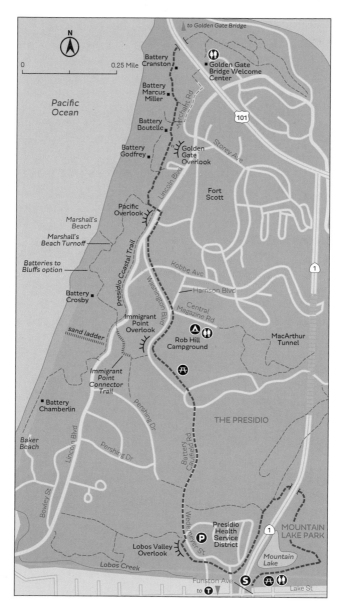

October 1775 with a caravan of 240 people. In March 1776, the weary crew stopped in Monterey, while Anza and a few others continued north, reaching the Golden Gate on March 27.

This hike follows the last stretch of Anza's journey in San Francisco from Mountain Lake to the Golden Gate. Aside from one moderate climb, this route is easy. Hikers can stop for picnics and enjoy three overlooks—Immigrant Point Overlook, the Pacific Overlook, and the Golden Gate Overlook. Anza's second expedition has been turned into the 1200-mile Juan Bautista de Anza National Historic Trail. To learn more, visit the Juan Bautista de Anza National Historic Trail section of the National Park Service's website. You can also visit the website of the Juan Bautista de Anza National Historic Trail.

GET MOVING

Start on Lake Street on a paved path sandwiched between Funston Avenue and Veterans Boulevard (Highway 1). Follow the path to the south shore of Mountain Lake, and turn right. When the path splits at 0.25 mile, stay left to follow the trail along Mountain Lake.

Follow the path along the lake for 0.3 mile, pass under Veterans Boulevard (Highway 1), and reach a T in the trail marked with white poles. Turn left and continue for 0.2 mile. After a short stint above and along the highway, pass a trail

IMPRESSIONS OF MOUNTAIN LAKE

Among those on Anza's trip to San Francisco was Father Pedro Font, who kept a detailed diary of the journey. Upon reaching Mountain Lake, he wrote: "This place and its vicinity has abundant pasturage, plenty of firewood, and fine water. Here and near the lake there are yerba buena and so many lilies that I almost had them inside my tent."

REMEMBERING OUR IMMIGRANTS

The Immigrant Point Overlook was created to celebrate our country's immigrants. At the site's dedication in May 2005, twenty-three foreign nationals from eighteen countries took the Oath of Allegiance to the United States of America. The overlook was made possible with a $1 million gift from Hungarian immigrant George Sarlo.

on the right with white poles. Turn right at the next paved path with a trail marker for the Park Trail and the Anza Trail (the trails overlap briefly here). Follow signs for the Anza Trail along Wedemeyer Street and around the Presidio Health Service District. In another 0.3 mile, a parking lot is on your right, Lobos Valley Overlook is to the left, and the former US Marine Hospital (Public Health Service Hospital) is ahead and to the right. (Read more about the overlook and hospital in Hike 22, Lobos Creek Valley Trail.)

The path drops you on Wedemeyer Street, where you cross and then turn left. After 0.1 mile the sidewalk ends, so cross back to the other side of the street, now Battery Caulfield Road. Continue uphill on Battery Caulfield Road for 0.3 mile to Washington Boulevard, where you'll cross the street and turn left to pick up a dirt trail. Walk by former military homes and continue past three picnic areas on your right as you approach Immigrant Point Overlook at 1.6 miles. You'll know you're at Immigrant Point Overlook when you reach a crosswalk across Washington Boulevard.

You soon reach a gravel trail on your right with a trail marker for Rob Hill Campground, the only overnight campground in San Francisco (see Hike 26, Presidio Bay Area Ridge Trail). Visit the campground or stay on Washington Boulevard for 0.4 mile, passing Central Magazine Road and Harrison Boulevard, and later Kobbe Avenue. When you arrive at Lincoln Boulevard, cross the street and turn right.

Eucalyptus leaves on a walkway on the Presidio Anza Trail

Reach the Pacific Overlook at 2 miles, and about 200 feet past the overlook, turn left at a sign for the Batteries to Bluffs Trail. Before you reach the Batteries to Bluffs steps on your left, turn right onto an unsigned trail after the fence on your right ends.

Continue on this trail until you see the first battery on this stretch, Battery Godfrey. As you walk past the battery, stairs on your right lead to a detour to the Golden Gate Overlook. Follow the trail downhill to Battery Boutelle. Before you reach a metal footbridge above your path, follow a sign for the Golden Gate Bridge (just 0.2 mile away) up a flight of stairs on a third battery, Battery Marcus Miller. At the top of the battery, turn right for sweeping views of the Golden Gate Bridge. Pass one last battery, Battery Cranston, on your way to the bridge. (Read more about coastal gun batteries in Hike 3, Batteries to Bluffs, and read more about Batteries Godfrey, Boutelle, Marcus Miller, and Cranston in Hike 25, Presidio Coastal Trail.)

As you near the bridge, the path narrows to make room for bike lanes on your right. Pass under the bridge and then take a crosswalk to turn right onto the pedestrian path that takes you to the bridge. Return the way you came.

A MOVING VIEW

Below the bridge, somewhere near Fort Point, Juan Bautista de Anza erected a cross to mark the site of the new Presidio. In his diary, Father Font wrote: "From this tableland, one enjoys a most delicious view; for from there one observes a good part of the bay and its islands as far as the other side, and one has a view of the ocean as far as the Farallones . . . so far as I have traveled, I have seen very good places and beautiful lands, I have yet seen none that pleased me so much as this. I do believe that, if we could be well populated, as in Europe, there would be nothing more pretty in the world."

GO FARTHER
You can vary your roundtrip (and add just 0.2 mile) by taking the Batteries to Bluffs Trail (Hike 3) or a portion of the Presidio Coastal Trail (see Hike 25). Either way, after about a mile, and just south of the Batteries to Bluffs southern trailhead, cross Lincoln Boulevard and take the Immigrant Point Connector Trail (a stairway) back to the Anza Trail.

Next page: Hikers enjoy San Francisco skyline
views on Angel Island's North Ridge Trail.

ISLAND HOPPING

In addition to San Francisco's mainland, the city owns (at least partially) a number of islands in the San Francisco Bay: Angel, Alcatraz, Treasure, and Yerba Buena.

Angel Island, the "Ellis Island of the West," has 13 miles of trails, camping, and a peak you can climb: Mount Livermore. The Agave Trail on Alcatraz Island is a short, but seasonal hiking trail packed with views that many overlook on their visits to the island. Treasure and Yerba Buena islands don't have official hiking trails (yet), but they do have parks and bay-front walks. Both islands are undergoing transformations that, over the course of the next decade, will bring new housing, restaurants, retail activity, and parkland. (At this writing, Yerba Buena Island's roads and parks are closed to the public.)

28 Angel Island

DISTANCE:	5.1 miles
ELEVATION GAIN:	880 feet
HIGH POINT:	790 feet
DIFFICULTY:	Moderate
TIME:	2 hours 30 minutes
FITNESS:	Walkers, hikers
FAMILY FRIENDLY:	May be too strenuous for young children, but children may enjoy a tram tour
DOG FRIENDLY:	No
AMENITIES:	Restrooms near ferry terminal; restaurants and bike rental companies open seasonally; in fall and winter, bring a picnic lunch
CONTACT:	California Department of Parks and Recreation
GPS:	37° 52' 6.5460" N 122° 26' 4.3332" W
MAP TO:	Angel Island State Park

GETTING THERE

Public Transit: *For the Pier 41 ferry:* MUNI F train to the Embarcadero and Stockton St.; MUNI bus 47 to the intersection of Powell and Beach streets; MUNI buses 8, 8X, and 39 to Powell and Bay streets. *For Angel Island:* The Blue and Gold Fleet takes you from Pier 41 to Angel Island. (If you're traveling from Tiburon, take the Angel Island Tiburon Ferry.) Schedules vary seasonally. Tideline Water Taxi provides on-demand service year-round. Reservations are suggested.
Parking: Parking near the ferry can be difficult. Pier 39, at 2350 Stockton St., offers a paid lot that's open twenty-four hours a day, seven days a week.

At 740 acres, Angel Island is the second-largest island in the bay after Alameda Island. While most of the island lies in Tiburon, Fort McDowell, on the eastern side of the island, is owned by the City and County of San Francisco. Angel Island is a perfect place to take in views of the Bay Area. On a clear

Ayala Cove and Tiburon from Angel Island

day, you can see as far as Napa and Sonoma counties to the north and San Jose to the south.

The former military base has 13 miles of trails and a lot of military history. This particular hike explores the North Ridge and Sunset trails that often remain empty even when throngs of visitors head to the island in the summer. For most of the year, there is only one boat you can take to the island in the morning, so I start my hikes early and then have a picnic lunch at the summit of Mount Livermore (788 feet). Mount Livermore is named after Caroline Livermore, the conservationist who led the campaign to create Angel Island State Park.

GET MOVING

From the ferry terminal, walk past the information booth and to your left to reach the North Ridge trailhead. After a short, but steep 0.1-mile climb, reach a picnic bench and the start

, a long flight of stairs. Climb more than one hundred stairs to reach the paved Perimeter Road. Catch your breath in the shade of some eucalyptus trees, knowing that the hardest part of the hike is over.

Cross the Perimeter Road and look right to locate the North Ridge Trail. For the next 1.7 miles, the trail winds gently uphill to the north and then to the center of the island, taking you through sun-drenched sections littered with chaparral as well as fern- and moss-covered areas lined with coast live oak. At 0.9 mile turn left on the Fire Road and take a right to continue on the North Ridge Trail toward Mount Livermore.

At 1.8 miles, reach a junction with the Sunset Trail and get your first downtown views of San Francisco. Turn right on a spur trail to reach Mount Livermore. At 2 miles you will start seeing picnic benches along the trail (if these are full, there are more beyond the summit), and at 2.1 miles, you reach the summit of Mount Livermore. From here, you're rewarded with views of San Francisco, the Golden Gate Bridge, Tiburon, Mount Tamalpais, Mount Diablo, Treasure Island, the Bay Bridge, and more.

A LITTLE OFF THE TOP

In the 1950s, dirt from Mount Livermore's summit was removed—actually not fully removed, just pushed aside—to make way for a Nike missile site. In 2002 the dirt was pushed (approximately) back into place and the summit was repaired—making Mount Livermore 788 feet tall, 16 feet taller than before.

Return the way you came to reach the junction with the Sunset Trail at 2.4 miles, and turn right. In 0.1 mile bear left at the paved Fire Road (Ida Trail, unsigned), and then immediately turn right to stay on the Sunset Trail. For the next 0.2 mile, you will be on exposed trails that give you unobstructed

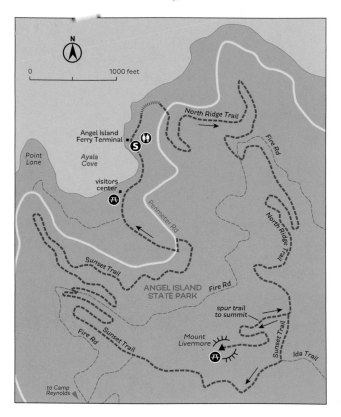

views of the Golden Gate Bridge. Along some of the grassy hills on the south side of the island, you will see charred trees, a reminder of the fire that burned one-third of the island in October 2008. As the trail wraps around the west side of the island, glimpse down at Camp Reynolds. Built during the Civil War, more than 2000 soldiers were stationed here by 1876.

At 3.2 miles, head back into the tree cover, and at 3.6 miles, take a right at a junction with the Fire Road and then a quick left. Follow the narrow trail (unsigned, but still the Sunset Trail) along a few long switchbacks through the woods

Stunning views of Alcatraz and the San Francisco skyline from Angel Island

THE ELLIS ISLAND OF THE WEST

The Coast Miwok were the first inhabitants of Angel Island and used the area as a seasonal hunting and fishing site. In August 1775, Lt. Juan Manuel de Ayala, a Spanish naval officer, anchored in today's Ayala Cove and spent a month mapping out the bay. He named the island for the Catholic feast day closest to his discovery. The feast day of Our Lady of the Angels of Portiuncula was shortened to Isla de Los Angeles, or Angel Island.

Camp Reynolds was built in 1863 to protect the island from a Confederate attack, and in 1899 Fort McDowell was built to house troops affected by contagious diseases. In 1905 the Angel Island Immigration Station was built, and Angel Island became known as the Ellis Island of the West. Between 1910 and 1940, the island welcomed a half million immigrants from eighty countries, including many people from China and Japan. During World War II, Fort McDowell was used as a port of embarkation for more than 300,000 soldiers, and the old immigration barracks housed prisoners of war before they were sent to inland camps. Fort McDowell was closed in August 1946, and the island was declared surplus by the War Department. The entire island, except for the Coast Guard facility on Point Blunt, was turned over to California in 1962 for use as a state park.

for 1.2 miles until you reach the Perimeter Road. Cross the road to continue on another paved road in front of you and to the left of the bike route. Follow the road downhill for 0.2 mile to the visitor center and the Ayala Cove area. With the water in front of you, turn right onto a paved path and continue a final 0.1 mile to your start.

GO FARTHER

Explore the island on foot or by bike on the Perimeter Road. Bikes are available seasonally on the island, so depending on the time of year, you may want to bring your own or rent one in San Francisco. On your tour, visit any number of historical sites, including Camp Reynolds, Fort McDowell, the US Immigration Station, and batteries Ledyard, Drew, and Wallace.

---

29 Wine Tasting on Treasure Island

DISTANCE:	3 miles
ELEVATION GAIN:	None
DIFFICULTY:	Easy
TIME:	1 hour 15 minutes
FITNESS:	Walkers, hikers, runners, bikers
FAMILY FRIENDLY:	Yes, flattest hike in this book
DOG FRIENDLY:	On leash, dogs welcome at most wineries
AMENITIES:	Restrooms in wineries; benches along waterfront
CONTACT:	Treasure Island Development Authority
GPS:	37° 48' 57.9384'' N 122° 22' 16.4172'' W
MAP TO:	1 Clipper Cove Way

GETTING THERE

Public Transit: MUNI bus 25 to Treasure Island Rd. (Guard Station). **Parking:** There are plentiful free parking spots along Avenue A between 5th and 9th streets.

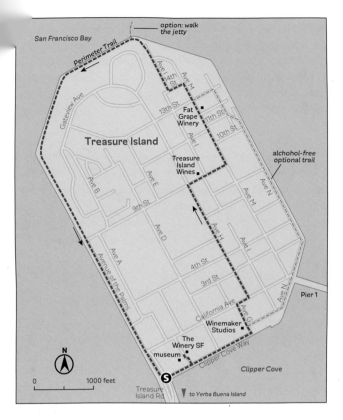

Treasure Island has an eerie postapocalyptic quality, which I find nothing short of fascinating. For every urban winery on the island, there are ten abandoned buildings. For every view of the San Francisco skyline, there is a barbed-wire fence surrounding a street of condemned buildings. The island feels empty: no cars in the parking lots, no people on the streets. The upside of all this? You'll feel like you have the whole place to yourself. Maybe you're the first person to discover the next best thing about San Francisco.

This route is designed to be done as an urban hike with wine tastings. Most wineries are open on weekends or by appointment only during the week, so take that into consideration when planning your visit. And, if you're not into wine, there's an alcohol-free hiking option too. Another fun way to do this route is to visit Treasure Island on two wheels. You can't ride your bike to the island, so you'll have to transport yours in a car or rent one there.

GET MOVING

Start your hike at the intersection of Clipper Cove Way and the causeway that leads from Yerba Buena Island to Treasure Island. Walk a block east on Clipper Cove Way to a large warehouse (a former naval hangar). This is The Winery SF. Continue straight on Clipper Cove Way, through a line of barrels, and then turn left to visit the winery. (The entrance is up a flight of stairs on the side of the building with "The Winery" painted on it in large letters.) The Winery SF produces all of its wine on-site in its 20,000-square-foot space.

After your tasting, head back to Clipper Cove Way. Walk past a second hangar, and turn left onto Avenue G (unsigned) after a barrel-lined bocce court. Here you can visit Winemaker Studios, a collection of four urban wineries: Howell Mountain Vineyards, Sol Rouge, Sottomarino, and VIE.

ALCOHOL-FREE HIKING

If you want to skip the wineries, take this palm-lined, waterfront alternative with stunning views of the bay, the Bay Bridge, and the East Bay. It adds about 0.1 mile to your hike. Stay on Clipper Cove Way until it becomes Avenue N. Follow Avenue N for 0.75 mile until you reach 13th Street. Take a left on 13th Street and then rejoin the route at the intersection of 13th Street and Avenue M.

In Clipper Cove, a sailboat's mast mimics the new tower of the Bay Bridge.

With the wineries at your left and a third hangar on your right, head to California Avenue. Take a right on California, and then your next left onto Avenue H, which you'll follow for 0.4 mile until you reach 9th Street.

Turn right on 9th Street and reach Treasure Island Wines at the corner of 9th Street and Avenue I. This was the first winery to open on the island in 2007. Today the company produces more than forty different wines on-site. Continue east on 9th Street, turn left on Avenue M, and when you reach 13th Street, visit Fat Grape Winery (entrance is on 13th Street). This family-owned operation is located in the former navy brig (jail) and specializes in sulfite-free wines. From 13th Street continue one block north on Avenue M to 14th Street. Turn left on 14th and right on Avenue I, an eerily abandoned block that dead-ends at a trail. When you reach the water, you can go right to walk along a rocky jetty (about 0.15-mile roundtrip) or turn left onto the Perimeter Trail for sensational views of the San Francisco skyline, the Golden Gate Bridge, Alcatraz, and Angel Island. Continue on the Perimeter Trail. After 1 mile the trail ends and becomes Avenue of the Palms. Continue another 0.3 mile on Avenue of the Palms to reach your start.

GO FARTHER

Visit the Treasure Island Museum to learn more about the island's history. If you've worked up an appetite, check out some of Treasure Island's restaurants. For a beachside picnic, head to Clipper Cove by walking along Treasure Island Road toward Yerba Buena Island. Partway along the causeway, take a left when you see signs for Clipper Cove.

AN ISLAND IN TRANSITION

Manmade Treasure Island was created with mud from the bay that was transported south from the Sacramento River Delta. Named for the gold that people thought might be hiding in its soil, it was supposed to become San Francisco's first airport, but in 1941, the navy traded Mills Field (now San Francisco International Airport) for Treasure Island. The island served as a naval base until 1996 when it was decommissioned and opened to the public. The navy is currently completing a radiological cleanup on the island (affected areas are well labeled), and when that's done, the navy will transfer the land to the Treasure Island Development Authority (TIDA), a nonprofit dedicated to the economic develop-ment of the island.

While Treasure Island is definitely a work in progress, it is now home to the annual Treasure Island Music Festival and a monthly food and antique fair, Treasure Island Flea. In the coming years, TIDA plans to create up to 8000 homes, 140,000 square feet of retail space, 100,000 square feet of office space, 3 hotels, and 300 acres of parks and open space. There may be gold in the soil after all.

30 Alcatraz Agave Trail

DISTANCE:	0.4 mile
ELEVATION GAIN:	75 feet
DIFFICULTY:	Easy
TIME:	15 minutes
FITNESS:	Walkers, hikers
FAMILY FRIENDLY:	Yes
DOG FRIENDLY:	No
AMENITIES:	Restrooms near ferry terminal and cellhouse; picnic area near dock; benches along trail
CONTACT:	Alcatraz Island, National Park Service; Golden Gate National Recreation Area
GPS:	37° 49' 35.2776" N 122° 25' 14.8872" W
MAP TO:	Alcatraz Island

GETTING THERE

Public Transit: *For the Pier 33 ferry:* MUNI F streetcar to the Embarcadero and Bay St. *For Alcatraz:* Alcatraz Cruises is the official ferry line for Alcatraz and departs from Pier 33. You can purchase tickets up to ninety days in advance. If tickets are sold out, you can show up at the ticket booth starting at 7:30 AM for day-of tickets (not a reliable option) or buy a package tour from a third-party provider (often significantly more expensive). *Note:* if you're not renting an audio guide while on the island, you can get a refund for a portion of your ticket from the supervisor at the cellhouse entrance; no refund option for the night tour. **Parking:** On-street parking in the Fisherman's Wharf area can be hard to find and expensive. Fifteen commercial lots are within five blocks of Pier 33 with more than 3000 spaces. The closest lot is one block from Pier 33 at Francisco and Kearny streets.

For Bay Area locals, it can be easy to overlook Alcatraz. I... something you already did or something you continue to put off for later. But when a friend or family member visits, you decide to venture into the bay. Before joining the throngs of people making a beeline for the prison, take a fifteen-minute break to walk the little-known Alcatraz Agave Trail. This lovely, manicured path meanders along the south side of the island. It features four species of agave plants and sensational views of San Francisco, the bay, and the Bay and Golden Gate bridges.

Plan your hike between October and February. Alcatraz's Parade Ground is one of the largest western gull nesting sites on the West Coast, and the trail is closed most of the year to protect nesting birds. Exact opening dates vary, so call before your visit to make sure the trail is open (see the appendix for contact information).

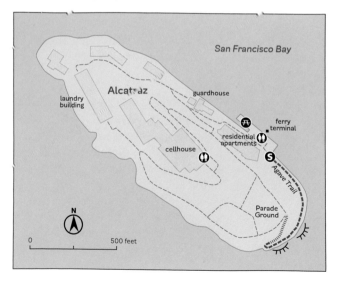

Skyline views abound on the short, but sweet Alcatraz Agave Trail.

GET MOVING

To find the trailhead, head left (opposite direction of the main sights) once you disembark from the ferry. You should quickly see the start of the wide dirt walkway that guides you along the water's edge to the south side of the island. Benches are along the trail for resting and contemplation, and tall agave stalks jut out alongside the trail. You'll have breathtaking views of the city minus the crowds, who will all have made a beeline for the prison. At the trail's western end, you'll overlook tide pools, and then climb 110 stone steps to the Parade Ground, a site used by the US military for drills and training in the 1960s. Return the way you came.

A LABOR OF LOVE

The agave plants on this island date back to the early twentieth century when Alcatraz was an active prison. Some say agave was planted to prevent erosion, others argue that the plants' spikes kept prisoners from escaping, and yet others claim that guards and their families planted agave to beautify the island since succulents can thrive in dry, rocky soil (and with little maintenance).

By the early 1990s, there was no pedestrian access to the plants that still lined the south edge of the island, but in 1994, the National Park Service renovated the area and built the Agave Trail. The creation of this trail was no small feat: materials were brought to the island on boats as large as football fields.

GO FARTHER

Turn your hike into a loop by continuing through the Parade Ground to visit the prison and listen to the cellhouse audio tour, narrated by former prisoners and guards. Then head downhill to reach the ferry terminal.

Next page: View of Twin Peaks Scenic Overlook and the Sutro Tower from Kite Hill

TALES OF
THE CITY

This section takes you on 10 hikes through San Francisco's diverse neighborhoods—taking advantage of any combination of the city's 670-plus stairways, 40-plus hills, and 70 miles of hiking trails. The first three routes in this chapter explore three periods of San Francisco's history. The Old Mission Road traces a walking and horse trail that dates back to the Spanish period of the late eighteenth century. The Barbary Coast Trail commemorates the raucous period between the gold rush and the 1906 earthquake when San Francisco was overrun with saloons, sailors, and prostitutes. And Bay to Breakers, once called the Cross City Race, remembers a race created to lift the spirits of San Francisco residents after the 1906 earthquake. Thousands run the course each May.

The next seven hikes venture into diverse neighborhoods from the Castro to Potrero Hill to the Sunset and more, with the goal of turning your walk into an adventure. On these routes, just some of the quirky sights you'll see are public slides, dirt roads, mosaic stairways, and gravestone-lined walkways. Many of these routes are reminiscent of those in *Stairway Walks in San Francisco* by Adah Bakalinsky and Mary Burk, but they are all of my own design. My goal with these hikes is to give you an exciting burst of novelty and to instill in you the belief that when it comes to San Francisco, there's always more to see.

31 Old Mission Road

DISTANCE:	4 miles one way
ELEVATION GAIN:	460 feet
HIGH POINT:	330 feet
DIFFICULTY:	Moderate
TIME:	2 hours
FITNESS:	Walkers, hikers, runners
FAMILY FRIENDLY:	Shorten the route by turning around at the end of Alamo Square Park (2.8 miles roundtrip)
DOG FRIENDLY:	On leash
AMENITIES:	Restrooms in Mission Dolores, Alamo Square, and the Presidio Officers' Club; benches and a playground in Duboce Park
CONTACT:	Mission Dolores; San Francisco Recreation and Park Department; Presidio Trust
GPS:	37° 45' 50.8644" N 122° 25' 35.1660" W
MAP TO:	Mission Dolores, San Francisco

GETTING THERE

Public Transit: MUNI bus 22 to 16th and Dolores streets; MUNI bus 33 to 18th and Dolores streets; MUNI bus 37 to 14th and Church streets; MUNI F streetcar to Market and Church streets; MUNI J train to 16th and Church streets; MUNI KT, L, and M trains to Church Street Station. **Parking:** Free street parking near the hike start, but most spaces are limited to two hours; some unrestricted spots near Dolores Park.

When the Spanish arrived in Yerba Buena (present-day San Francisco) in the late 1700s, they had two priorities: to establish a mission and to defend the area from outside attack. To these ends, they constructed Misión San Francisco de Asís (now Mission Dolores) and the Presidio. Connecting these two centers of activity—and connecting California's missions to one another—was the Old Mission Road, or El Camino Real. El Camino Real was known as the Royal Road

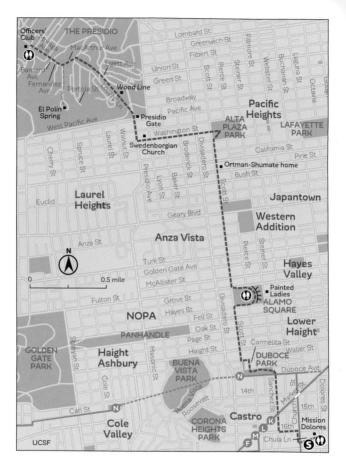

and the King's Highway. In Yerba Buena, it followed the natural contours of the land, running through the center of town and avoiding sand dunes to the west and marshy land to the east.

This section of the Old Mission Road starts at Mission Dolores and ends at the Presidio Officers' Club. In between, you'll visit Duboce Park, Alamo Square, Alta Plaza Park, and Lovers' Lane. Although you're walking through a modern city, remember that you also are following a path that has existed for nearly 250 years.

GET MOVING

Start your hike in front of Mission Dolores on Dolores Street between 16th Street and Chula Lane. You can enter the church to see its hand-carved wooden altar and a beautiful chevron pattern painted on the ceiling. Mission Dolores's cemetery is a final resting place for more than 5000 people including Native people, founders of the mission, and California pioneers.

MISIÓN SAN FRANCISCO DE ASÍS

Misión San Francisco de Asís was founded on June 29, 1776, making it the sixth of California's twenty-one missions. It was named for St. Francis of Assisi, the founder of the Franciscan Order. A temporary mission was likely built near present-day 14th and Dolores streets, and construction for the present church was started in 1788. It was dedicated in 1791, making it the oldest intact building in San Francisco. The church is known as Mission Dolores for a creek and lake that used to exist here called Arroyo de los Dolores (Creek of Sorrows) and Laguna de Nuestra Senora de los Dolores (Lake of our Lady of Sorrows). The creek and lake were named by the Spanish for the day they were discovered, Viernes de Dolores (Friday of Sorrows), the Friday before Palm Sunday.

Walk down Chula Lane, to the south of the church, and turn right on Church Street when Chula ends. Go left on 16th Street and right on Sanchez Street. Stay on Sanchez Street as you cross Market Street and continue to Duboce Avenue. Turn left and walk toward Duboce Park. Walk west through the park for 0.15 mile, take a right to exit on Carmelita Street. Then go left on Waller Street and right on Scott Street. Follow Scott for 0.3 mile to Alamo Square, entering the park at 1.3 miles.

A WATERING HOLE ALONG THE WAY

Alamo Square gets its name from a cottonwood tree that used to sit atop Alamo Hill. *Alamo* means poplar tree in Spanish, and during the Spanish period, the cottonwood marked the spot of a watering hole along the horseback trail from Mission Dolores to the Presidio.

Today, on the Steiner Street side of the park, you can visit the Painted Ladies, a row of well-maintained Victorian homes that were featured in the opening credits of the 1980s sitcom *Full House*. The houses are also called Postcard Row for the picture-perfect view they (and the skyline behind them) offer from Alamo Square.

After visiting the park, continue another mile on Scott Street, watching the neighborhoods transition from Alamo Square to Lower Pacific Heights to Pacific Heights. A number of houses on this street appear on the National Register of Historic Places. The houses at 1239–1245 Scott Street were built around 1882, 1249 was built in 1868, 1321 was built around 1885, and 1331–1335 were built around 1888. These houses were moved from their original locations in the 1970s when the San Francisco Redevelopment Agency razed much of Western Addition. At 1901 Scott Street (at Pine Street), you reach the Ortman-Shumate home, built by John Frederick Ortman in 1870. This house sits on a 19,000-square-foot lot, the equivalent of more than seven standard city lots.

At 2.6 miles arrive at Alta Plaza Park, which was a rock quarry until 1877. Today the park offers panoramic views and Pug Sunday once a month. Midway through the park on its west side, turn left on Washington Street. Continue on Washington, taking notice of the Swedenborgian Church, built in 1895, at the intersection of Washington and Lyon streets. Take a right on Presidio Avenue and continue past Pacific Avenue and through the Presidio Gate.

Just past the left side of the gate, pick up a paved path, Lovers' Lane. This section of the original Old Mission Road

A serene sunset from Alta Plaza Park

earned its name in the late 1800s when the Presidio was a US military post. Soldiers would frequently use Lovers' Lane to head into town to visit their sweethearts. Cross West Pacific Avenue and pick up the path on the other side, or take a detour to your right to visit *Wood Line*, a 1200-foot-long artwork by Andy Goldsworthy (see Hike 24, Goldsworthy Gallery Tour). You'll want to return to Lovers' Lane near Liggett Avenue and continue following it downhill until the next intersection, MacArthur Avenue. Turn left and stay on MacArthur past Portola Street, which branches off to the left. When you reach two crosswalks, bear right at the second one to pick up Fernandez Street at 4.1 miles, and climb a steep one-block hill.

Or from the intersection of MacArthur and Fernandez, take a 0.35-mile roundtrip detour to the left to visit El Polín Spring (see Hike 24). This is a prime area for bird-watching.

Fernandez Street ends at Barnard Avenue, which you'll cross and then climb a stairway that leads to Moraga Avenue.

Pass the Inn at the Presidio and continue 0.1 mile until you reach the Presidio Officers' Club. The Officers' Club is located on the site of the original Spanish Presidio (built in 1776). Many of the fort's buildings were destroyed during a storm in 1779 and were rebuilt only to be damaged again during earthquakes in 1808 and 1812. In the building's Mesa Room, you can see an exposed section of an adobe wall that dates back to the 1810s.

To return via public transit, walk to the Presidio Transit Center at the intersection of Lincoln Blvd. and Graham St.

GO FARTHER

From here, check out the Presidio Officers' Club's exhibits on San Francisco history, visit Andy Goldsworthy's *Earth Wall* (see Hike 24), or get a bite at one of the Main Post's restaurants.

32 Barbary Coast Trail

DISTANCE:	4.4 miles one way
ELEVATION GAIN:	250 feet
HIGH POINT:	170 feet
DIFFICULTY:	Easy
TIME:	2 hours
FITNESS:	Walkers, hikers
FAMILY FRIENDLY:	Parents of young children can shorten the hike by starting at Washington Square Park
DOG FRIENDLY:	On leash
AMENITIES:	Benches and restrooms in Union Square, Portsmouth Square, Washington Square Park, and Pier 39; restrooms in the Argonaut Hotel and the Maritime Museum
CONTACT:	San Francisco Museum and Historical Society; San Francisco Recreation and Park Department; National Park Service
GPS:	37° 46' 58.8252" N 122° 24' 25.1568" W
MAP TO:	5th St. and Mint Plz., San Francisco

GETTING THERE

Public Transit: BART; MUNI trains F, J, KT, L, M, and N; and MUNI buses 5, 5R, 6, 7, 7R, 7X, 9, 9R, 21, 31 to Market and 5th streets. MUNI buses 8, 8AX, 8BX, 14R, 14X, 27, 30, 38, and 45 also serve the area. If you're starting at Washington Square, take MUNI bus 30 to Columbus Ave. and Filbert St.; MUNI buses 8 and 45 to Union St. and Columbus Ave.; Powell-Mason cable car to Columbus Ave. and Filbert St. **Parking:** Street parking is difficult. You may want to park in a garage. SFMTA Fifth and Mission Parking Garage is at 833 Mission St. If you're starting at Washington Square, you can park at the American Parking Management lot, 721 Filbert St.

The Barbary Coast Trail commemorates the rollicking period between the gold rush and the 1906 earthquake. Just one year after James W. Marshall discovered gold at John Sutter's lumber mill in 1848, San Francisco transformed from a sleepy village of fewer than a thousand to a booming city of 25,000. Flush with men free from wives and children, the city became a breeding ground for saloons, gambling, and prostitution. Much of this activity was concentrated around the Barbary Coast—an area bounded roughly by the Embarcadero (formerly East Street and the waterfront) to the east, Clay and Commercial streets to the south, Grant Avenue to the west, and Broadway to the north.

With the gold rush and the subsequent 1859 silver boom in Nevada, riches flowed downstream to San Francisco. Commercial buildings popped up around Jackson Square, and homes and luxury hotels were built too. Then, with an estimated 7.9- to 8.3-magnitude jolt on April 18, 1906, more than 28,000 buildings were destroyed, leaving 225,000 homeless. A bust in the now-familiar boom-and-bust cycle had arrived, and the city abruptly sobered up.

This route crosses through the Financial District, Chinatown, Portsmouth Square, North Beach, the Embarcadero,

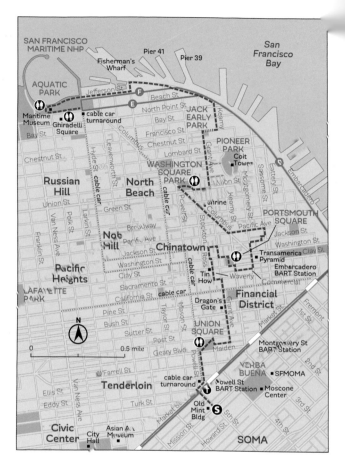

Fisherman's Wharf, and San Francisco Maritime National Historical Park—with bronze Barbary Coast Trail medallions embedded in the sidewalk to keep you on the route.

GET MOVING

Start your hike at the old San Francisco Mint on 5th Street between Mission Street and Mint Plaza. Built in 1874, this is the oldest federal building on the West Coast. On the day of the 1906 earthquake, mint workers and soldiers protected the building and the $200 million of gold in its vaults. When most other banks in the city burned down, the mint was able to serve as a central bank, giving people much-needed access to money after the disaster.

Walk northwest to Market Street, cross Market, and turn right. Turn left at the Powell-Market cable car turnaround. Continue three blocks on Powell Street to Geary Boulevard, and climb the stairs at the corner to enter Union Square at 0.3 mile. The square earned its name during the Civil War when it was a gathering spot for celebrating Union victories. Walk diagonally through the square, exiting at the northeast corner. Turn right on Stockton Street and take a left on Maiden Lane, which was full of brothels in the late 1800s. After one block on Maiden Lane, turn left onto Grant Avenue (unsigned). Pass Post and Sutter streets to arrive at Bush Street, where you'll pass through Dragon's Gate, the entrance to Chinatown. Built in 1970, its sign reads "All under heaven is for the good of the people."

Continue on Grant Avenue to Sacramento Street. Cross and turn left on Sacramento Street, and then take your first right onto Waverly Place. At 125 Waverly Place, look for Tin How, the first Buddhist temple in the United States, dating back to 1852. Continue two blocks to reach a T with Washington Street where you'll turn left. Take a quick right onto Ross Alley (no crosswalk), a right on Jackson Street (unsigned), and a right again on Grant Avenue. Take a left on Washington Street, and midway through the block, enter Portsmouth Square on your right at 1.3 miles. This was the city's first public square and the site where the gold rush started when James Marshall announced to San Francisco that he had found gold on the American River.

Walk one block right through Portsmouth Square to Clay Street and turn left. Turn right on Kearny Street, cross to the

Old and new San Francisco mix on the Barbary Coast Trail.
(photo by Brett Lider)

far side of the street, and take a left on Commercial Street (unsigned). Midway through the block, you'll come across adorable Empire Park on your left. Empire Park is a privately owned public open space (or POPOS) created and maintained by the owners of 505 Montgomery Street. Empire Park gets its name from the spire atop 505 Montgomery Street, which is a replica of that of the Empire State Building.

At the end of the block, turn left on Montgomery Street and pass the Transamerica Pyramid, the city's tallest building at 853 feet. Across the street, at 601 Montgomery, is the former headquarters of the Pony Express, which, from 1860 to 1861, delivered mail cross-country in ten to thirteen days. For a quick detour, head to Transamerica Redwood Park on the east side of the pyramid between Washington and Clay streets.

Continue on Montgomery Street to its intersection with Jackson Street, staying right when the road splits. Take a right on Jackson Street, a left on Balance Street, and the next right on Gold Street (unsigned). This was the site of the first gold rush assaying office where miners tested their gold for purity and then traded their findings for cash.

Take a left on Sansome Street (unsigned) and another left on Pacific Avenue. This area is the heart of the Barbary Coast. In the mid- to late 1800s, it housed brothels, dance halls, and music venues. Four blocks east, at 33 Pacific Avenue, was Shanghai Kelly's boarding house. In the days of the Barbary Coast, captains needed men to work on their ships, but sailors landing in San Francisco were hungry for gold and didn't want to go back to sea. Men were sometimes drugged, kidnapped, and put back on the boats to work, a practice that came to be known as "shanghaiing." (Shanghai was chosen as the verb because it was hard to secure a return trip on the San Francisco to Shanghai route.) Irishman James "Shanghai" Kelly was notorious for this practice.

Go right on diagonal Columbus Avenue. Between Pacific Avenue and Broadway, look for City Lights Bookstore. Founded in 1953 by Lawrence Ferlinghetti and Peter D. Martin, City Lights was the first paperback-only bookstore in the United States. Ferlinghetti went on to create City Lights Publishers to publish the works of the Beat poets.

Check out Cafe Trieste, the first espresso coffee house on the West Coast (established in 1956). The church at the corner of Columbus and Vallejo was built in 1849 and is the National

Shrine of Saint Francis of Assisi (the saint for whom San Francisco is named). Head back to Columbus Avenue, go right, and walk past Union Street and through Washington Square Park at 2.4 miles total. Arc through the park to see Saints Peter and Paul Church and then head to the corner of Union and Stockton streets. (Learn more about Saints Peter and Paul Church in Hike 36, Stairways to Heaven.) Take a left on Union Street and a left on Grant Avenue. At Filbert or Greenwich streets, you can add 0.5 mile roundtrip by taking a detour to Coit Tower (learn more about Coit Tower in Hike 36). Continue on Grant past Chestnut Street. When Pfeiffer Street is on your left, look for stairs on your right that lead up to Jack Early Park (see Hike 36). Optionally, head up to visit the scenic overlook at the top.

Back on Grant, continue downhill, turn right onto Francisco Street, and head down the extensive wooden stairs. Walk through the apartment complex courtyard and take your first left on Kearny Street, which leads you to the Embarcadero after two blocks. To get to the bay side of the Embarcadero, turn left at North Point Street and cross at a crosswalk. You are now in a massive tourist hub. Continue west for 0.7 mile past Pier 39, Pier 41, and Fisherman's Wharf. Turn left on Taylor Street when you reach signs for Alioto's and Fisherman's Grotto. Take a right on Jefferson Street, which ends in San Francisco Maritime National Historical Park. Follow the path along the water. Just after some bleachers, pass the Maritime Museum, which looks like a ship. Walk to the back of the museum to reach Beach Street. The route ends at Beach and Hyde streets at the Powell-Hyde cable car turnaround.

Take a cable car ride back to your starting point at Powell and Market. For a faster journey, the nearest MUNI stop is at North Point and Hyde streets.

GO FARTHER

If you liked this hike, read *Walking San Francisco on the Barbary Coast Trail* by Daniel Bacon.

33 Bay to Breakers

DISTANCE:	7.5 miles one way
ELEVATION GAIN:	310 feet
HIGH POINT:	270 feet
DIFFICULTY:	Moderate
TIME:	1 hour 15 minutes (running)
FITNESS:	Walkers, hikers, runners
FAMILY FRIENDLY:	This long route may not be interesting for children
DOG FRIENDLY:	On leash
AMENITIES:	Benches and restrooms in Alamo Square and Golden Gate parks; restrooms at the conservatory, Rose Garden, Spreckels Lake, North Lake, and Beach Chalet
CONTACT:	Zappos.com Bay to Breakers
GPS:	37° 47' 26.1888" N 122° 23' 36.0960" W
MAP TO:	Howard and Main streets, San Francisco

GETTING THERE

Public Transit: MUNI trains J, KT, L, M, and N and BART to Embarcadero Station; F streetcar and MUNI bus 14 to Market and Main streets; MUNI bus 30X to Howard and Main streets. Additional lines also serve the nearby area. **Parking:** There are metered spaces near the route start at Howard and Main streets, but most spots are two hours or less. Parking is free in this area on Sundays.

After the 1906 earthquake and fire destroyed most of San Francisco, the city was in need of a major morale boost. As repairing and rebuilding began, the city created events to cheer up despondent San Franciscans. As a prelude to world-class athletic events to be held at the Panama Pacific Exposition in 1915, the first Cross City Race took place on January 1, 1912, with 186 runners and 121 finishers. Now known as Bay to Breakers—and run in May—the race has become a tradition with 40,000 to 50,000 registered participants each year.

Bay to Breakers participants run through Golden Gate Park.

Today, the race has a party atmosphere with many runners wearing costumes, and as many as 100,000 people cheering from the sidelines. Music blasts out of homes along the route and live bands play in Golden Gate Park. While you can never re-create the energy of race day, this route will help you get in the spirit (and train for next year's race)!

GET MOVING

Start your "race" at the intersection of Howard and Main streets, and head down Howard Street for 1.5 miles until you reach 9th Street. Take a right on 9th Street and a left on Hayes Street immediately after crossing Market Street. Here, the famed Hayes Street Hill kicks in and continues for two-thirds

THE HAYES STREET HILL

The infamous Hayes Street Hill hits at 2 miles into the race. While the average grade is 5.5 percent, the steepest section, between Fillmore and Steiner streets, averages 11 percent. This hill wasn't part of the original race course but was introduced in 1968 in order to bypass construction work on BART. In 2016, the man and woman to climb the hill the fastest were each awarded a cash prize of $2500. At the top of the hill, you're at Alamo Square, where you can turn around to see the famous Painted Ladies as well as a fantastic view of downtown.

of a mile, ending at Pierce Street midway through Alamo Square. Continue on Hayes and take a left on Divisadero Street at 3 miles. Take a right onto Fell Street, and two blocks later, at the intersection with Baker Street, enter the Golden Gate Park Panhandle.

During the race, the streets are closed to cars, and you'd continue on Fell Street. But since the streets won't be closed for you, head south toward Oak Street, where you'll follow a pedestrian-only path through the Panhandle. At the end of the Panhandle, cross Stanyan Street to enter Golden Gate Park. Continue on a path along John F. Kennedy Drive for 2.9 miles, passing along the way: the Conservatory of Flowers, the Rose Garden, Lloyd Lake, and Spreckels Lake—all on the right side of the road.

Toward the end of this stretch, you'll pass the Bison Paddock and then the Golden Gate Park Golf Course. Though you can't see much of the course from the path, it starts just after Chain of Lakes Drive East. Just before JFK Drive bends to the right in front of you at 7 miles, look for a dirt path on your left with wooden stairs. Descend the stairs and use the crosswalk to cross John F. Kennedy Drive, then use another crosswalk on your right to cross Bernice Rodgers Way (unsigned). Follow Bernice Rodgers Way until it intersects with Martin Luther

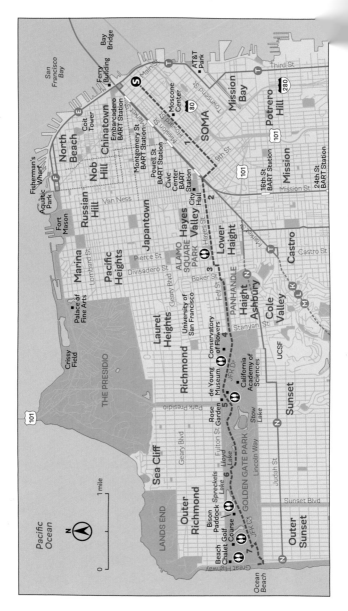

ing Jr. Drive, where you'll take a right. Follow Martin Luther King Jr. Drive for 0.3 mile to Lincoln Way, where you take a right and then another right on Great Highway. The official race continues about 0.1 mile north on Great Highway. As you reach the end, celebrate your victory and sign up for next year's race.

To return to the start, take one of the MUNI lines that operates near La Playa Street.

GO FARTHER

If you have energy after 7.5 miles, take a walk along Ocean Beach. Or, take a more leisurely hike through Golden Gate Park.

BAY TO BREAKERS TIMELINE AND RECORDS

The men's course record is held by Sammy Kitwara at 33:31 (2009), and the women's course record is 38:07 by Lineth Chepkurui (2010).

1912: First Cross City Race is run. The winner is Bobby Vlught with a time of 40:59.

1940: Bobbie Burke, disguised as a man, is the first woman to run the Cross City Race. The first costumed runner, dressed as Captain Kidd, was the last to cross the finish line.

1963: Cross City Race registration hits a low with just 25 official participants.

1965: Race name changes to Bay to Breakers.

1968: Hayes Street Hill is incorporated into the race route.

1971: Women are officially allowed to participate in Bay to Breakers. The top female finisher, Frances K. Conley, finishes in 50:45.

1978: The first centipede (runners tied together) runs the race with 13 people.

1986: Bay to Breakers reaches a record 110,000 official participants, earning a Guinness Book of World Records award for the largest footrace in the world.

2000: The oldest participant to cross the finish line is Stefan Arcelona at age ninety-nine.

34 Castro to Twin Peaks Loop

DISTANCE:	4.8 miles
ELEVATION GAIN:	840 feet
HIGH POINT:	910 feet
DIFFICULTY:	Challenging
TIME:	2 hours
FITNESS:	Hikers
FAMILY FRIENDLY:	May be too challenging for some children, but they will love the Seward Street slides
DOG FRIENDLY:	On leash
AMENITIES:	Benches on Kite Hill and Tank Hill; restrooms at Christmas Tree Point
CONTACT:	San Francisco Recreation and Park Department
GPS:	37° 45' 43.3188" N 122° 26' 5.1324" W
MAP TO:	429 Castro St., San Francisco

GETTING THERE

Public Transit: MUNI trains K, L, and M to Castro Street Station; MUNI buses 35 and 37 or MUNI F streetcar to Market and Castro streets; MUNI bus 24 or 33 to Castro and 18th streets. **Parking:** Parking is tough in this neighborhood as most parking spots are two hours only. I recommend taking public transit if at all possible. There is a California Parking lot located at 2351 Mission St., but it is just over a mile from the hike start.

On this hike, you'll climb from the Castro District to Twin Peaks—and back—in about 5 miles and two hours. You'll summit three hilltops with panoramic views of the city, bridges, and bay. Along your route, you'll visit a late nineteenth-century mansion, slide down the Seward Street slides, climb epic stairways to the top of Twin Peaks, stand at the foot of Sutro Tower, and walk alongside a peaceful eucalyptus rest. This hike has some sensational views, so make sure you're hiking on a sunny day.

GET MOVING

Start your hike at the Castro Theatre at 429 Castro Street. Built in 1922, the movie theater was designed by architect Timothy Pflueger, a native San Franciscan born to German parents. The theater's iconic neon sign was added in 1937. Look for this sign and the theater from all the hilltops on your hike.

From the theater, head down Castro to 18th Street and turn right. Take a left onto Douglass Street, and a right onto Caselli Avenue. At the corner of Douglass and Caselli, you'll see a beautiful Queen Anne Victorian mansion.

NOBBY'S FOLLY

Alfred E. "Nobby" Clarke came to San Francisco from Ireland in 1850 during the gold rush. He didn't make it big in gold, so he joined the police force in 1856 and eventually became the chief of police. By the time he left his position in 1887, he had amassed a fortune of $200,000, half of which he spent building this mansion. It was called Nobby's Folly, as people thought he was crazy for building a home so far outside what was then the city center.

After Nobby's death, the house became California General Hospital in 1904. Today, it houses fourteen apartments. Look at the gold knobs atop the house's towers. Like the Castro Theatre, you can see these from all of the hilltops on this hike.

Continue on Caselli for a half block. Between 97 and 101 Caselli Street, look for a stairway, signed as Clover Lane, on your left. Climb the stairs for two blocks until you reach 19th Street (unsigned), where you'll turn left. Take your first right on Seward Street, and when you reach the Seward Mini Park on your right (after 39 Seward Street) enter the park to find the Seward Street slides. Climb the steep stairs to the left of

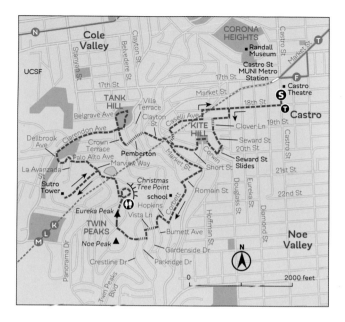

the slides, turn right, and continue up the steep hill until you reach a T intersection with Corwin Street (unsigned). Turn right and follow Corwin Street to the end of the block to reach Kite Hill Open Space at 0.8 miles. Climb to the top of Kite Hill, enjoying the views. (Can you see the Castro Theatre and Nobby's mansion?) Then look to the southwest for wooden stairs going down the hillside. Exit the park using those stairs and take a left on Yukon Street (unsigned). Continue uphill on Short Street instead of bearing left to stay on Yukon. Stay straight to reach a stairway that leads to Market Street. Turn right onto Market Street and walk to the traffic light at Clayton Street (unsigned). Cross Market using two crosswalks and turning left and uphill on a walkway bordered by a green wall.

At the intersection of Market and Romain streets (with a pedestrian bridge across Market on your left), turn right on Romain. At the end of Romain, turn left on Corbett Avenue.

Pass the Rooftop School and take your next right on Hopkins Avenue. After a short but steep climb on Hopkins, take a left onto Burnett Avenue. Across from 535 Burnett Avenue, you'll see Vista Lane stairway, which you'll climb four blocks to Parkridge Drive. Turn left on Parkridge Drive and climb the last two blocks of Vista Lane to Crestline Drive.

Turn right, and take the stairway built into the hillside on your left up to Twin Peaks Boulevard. Hop the wall lining Twin Peaks Boulevard, and go right to climb the stairs to the summit of Eureka Peak at 2.0 miles. Here you are treated to panoramic views spanning from the bay to the ocean.

Descend a stairway on the other side of the peak and turn right to pick up Christmas Tree Point Road, keeping a building and two towers on your left. (To learn more about Twin Peaks, see Hike 14, Creeks to Peaks.) Stay on Christmas Tree Point Road as it loops back to Twin Peaks Boulevard, as you take in great views of downtown and the Golden Gate Bridge. Turn right onto Twin Peaks Boulevard and walk along the far side of the road, carefully facing traffic for 0.1 mile until you see a narrow trail on your left near a reservoir. Jump the guardrail here, take the paved trail until it ends, and then follow the dirt trail downhill to Marview Way. From here, look for a dirt path across the street and to your right. Follow this path to the foot of Sutro Tower at 2.5 miles (there is a faint trail to the right early on but don't take it). Sutro Tower was built to give San Francisco good television reception (the city's many hills previously caused interference). The tower was built between 1971 and 1972, and reaches to 977 feet at the top and 1811 feet above sea level. The top of the tower is the single highest point in San Francisco.

From Sutro Tower, walk back to Marview, and turn left. Then take your first left onto Palo Alto Avenue. Follow the street to its end, and walk behind a fence to reach La Avanzada Street. Turn right here and walk downhill to Clarendon Avenue. Cross Clarendon carefully, turn right, and continue on Clarendon

A rustic, elegant flight of the Pemberton Place Steps

Avenue for 0.3 mile. When you reach the intersection with Twin Peaks Boulevard on your right and a firebox is just ahead, turn left onto Bigler Avenue (unsigned), a dirt road. Bigler Avenue ends at Belgrave Avenue, where you turn right and climb a wood and dirt stairway to Tank Hill. Tank Hill is 650 feet tall and was the former site of the Clarendon Heights water tank, which was built in 1894 to store drinking water pumped from the Laguna Honda Reservoir. The tank was removed in 1957, but the concrete base where the tank stood remains.

From the top of the stairway, walk to the rock formation and bench to enjoy sweeping views, including the Castro Theatre and Nobby's mansion. Then locate the large concrete base where the water tank stood. On the opposite side of the hill from where you entered the park, look for a stairway that leads down to Twin Peaks Boulevard. Cross Twin Peaks Boulevard to reach Crown Terrace (crosswalks are uphill by Bigler Avenue), and take Crown Terrace to a stairway on your left, Pemberton Place. Descend Pemberton three blocks until you reach Clayton Street (unsigned) and go right. At the stop sign, cross Corbett Avenue, turn left, cross Clayton Street, and make a right. Continue on Clayton Street and go down the stairway next to the last house on your left before Market Street.

At the bottom of the stairs, turn right on Market Street. When you reach the light where you crossed before, cross Market, turn right, and take your first left on Mono Street (a stairway). Stay on Mono another block as it becomes a paved path. When the path ends, take a right on Caselli Avenue and take a left down Clover Street. Turn right on 18th Street, and stay on 18th until you reach Castro Street, where you'll see the Castro Theatre on your left.

GO FARTHER

Walk down to 573–575 Castro Street, the former location of Castro Camera, Harvey Milk's photography shop and campaign headquarters. Milk also lived here from 1975 to 1978. If you want to continue hiking, do the 500 Club (see Hike 35).

35 | The 500 Club

DISTANCE:	3.1 miles
ELEVATION GAIN:	770 feet
HIGH POINT:	560 feet
DIFFICULTY:	Moderate
TIME:	1 hour 15 minutes
FITNESS:	Hikers
FAMILY FRIENDLY:	Some steep climbs, but hike is short
DOG FRIENDLY:	On leash
AMENITIES:	Benches in Saturn Street Steps Park, Buena Vista Park, and Corona Heights Park
CONTACT:	San Francisco Recreation and Park Department
GPS:	37° 45' 45.3528" N 122° 26' 6.5364" W
MAP TO:	Market and Castro streets, San Francisco

GETTING THERE

Public Transit: MUNI K, L, and M trains to Castro Street Station; MUNI buses 24, 35, and 37 to Market and Castro streets; MUNI bus 33 to 18th and Castro streets. **Parking:** Street parking can be difficult to find in the Castro. Some free one- and two-hour spots are available near the hike start.

The 500 Club earns its name as this short route includes three hills between 500 and 600 feet tall: Mount Olympus, Buena Vista Park, and Corona Heights Park. Mount Olympus has a sixty-year-old mystery concerning a missing statue. And Buena Vista Park and Corona Heights Park are what I call "fraternal twin peaks." While close in proximity and similar in elevation, these two hills look completely different. Buena Vista Park features sandy trails under a canopy of cypress and eucalyptus, while Corona Heights Park is made of exposed chert with a jagged rock formation at its summit. When you're not busy summiting hills, you'll enjoy walking through upscale sections of Ashbury Heights, Corona Heights, and the Castro.

GET MOVING

Start your hike at the southwest corner of Market and Castro streets. Start to cross Market and then turn left on the median between 17th and Market streets. Just behind a bus shelter, you reach Pink Triangle Park.

LGBT REMEMBRANCE IN WORLD WAR II

This is the first permanent, freestanding monument in the United States dedicated to the LGBT experience during World War II. The fifteen granite pylons decorated with pink triangles memorialize the estimated 15,000 LGBT individuals sent to concentration camps during the war. Just as the yellow star was used to identify Jews, the pink triangle was used in the camps to identify gay people.

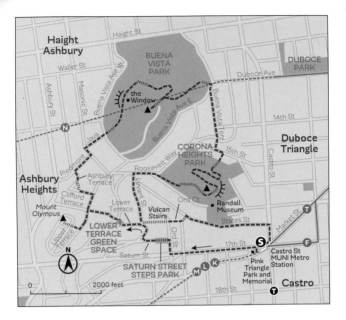

Exit the park on 17th Street and walk uphill. Take a right onto Ord Street, and take a left to head up Saturn Street through Saturn Street Steps Park. At the top of the steps, continue on Saturn Street, taking a stairway lining the right side of the road. At the end of the rock wall on your right, climb a stairway on the right to Lower Terrace. Follow Lower Terrace past the intersection with Levant Street, and then take a right up a stairway just past 180 Lower Terrace. At the top, cross Roosevelt Way (unsigned) to turn left onto steep Clifford Terrace. Take a left on Upper Terrace. Across from 227, take a right up a stairway to visit Mount Olympus (look for a blue Bay Area Ridge Trail sign) at 0.7 mile.

Descend the same stairs you ascended and turn left on Upper Terrace. Pass Clifford Terrace and take a left on Ashbury Terrace. Next to 64 Ashbury Terrace, take a stairway to the lower part of the street and turn right. At the end of the block, go right on Piedmont Street, left on Masonic Avenue, and right on Java Street. Cross Buena Vista Avenue West and continue straight up a wooden stairway in Buena Vista Park.

A DECADES-OLD MYSTERY

Reaching an elevation of 570 feet, Mount Olympus was one of Adolph Sutro's many land holdings. On Thanksgiving Day 1887, he dedicated a statue at this site. The statue, a copy of Belgian sculptor Antoine Wiertz's *The Triumph of Light*, depicted the Goddess of Liberty prevailing over a male figure symbolizing despotism, who is reaching up toward her. Over time the statue fell into disrepair, and many forgot about it completely. During the 1950s, the statue disappeared, and to this day, no one knows what happened to it.

Bear left when your path splits at an overlook, the Window, with views of St. Ignatius Church and the Golden Gate Bridge. Continue 0.1 mile and climb the first wooden stairway in the hillside to your right until it ends. Pick up a faint dirt trail in front of you. As the path plateaus, turn right on a path lined with thin logs. This path turns into a paved path, which heads uphill and brings you to a stairway to the park's summit at 1.5 miles.

After enjoying the views from the summit, descend the stairway you just took and head back to the paved path. When you get to an intersection, take the path along a stone wall to the left of the one that looks like a sidewalk. After 0.1 mile, take a right on a paved path and then descend a stairway to Buena Vista Avenue East at Duboce Avenue.

Cross Buena Vista Avenue East and turn right onto Buena Vista Terrace. Stay here past 14th Street and Roosevelt Way (a busy road with no crosswalk) until you reach a T with 15th Street. Cross the street (no crosswalk), take a left, and just before the tennis courts, take a right on a paved path to enter

Corona Heights Park. Corona Heights Park covers thirteen acres and shoots 540 feet into the air. In the late nineteenth century, this park was a rock quarry owned by the infamous Gray Brothers (learn more about the brothers in Hike 37, Walk on the Wild Side).

THE OLDEST PARK IN THE CITY

Thirty-six-acre Buena Vista Park is the oldest park in San Francisco. With an elevation of 589 feet, it was first established as Hill Park in 1867 but was renamed Buena Vista in 1894. As you continue into the park, white stones line the gutters. Many of these stones are broken headstones from cemeteries that were cleared in the early to mid-twentieth century to make room for further development. If you look closely, you'll see that some of the stones were placed with their inscriptions face up.

When the paved path ends, climb two flights of stairs and turn left to continue up the tree-covered hillside. After 0.2 mile, emerge from the trees and reach a T with a wooden fence-lined path and turn left. Then, after about 250 feet, climb a small flight of stairs and then continue up more stairs to the right. When you reach a clearing, turn right up the path and stairs toward the rock formation at the summit at 2.3 miles. Walk past one part of the rock formation and take a left before the second part. Descend a long stairway, and at an intersection with another path, turn right and head down more steps to the park exit ahead to your left.

At the exit take the crosswalk to the left and pick up Roosevelt Way by heading right. Take a left on Levant Street, pass States Street (no crosswalk), and continue until you reach the Vulcan Stairs. At the bottom take a left on Ord Street and then a quick right on Ord Court. Follow Ord Court to its end and climb the stairs on your left to States Street.

Mount Olympus's missing statue is an intriguing mystery.

Turn right and follow States Street for 0.2 mile until you reach Castro Street (this stretch of States Street that started at Levant Steet is the city's longest continuous block without an intersection). Go right on Castro to return to your start.

GO FARTHER

Walk down to 573–575 Castro Street, the former location of Castro Camera, Harvey Milk's photography shop and campaign headquarters. Milk also lived here from 1975 to 1978. If you have a lot of leftover energy, do the Castro to Twin Peaks Loop (see Hike 34).

36 Stairways to Heaven

DISTANCE:	4 miles
ELEVATION GAIN:	1000 feet
HIGH POINT:	295 feet
DIFFICULTY:	Challenging
TIME:	2 hours 25 minutes
FITNESS:	Hikers
FAMILY FRIENDLY:	May be too challenging for some children
DOG FRIENDLY:	On leash
AMENITIES:	Restrooms in Levi's headquarters, at Coit Tower, and in Washington Square Park
CONTACT:	San Francisco Recreation and Park Department
GPS:	37° 48' 7.6284'' N 122° 24' 7.1388'' W
MAP TO:	Battery and Filbert streets

GETTING THERE

Public Transit: MUNI F train to the Embarcadero and Greenwich St.; MUNI bus 82X to Sansome and Filbert streets. **Parking:** Street parking is often limited to two hours near the start of the hike; the best garage for this hike is the Levi's Plaza garage located on the corner of Sansome and Greenwich streets.

This urban hike winds and wanders through multiple stairways, alleyways, and hilltops in the North Beach, Telegraph Hill, and Russian Hill neighborhoods. On this route, you'll visit the Filbert and Greenwich Street steps up and down from Coit Tower, climb the curvy section of Lombard Street, and explore multiple little-known parks. In addition, you'll learn the history of your Levi's, discover one of the most romantic spots in the city in Jack Early Park, stroll Macondray Lane (the real Barbary Lane from the book series *Tales of the City*), and see where Marilyn Monroe and Joe DiMaggio took their wedding photos. This route is short, but has some serious elevation gain. Take your time and stop on the hills to catch your breath as you see fit.

GET MOVING

Start your hike at Battery and Filbert streets in Levi's Plaza, at Levi's headquarters. Look for the Filbert Street Steps climbing the hillside to the west and take the stairs—almost 400, if you're counting—to Coit Tower.

KNOW YOUR LEVI'S

Levi Strauss was born in Bavaria in 1829. He moved to New York in 1848 and left for San Francisco in 1853 with hopes of making a fortune in the gold rush. When that didn't happen, he opened a West Coast branch of his family's dry goods store, calling it Levi Strauss & Company. Around 1872, one of his customers, Jacob Davis, a tailor from Reno, sent Strauss a letter telling him about making work pants with a new element, rivets, to reinforce them at points of strain. He wanted to patent his new idea but needed a business partner. Strauss and Davis applied for a patent, and on May 20, 1873, Levi Strauss & Company received patent #139,121 from the US Patent and Trademark Office. The rest is history.

On the flights of stairs between Sansome and Montgomery streets, there are two official city streets that you can explore, Napier Lane and Darrell Place. On this same section, enjoy the beautiful public gardens created in 1949 by former Hollywood stuntwoman and Telegraph Hill resident Grace Marchant.

Cross Montgomery Street and continue your ascent. When you reach the very top of the stairs, turn right to walk alongside Telegraph Hill Boulevard until you reach the north side of the Coit Tower parking area.

Walk all the way around the parking area to locate the public restroom and a stairway. Head down one flight of stairs and then turn right on a paved path. At the end of the path, descend another stairway to end up on Lombard Street. Pass by Kearny Street, go right on Julius Street, left onto Whiting

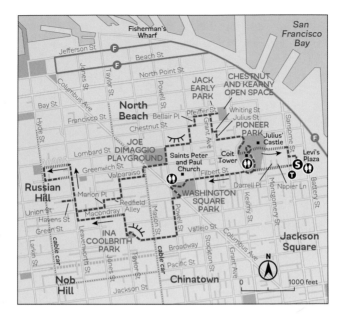

Street, and then right onto Grant Avenue. Cross Chestnut Street and continue downhill on Grant. Look for a stairway on your right, across from Pfeiffer Street on your left, and climb the stairs to explore Jack Early Park at 0.7 mile.

FROM A DREAM TO A PARK

In 1962 North Telegraph Hill resident Jack Early had an idea to transform a strip of city-owned land near his home. After gaining clearance from the city, he planted shrubs and trees, including a eucalyptus and a Monterey cypress. At first, he painstakingly watered his flora by carrying buckets of water up to the hill where the park sits. Eventually, he used donated railroad ties to build a set of steps. After twenty-five years of hard work, the city made Jack Early Park official in 1987. Jack Early died in 1997 at the age of eighty-two.

COIT TOWER AND FIREBELL LIL' (1843–1929)

Coit Tower is named for Lillian (Lillie or Firebell Lil') Hitchcock Coit, who moved to Telegraph Hill with her family in 1851. When she was fifteen, she was coming home from school when a fire broke out in her neighborhood. She saw the local fire company, Knickerbocker Engine Company No. 5, trying to get up the hill. She threw down her schoolbooks and began pulling on a tow rope to get the truck up the hill while calling out to bystanders to help. With the extra help, the engine was the first to reach the fire.

In 1863, Lillie was elected an honorary member of the fire company. That same year, she married the wealthy Howard Coit of the San Francisco Stock and Exchange Board. They separated in 1880, and he died in 1885 at the age of forty-seven. When Lillie Coit died in 1929, she left $125,000 to the city. Two memorials were created with her bequest: Coit Tower and a statue of San Francisco firemen in Washington Square Park.

Coit Tower was completed in 1933. The 210-foot tower was built with reinforced concrete, and the interior features frescoes painted by twenty-seven on-site artists plus two additional paintings that were created off-site.

After enjoying the park, head across Grant to Pfeiffer Street and continue on Pfeiffer to the almost-hidden Bellair Place (unsigned) and go left. (Look for three metal poles that mark the start of the street.) At the end of Bellair, turn right onto Chestnut Street, left onto Stockton, and right onto Lombard. As you walk down Lombard, look for Tuscany Alley on your left, where you're treated to a great view of one of the spires of Saints Peter and Paul Church.

Continue to Powell Street, turn left, and in one block, turn right onto Greenwich Street. Cross Columbus Avenue at the crosswalk to reach a small traffic island with a tree on it. From the island, turn left at a crosswalk and then turn right and cross Mason Street (the one with the cable car tracks). Turn

A cobblestone walkway on Macondray Lane, home base of the book series,
Tales of the City

left on Mason, take a right on Valparaiso Street, and then a left
on Taylor Street. Cross to the far side of Taylor and then cross
Filbert Street. Half a block past Filbert, turn right on Redfield
Alley. Follow the alley as it turns into a dirt road, hooks left,
and becomes Marion Place. This not-yet-official park is called
Molinari Mana Park by the locals (there's even a sign!).

Marion Place leads to Union Street, where you'll take
a right and continue on Union until you reach Leavenworth
Street. Go right on Leavenworth, head downhill, and in three
blocks you reach the curvy part of Lombard Street at 1.8
miles. Lombard Street's distinctive design was first proposed
by property owner Carl Henry. In the early 1920s, the street
had a 27 percent grade, which was too steep for the vehicles
of the day. When the current curvy design was implemented,
the grade was reduced to 16 percent. Despite Lombard's fame

as the "Crookedest Street in the World," Vermont Street in Potrero Hill is actually curvier (see Hike 39, Peaks of Potrero).

Climb the stairs along this crooked block and after you catch your breath at the top, take a left on Hyde Street and then a left on Greenwich Street. At the end of the block, stay left and pick up a path that zigzags through a garden to Leavenworth Street. Take a right and head two blocks uphill to Union Street. Option: Along your way, take a right to explore Buddha-filled Havens Street.

Cross Union Street and Leavenworth, and continuing south on Leavenworth, take your first left onto an unmarked street (Macondray Lane). At the end of the block, take a sidewalk on the right side of the street to Jones Street. Cross Jones and walk under a trellis to continue on Macondray Lane. In *Tales of the City*, much of the action takes place at 28 Barbary Lane, which, the author Armistead Maupin says, is based on Macondray Lane (sadly, 28 Macondray Lane is fictional).

The last section of Macondray Lane involves uneven cobblestones and a stairway. Descend the stairway, turn right on Taylor Street, pass Green Street, and take a left into Ina Coolbrith Park at 2.6 miles. The park is at the top of a hill at the intersection with Vallejo Street. Walk left on a paved path instead of taking the stairs in front of you. When you reach a stairway on your right, descend as far as you can and then turn right along a paved path to take in an amazing downtown view. When you reach another stairway, descend and exit the park on Vallejo.

Follow Vallejo two blocks to Powell Street and go left to take Powell to Union Street. Cross Union and turn right. Then cross Columbus Avenue and turn left. You're now walking along Washington Square Park at 3.1 miles. As you head toward Filbert Street, look for the statue of the San Francisco firemen from the bequest of Lillie Hitchcock Coit. Then walk through the park to face Saints Peter and Paul Church.

A CHURCH TOUCHED BY CELEBRITY

Saints Peter and Paul Church was first built in 1884 on Filbert Street and Grant Avenue, but it burned down in the 1906 earthquake. The present church was completed in 1924.

Joe DiMaggio and Dorothy Arnold were married in the church in 1939, but they later divorced. In 1954 DiMaggio married Marilyn Monroe at City Hall, and after the ceremony, they visited the church to take their wedding photos. DiMaggio's funeral took place at the church in 1999.

Continue on Filbert Street uphill all the way to Telegraph Hill Boulevard. At the top of the last flight of steps, follow the road left toward the parking area. When the steps up to Coit Tower are on your left, turn right on Greenwich Street to start your descent of 400 or so steps. At Montgomery Street, you'll pass Julius' Castle, a former restaurant, on your left. Go right on Montgomery and stay on the lower (left) side of the street when it forks. Look for a continuation of the Greenwich Street steps on your left. Follow the steps down to Sansome Street, cross Sansome, and head right to enter Levi's Plaza and return to the start.

37 Walk on the Wild Side

DISTANCE:	4.1 miles
ELEVATION GAIN:	1050 feet
HIGH POINT:	605 feet
DIFFICULTY:	Challenging
TIME:	1 hour 30 minutes
FITNESS:	Hikers
FAMILY FRIENDLY:	May be too strenuous for young children, but families can enjoy a walk around Glen Canyon Park

DOG FRIENDLY:	On leash
AMENITIES:	Picnic areas and restrooms at Glen Park Recreation Center; benches in Walter Haas Playground
CONTACT:	San Francisco Recreation and Park Department
GPS:	37° 44' 0.5100" N 122° 26' 2.9832" W
MAP TO:	Glen Park BART Station

GETTING THERE

Public Transit: BART to Glen Park Station; MUNI buses 23, 36, 44, and 52 to Bosworth and Diamond streets; MUNI J train to San Jose Ave./Glen Park Station. **Parking:** Street parking is available near the Glen Park BART Station. Parking time limits are longer a few blocks away from the station.

This hike traverses three neighborhoods in just 4 miles: Glen Park, Diamond Heights, and Noe Valley. The route starts with a quick walk through Glen Park to reach sixty-acre Glen Canyon Park, a major highlight of this area of the city. Once in the park, you'll take the new Coyote Crags Trail to walk high above the canyon. Then, you'll explore Duncan-Castro Open Space and the stairways of Noe Valley. As you meander into Diamond Heights, you'll explore Harry Street—Diamond Heights' most epic stairway—and Billy Goat Hill with fantastic downtown views. From there, you'll take a trail to Walter Haas Playground and finally explore three Glen Park dirt roads that make you feel like you're in a small town, not a big city.

GET MOVING

Start your hike at the Glen Park BART Station at the corner of Bosworth and Diamond streets. Walk one block north on Diamond Street (toward downtown Glen Park), and take your first left on Kern Street. Cross Brompton Avenue to pick up a dirt path slightly to your left. Continue on this path through Bosworth Street Open Space for three blocks until you reach Burnside Avenue. Go right on Burnside and left on Paradise Avenue. After one block, turn right on Elk Street, pass Glen Canyon Park's main entrance, and take a left just past the

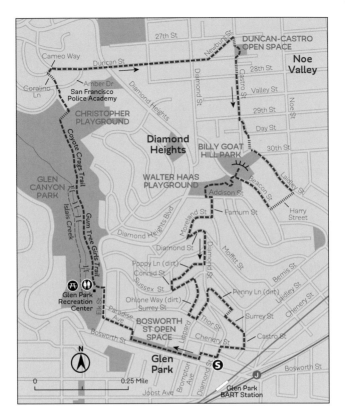

tennis courts into the park. This trail turns into the Gum Tree Girls Trail after you pass the recreation center. (To learn more about Glen Canyon Park, see Hike 14, Creeks to Peaks.)

About 0.1 mile after the recreation center, you'll reach a trail marker pointing to Christopher Playground. Take a right up a stairway embedded in the hillside. Continue following the path and stairs, and just as you're starting to reach the first of Glen Canyon's rock formations, you'll reach another trail marker and the Coyote Crags Trail. Continue straight here past a large rock formation on your right and a smaller one on your left. At a third trail marker pointing to Christopher Playground, stay right and head uphill toward more paths and stairs. At the fourth trail marker, stay left and follow the arrow to Crags Court. At the fifth trail marker, which points up a stairway to Christopher Playground, remain on the Coyote Crags Trail. When the path splits, stay right and climb a number of flights of stairs.

At the top of all the stairs, take a left to exit the park and walk right toward the Amber Drive sign. Cross Amber Drive and to the right of 289 Amber Drive, locate Coralino Lane, a stairway that leads to Cameo Way (unsigned), where you turn right. At the next intersection, take a right on Duncan Street, which you'll follow for 0.4 mile to Newburg Street. The first block of Duncan is relatively flat and passes a large community garden and St. Nicholas Orthodox Church. After Diamond Heights Boulevard, Duncan becomes a steep downhill with some great city views. At Newburg Street, take a left for even better city views. Take the stairway on your right as you reach the intersection with 27th Street. At the top of the concrete stairs, continue right up a wooden stairway. (A neighbor has put some whimsical metal art in their yard.) Take a right at the top of the stairs to enter Duncan-Castro Open Space at 1.7 miles. A steep path goes to the top of the hill and then down to the intersection of Duncan and Castro streets.

Take Castro Street one block to a stairway. Descend the stairway and pass 28th and Valley streets. When you reach the intersection with 29th Street, you have four options. Cross the street and pick up the lower part of Castro Street. In one block, Castro Street turns into a concrete path and then a stairway. Climb the stairway and take a left on 30th Street (unsigned). Billy Goat Hill is on your right. When the road forks, stay right to pick up Laidley Street. After 0.1 mile, turn right onto Harry Street—the entire "street" is a stairway. Climb the 236 steps and turn right on Beacon Street. After

0.1 mile turn right to enter Billy Goat Hill Park at 2.4 miles. Descend the stairs to the viewing platform (and the swing if it's there) and enjoy the scenery.

FROM QUARRY TO PARK

Billy Goat Hill was likely named for the goats that used to graze here in the 19th century. At the turn of the twentieth century, the Gray Brothers ran a quarry here. They were known for unsafe practices, overblasting hills, and failing to pay employees. In 1914 a disgruntled employee, Joseph Lococo, shot and killed one of the brothers, George Gray, on this very hill, effectively ending the quarrying operation. When Lococo was acquitted, the courtroom cheered.

Exit the park the way you entered, cross Beacon Street, and look for a trail across the street that climbs through a wooded area. Emerge from the woods and take a right on a paved path when you enter Walter Haas Playground at 2.6 miles. Look for a bench next to the playground area for a great view. Continue on the paved path along the basketball court, and head slightly right to exit the park on Addison Street (unsigned). Take a left on Addison and a right onto Farnum Street. From here, you'll be making a lot of turns in short succession with the goal of getting you to Glen Park's dirt roads: Penny, Poppy, and Ohlone lanes. They were named at some point in the 1990s upon the fire department's insistence.

From Farnum take your first right onto Moreland Street. Follow Moreland until it ends in a T. Take a left on Diamond Street (unsigned) and follow it as it bears right. When you reach a stop sign, stay right to continue on Diamond Street. Take a right on Poppy Lane to visit your first dirt road. (This side of Poppy Lane is unsigned, but there is a sign across the street.)

Chert outcroppings in Glen Canyon Park

At the end of Poppy Lane, turn left onto Conrad Street (unsigned) and take a left onto Sussex Street. Take your second right onto a dirt road, Ohlone Way, and when you reach a T at the end of the road, head left onto Surrey Street (unsigned). When you reach the next intersection, take another left to stay on Surrey Street (street sign on your right will say Lippard). Pass Thor Avenue on your right and then reach an intersection with Diamond Street. Go left on Diamond, take a right onto the third dirt road, Penny Lane, and follow it to its end as it descends a few stairs to Surrey Street (unsigned). Take a left on Surrey Street and a right on Castro Street. From Castro take a right onto Chenery Street, a left onto Diamond Street, and in a few blocks you're back at your start.

GO FARTHER
Check out Glen Park's small downtown for shops and restaurants.

38   Beauty of Bernal

DISTANCE:	2.9 miles
ELEVATION GAIN:	720 feet
HIGH POINT:	445 feet
DIFFICULTY:	Moderate to challenging
TIME:	1 hour 15 minutes
FITNESS:	Hikers
FAMILY FRIENDLY:	Playground in Holly Park and slides on Esmeralda Ave. and Coleridge St.; hills can be challenging
DOG FRIENDLY:	On leash
AMENITIES:	Benches in Bernal Heights Park, in parks along Esmeralda Ave.; picnic area, benches, and restrooms in Holly Park
CONTACT:	San Francisco Recreation and Park Department
GPS:	37° 44' 49.5924" N 122° 24' 48.7080" W
MAP TO:	Folsom St. and Precita Ave., San Francisco

GETTING THERE

Public Transit: MUNI buses 12 and 27 to Cesar Chavez and Folsom streets; MUNI buses 14 and 49 to Mission St. and Precita Ave.; MUNI bus 67 to Folsom St. and Precita Ave.

Parking: Free parking is available near the hike start. There are a few parking spots at the entrance to Bernal Heights Park; if you park here, subtract 0.4 mile from the total distance.

Bernal Heights was once part of a 4446-acre land grant given to José Cornelio de Bernal, a grandson of a soldier in Juan Bautista de Anza's 1776 expedition (see Hike 29). The grant extended from present-day Cesar Chavez Street to Daly City. In the mid-nineteenth century, Irish, Scottish, and Scandinavian immigrants moved into the neighborhood, and Bernal Hill was used for cattle ranching and dairy farming. In May 1876, with gold fever still in the air, Frenchman Victor Resayre announced that he had found gold on Bernal Hill. For several days the hill was the site of extensive mining efforts; however, it turned out that Resayre had found quartz, not gold.

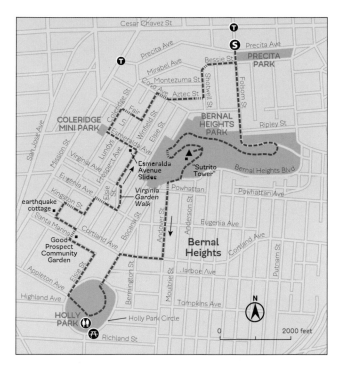

On your walk, you'll visit two major parks—Bernal Heights and Holly—plus the neighborhood's main drag, Cortland Avenue. You'll also visit the nooks and crannies of the neighborhood—stairways, mini parks, a community garden, slides—all the little things that make this cozy enclave so special.

GET MOVING

Start your hike at the corner of Folsom Street and Precita Avenue. Climb nearly 200 feet as you head up Folsom for 0.2 mile. Continue following Folsom as it goes left to the Bernal Heights Park entrance, where you'll head right on the paved road. Stop at any of the several benches for a panoramic view of the city. After 0.3 mile on this path, take a left on a stairway built into the hillside. (There is also a stairway on your right.)

Bernal Hill's views stretch from the skyline to the bay to the peninsula.

At the top of the twenty or so stairs, follow the path directly to your left along the edge of the hill. When the path forks, stay left and continue on along the south side of the hill for 0.1 mile. When the path fades away, look for a guardrail on your right. Turn right and walk along the guardrail and then a fence to visit the hill's summit at 0.8 mile. The summit is adorned with what the locals call "Sutrito Tower."

Take in the views around you, and when you've had your fill, retrace your steps to reach the guardrail. Turn right and walk down the hill on the paved road to Bernal Heights Boulevard. Turn right on Bernal Heights Boulevard and descend a stairway on your left next to a street light. (The stairway looks private, but isn't.)

From the bottom of the stairway, take Andover Street for two blocks and turn right on Cortland Avenue. Take a left at Bocana Street and continue for one block. Cross Holly Park Circle and take the stairway to enter Holly Park at 1.4 miles. Head left at the top of the stairs and then take a right off the main path and toward a picnic area. (There are two paths that branch off to your right; take the one directly adjacent to the picnic area.) Continue past the basketball court and a restroom, and exit the park where Holly Park Circle meets

Appleton Avenue. Turn right onto Holly Park Circle and stay left off the circle at Elsie Street. Follow Elsie past a reservoir and turn left onto Santa Marina Street. Look for a break in the houses on the right (between 83 and 101) and turn down the stairs into the Good Prospect Community Garden. At the end of the garden, take a left on Cortland Avenue and then a right on Coleridge Street. From the corner of Cortland and Coleridge, turn around and look for 48 Cortland Avenue, one of the few remaining earthquake cottages.

Continue on Coleridge and take your next right up Kingston Street, a stairway that turns into a path that you'll follow to the end of the block. Take a left on Prospect Avenue and a right up a stairway on Eugenia Avenue. Continue one more block on Eugenia Avenue and head left on Elsie Street (there will also be a sign for Virginia Avenue). When the street forks, stay right to stay on Elsie Street. At 2.1 miles, pick up the Virginia Garden Walk, a neighborhood beautification initiative, to the left of an adorable red house. Exit the walk and take a right on Winfield Street. Take a left onto Esmeralda Avenue to a park with slides. Follow Esmeralda past Prospect Avenue and Lundys Lane until you dead-end at Coleridge Street. Take a right and the Coleridge Mini Park, with a mini slide, is on your left. Continue on Coleridge Street and take a right on the Fair Avenue stairs. Cross Lundys Lane, continue a second block on Fair Avenue, then take your next left on Prospect Avenue.

A REMINDER OF 1906

During the 1906 earthquake, Bernal Heights fared better than other neighborhoods due to its sparse development and foundational bedrock. Across the city, some 5600 tiny "earthquake cottages" were built to shelter those made homeless after the quake. Only 21 confirmed earthquake cottages remain in the city and more than a dozen of them are in Bernal Heights.

Go right onto Coso Avenue, a steep uphill with stairs, and then left onto Aztec Street, another steep hill. Continue down the stairs at the end of Aztec and take a left onto Shotwell Street (unsigned). After passing Montezuma Street and Mirabel Avenue, take the stairs to the right down to Bessie Street (unsigned) and turn right. Follow Bessie Street two blocks to Folsom, and take a left to arrive back at your start at Precita Avenue.

GO FARTHER

Take a break in Precita Park or walk west to Mission Street, where there are many places to eat between Cesar Chavez and 29th streets.

39 Peaks of Potrero

DISTANCE:	2.3 miles
ELEVATION GAIN:	480 feet
HIGH POINT:	310 feet
DIFFICULTY:	Moderate
TIME:	1 hour
FITNESS:	Walkers, hikers
FAMILY FRIENDLY:	Hilly, but children will enjoy the playground at McKinley Square and curvy Vermont Street
DOG FRIENDLY:	On leash
AMENITIES:	Benches in several places; restrooms in the Potrero Hill Recreation Center
CONTACT:	San Francisco Recreation and Park Department; Starr King Open Space
GPS:	37° 45' 43.3080" N 122° 24' 18.9108" W
MAP TO:	18th St. and San Bruno Ave., San Francisco

GETTING THERE

Public Transit: MUNI buses 9 and 33 to Potrero Ave. and 18th St.; MUNI bus 19 to De Haro and 18th streets. **Parking:** Free street parking is available near the hike start.

Fog rolls into the city behind Bernal Hill.

In the late eighteenth century when space grew short near the Spanish mission, cattle were moved to this area, then called Potrero Nuevo (new pasture). In 1855 during the Mexican period, Potrero Nuevo was granted to the twin sons of Francisco de Haro. De Haro was the first *alcalde* (mayor) of San Francisco (then Yerba Buena) in 1835. In 1846, when the United States and Mexico were at war, the nineteen-year-old twins were shot dead for being suspected of carrying messages for the Mexican military.

During the gold rush, speculators began selling off Potrero Nuevo's land (even though the de Haro family's claims would be in the courts until 1878), but most decided the area was too remote to live in. In 1865, a bridge across Mission Bay helped connect the area with the city and bring in residents.

Today, US Highway 101 and Interstate 280 run on either side of Potrero Hill, isolating it somewhat from the rest of the city and giving it a small-town feel. Potrero offers some of the best views of downtown, the Mission, Twin Peaks, and Bernal Hill. On this hike you'll visit three parks, the actual curviest street in the city, numerous stairways, a dirt road, and four community gardens. While this route looks short, watch out as this neighborhood boasts some serious hills.

GET MOVING

Start your hike at 18th Street and San Bruno Avenue. On your right is the Benches Garden, which was founded in January 2010. Continue on San Bruno Avenue for two blocks to 20th Street and enter the Potrero Hill Community Garden on your right. Local resident Estelle West, known as the Goat Lady of Potrero Hill, used to graze her eighteen goats here. The garden offers sensational views of Twin Peaks, the Mission, and Bernal Hill.

Just under the street signs for 20th Street and San Bruno Avenue, take a paved path marked with two poles. The path quickly turns to dirt. When you reach stairs on either side of you, take the stairs up to your left to reach the curvy section of Vermont Street at 0.35 mile. Vermont—not Lombard—is the crookedest street in San Francisco. Cross to the far side of the road (no crosswalk) so that you can take a stairway alongside the entire street.

Follow Vermont Street until you reach its intersection with 22nd Street. Make a right on Kansas Street and then take a left onto 23rd Street. Go right onto Rhode Island Street and

THE REAL "CROOKEDEST" STREET

While Lombard Street has eight switchbacks and Vermont only seven, Vermont beats Lombard in sinuosity. Vermont Street has starred in two movies: *Magnum Force* and *Bullitt*. The street also hosts the annual Bring Your Own Big Wheel event on Easter Sunday when hundreds of people of all ages ride children's bikes and careen down the hill's curves.

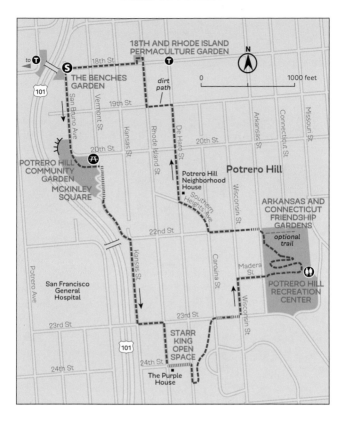

continue one block to 24th Street, where you take a left. On this corner, there's a purple Victorian dating back to the 1880s fittingly called "The Purple House."

Use either of the stairways along the street to climb this steep block. At the top, look for an unmarked paved path across the street to your right. Take the path, and at the top, turn left and walk to the end of the block to enter Starr King Open Space at 0.9 mile. Walk toward the right to pick up the main path through the park. When your path splits, stay left and follow it to the park's exit at Carolina and 23rd

THE ORATOR WHO SAVED THE NATION

Starr King Open Space is a swath of serpentine grassland—part of an ecosystem that runs from the southeast corner of the city to Inspiration Point in the Presidio. The open space was named for Thomas Starr King, a pastor and leader in the Unitarian Universalist Church. Abraham Lincoln called him the "orator who saved the nation" after his words helped persuade California to stay in the Union during the Civil War. Starr King became an open space in 1984, and today it's owned by a nonprofit, not the city.

streets. Take the stairway to your right, cross Carolina Street, and continue up steep 23rd Street. At the top of 23rd, take another stairway on your left to reach Wisconsin Street. Take a left on Wisconsin and then a right onto Madera Street.

At the end of Madera, cross Arkansas Street and pick up a paved path to the right of the Potrero Hill Recreation Center. O. J. Simpson grew up in this neighborhood, and the rec center's indoor basketball courts were built partly with donations from him. Take the path all the way around the rec center and almost back to Arkansas Street, but just before you reach the street, turn right to walk behind a fence and take a dirt path downhill for about 100 feet. Turn right at a T to follow the path farther downhill. When the path ends, make a sharp left and walk with the tennis courts on your right. Next, pass a playground and exit the park. Turn right onto Arkansas Street. After 100 feet, you can take a detour to the right (which adds about 0.1 mile to your hike) to explore the Arkansas and Connecticut Friendship Gardens.

Cross Arkansas Street to climb the stairs at the intersection with 22nd Street (unsigned). At the top of the stairs, continue past Wisconsin Street to Carolina Street. Cross to the far side of Carolina and turn right, and then stay left to pick up Southern Heights Avenue. At 1.7 miles, you'll pass the Potrero

Hill Neighborhood House (or simply the "Nabe") at the corner of Southern Heights and De Haro. Designed by Julia Morgan, the community center opened in 1922. Today, the Nabe offers free wellness classes and senior and children's programs. Cross to the west side of De Haro Street, turn right, and continue for two blocks to 19th Street (unsigned), where you'll take in great downtown views. Turn left to take a dirt path to the left of 698 De Haro. At the end of the dirt path, head right on Rhode Island Street for one block and cross the street to the northwest corner of the intersection, where you'll find the 18th and Rhode Island Permaculture Garden. This "lush food forest" has numerous places to sit and relax. After exploring the garden, continue west on 18th Street for three blocks to return to your start.

GO FARTHER

Anchor Brewing is on nearby Mariposa Street, and plenty of other restaurants and coffee shops are on 18th Street between Connecticut and Texas streets.

40 Sunset Stairway Stroll

DISTANCE:	2.7 miles
ELEVATION GAIN:	700 feet
HIGH POINT:	760 feet
DIFFICULTY:	Challenging
TIME:	1 hour 15 minutes
FITNESS:	Walkers, hikers
FAMILY FRIENDLY:	Short but may be too strenuous for young children
DOG FRIENDLY:	On leash
AMENITIES:	Benches in Grand View Park and Golden Gate Heights Park; playground in Golden Gate Heights Park
CONTACT:	San Francisco Recreation and Park Department
GPS:	37° 45' 42.4368" N 122° 28' 25.6512" W
MAP TO:	16th Ave. and Judah St., San Francisco

GETTING THERE

Public Transit: MUNI N train to Judah St. and 15th Ave.; MUNI bus 7, 7X, or 7R to Lincoln Way and 15th Ave.; MUNI bus 28 to 19th Ave. and Judah St. **Parking:** Free parking is available near the hike start.

In the mid-1800s, the Sunset was simply the "Outside Lands," an expanse of sand dunes thought to be virtually uninhabitable. While San Francisco incorporated in 1850, the Sunset didn't join the city until 1866. Three events eventually brought

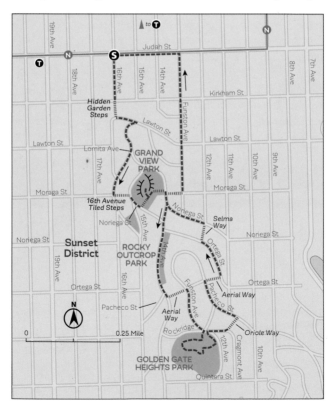

San Francisco's original mosaic stairway: the 16th Avenue Tiled Steps

people to the Sunset: the construction of Golden Gate Park starting in 1870; the 1906 earthquake, which moved people west from the damaged city center; and the opening of the Twin Peaks and Sunset tunnels, allowing people to take streetcars downtown to their jobs. Today, many San Franciscans enjoy the area as a quiet place to live with easy downtown access.

The Sunset features two impressive mosaic stairways that have beautified the area and attracted visitors and press. And of all the parks in the city, aptly named Grand View Park has some of the best panoramic views of the ocean, Golden Gate Park, the Golden Gate Bridge, Mount Sutro and Sutro Tower, and downtown San Francisco. Since there are such good views on this hike, do it on a sunny day.

GET MOVING

Starting at 16th Avenue and Judah Street, walk uphill one block south to Kirkham Street and climb the Hidden Garden Steps. Inspired by the 16th Avenue Tiled Steps Project (which you'll see later on this hike), the Hidden Garden Steps were conceived in January 2010 and completed in November 2013. The same artists from the 16th Avenue project created this

148-step mosaic depicting flora and fauna, including flowers, ferns, butterflies, and a salamander that extends up 26 stairs.

At the top of the steps, turn left on Lawton Street and take a right onto Lomita Avenue. At the next Lomita street sign, bear right and downhill. And at the next intersection when Lomita merges with 16th, follow 16th another 200 feet to the intersection with Moraga Street. Turn left and climb the 16th Avenue Tiled Steps.

At the top of the steps, turn right on 15th Avenue and take a stairway built in a concrete wall to your left to climb to Noriega Street. Go right on Noriega and climb the zigzag stairway on your left up to Grand View Park at 0.6 mile. At the top of the stairway, head left to a dirt path to the summit and take in what may be the best 360-degree view of the entire city. When you're done with the view, return to the dirt path, turn left toward the east side of the hill, and descend a concrete stairway on your right that leads to the intersection of 14th Avenue and Moraga Street. Turn right onto 14th Avenue

MOSAIC STAIRWAYS:
A NEIGHBORHOOD DRAW

The 16th Avenue Tiled Steps project began in early 2003 when neighborhood residents Jessie Audette and Alice Xavier conceived of the idea to bring people together and beautify the neighborhood. Later that year, project volunteers chose Aileen Barr and Colette Crutcher as the project artists. The 163-step mosaic depicts a landscape that goes from the bottom of the ocean, to land, and all the way to the sun in the sky. More than 300 neighbors participated in the creation of the panels. Work started on July 13, 2005, and the ribbon-cutting ceremony was held on August 27, 2005, which the mayor's office proclaimed "16th Avenue Tiled Steps Day."

The inspiration for the steps came from Selarón's staircase, a mosaic staircase in Rio de Janeiro named after artist Jorge Selarón. Jesse Audette discovered the staircase while living in that city.

and follow it for 0.3 mile, passing Rocky Outcrop Park, a great example of Franciscan chert, the city's bedrock.

Across from 14th Avenue's intersection with Pacheco Street take a left on the Aerial Way stairs—this one's a quad burner, as I like to say. At the top of the stairs, take a right on Funston Avenue (unsigned). When you reach Rockridge Drive after 0.15 mile, turn right to cross Rockridge and enter Golden Gate Heights Park on a paved path. When the path splits, turn right to walk along the west side of the park. Follow the path as it curves left in front of a grassy lawn. When you reach a playground, head right and continue to the park's 12th Avenue exit and take a left onto 12th. Take your first right onto Cragmont Avenue and then a left down Oriole Way stairway. At the bottom of the stairs, go left at Pacheco Street. Pass 11th Avenue on your right, and before you reach 12th Avenue on your left, you'll come to a community garden with a dune habitat.

Continue on Pacheco for another block and turn right to descend the Aerial Way stairs. At the bottom, turn left onto the upper part of Ortega Street, cross to the lower part of Ortega Street, and take your next right onto the Selma Way stairway. At the bottom, go left on the upper section of Noriega Street and after about 0.15 mile, Noriega Street meets up with 14th Avenue. Bear right on the lower section of 14th Avenue. After 175 feet, take the Moraga Street stairway on your right down to Funston Avenue. Turn left onto Funston and walk 0.3 mile to Judah Street; turn left and walk three blocks to 16th Avenue and back to your start.

GO FARTHER

If you're up for a bite, continue on Funston one more block to Irving Street and then head right. There are seemingly limitless food choices between 12th and 5th avenues.

Next page: Sixty-foot-tall letters decorate
Sign Hill in South San Francisco.

SOUTH OF
THE BORDER

This section includes four hikes south of San Francisco. One hike explores the South San Francisco sign on Sign Hill, and the others cover five of San Bruno Mountain's nine trails. San Bruno Mountain encompasses 2326 acres and its summit reaches 1314 feet. Located on the northern end of the Santa Cruz mountain range, it is both a state and county park. The mountain's proximity to the Pacific Ocean results in frequent fog and westerly winds, with speeds up to 30 miles per hour. Once a Costanoan habitat, the area was used for sheep and cattle grazing during the Spanish Mission period. Under Mexican rule, this was part of Jacob P. Leese's Rancho Cañada de Guadalupe la Visitación y Rancho Viejo.

In the 1870s, railroad magnate Charles Crocker bought the property and it was transferred to the Crocker Land Company after his death. A Nike missile site was installed in 1950; although today it is in ruins. Over the next few decades, land conservationists and real estate developers fought over the land, and in 1982, Edward J. Bacciocco Jr., a member of the San Mateo Board of Supervisors, got the two sides together for discussion. Eventually the San Bruno Mountain Habitat Conservation Plan was created. Some parts of the mountain were set aside for housing, but the housing had to be built in a way to protect endangered plant and butterfly habitats. Today the group San Bruno Mountain Watch works to protect the mountain, which is officially managed by the San Mateo Department of Parks.

41 San Bruno Mountain North Loop

DISTANCE:	2.9 miles
ELEVATION GAIN:	290 feet
HIGH POINT:	825 feet
DIFFICULTY:	Easy
TIME:	1 hour
FITNESS:	Walkers, hikers, runners
FAMILY FRIENDLY:	Families wanting a shorter route can do the Bog Trail, 0.8-mile roundtrip alternative
DOG FRIENDLY:	No
AMENITIES:	Restrooms, picnic sites with benches, and barbecue pits near main park entrance
CONTACT:	California Department of Parks and Recreation; San Mateo County Parks Department
GPS:	37° 41' 49.6176" N 122° 26' 3.5484" W
MAP TO:	555 Guadalupe Canyon Pkwy., Brisbane

GETTING THERE

Public Transit: The closest BART stop is Daly City (2.6 miles from trailhead); otherwise, there are no great public transportation options. **Parking:** There is a six-dollar fee for each vehicle entering San Bruno Mountain State and County Park. Pay your fee at the self-registration station in the parking lot at 555 Guadalupe Canyon Pkwy.

This hike's three trails show off three different facets of San Bruno Mountain in just under three miles. The Bog Trail eases you into the hike on a narrow dirt path that winds along scrub, shrubs, and trees. From here, you head to the paved Old Guadalupe Trail, where you'll find walkers and bikers enjoying the serene shade of eucalyptus trees. And then you meet up with the Saddle Loop, where you'll spend the majority of this hike. This expansive grassland area with wide trails gives

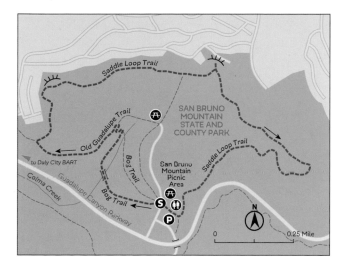

you spectacular views that start at the San Francisco skyline, move down to the peninsula and the bay, and reach the San Bruno Mountain summit. Stay aware of your surroundings as horses are allowed on the Old Guadalupe and Saddle Loop trails and bicycles are allowed on the Old Guadalupe Trail.

GET MOVING

Start your hike on a paved road behind the "authorized vehicles only" gate. Almost immediately, take a dirt path on your left marked as the Bog Trail. After 150 feet or so, the Bog Trail splits. The section of the Bog Trail to your left is wilder and narrower and can be muddy after a rainstorm. The trail ahead of you is more manicured and has benches along the way. You can go either way, but for this hike you'll go left.

As you walk parallel to Guadalupe Canyon Parkway, you are in a grassland area punctuated with bushes, trees, and plenty of blackberries to pick in the summer. At 0.3 mile, enter a tree-covered area and cross a wooden bridge over Colma

Hikers on the Saddle Loop Trail

Creek. After another 0.2 mile, join up with the other side of the Bog Trail.

Stay straight at the trail marker and continue toward the Old Guadalupe Trail as eucalyptus trees start to line the left side of your path. Follow the trail as it hooks left at a rest area with a bench. You are soon in the eucalyptus grove you just walked by. At 0.6 mile, turn left when you reach the Old Guadalupe Trail. Enter into a clearing where you can see the towers of San Bruno Mountain in the distance on your left. Head into a second and then a third eucalyptus grove. In the third grove, pick up the Saddle Loop Trail, a wide gravelly trail on your right.

The Saddle Loop Trail climbs gently uphill through a grassy meadow dotted with shrubs and trees. You will soon see houses on your left rising up from the horizon. As you continue the climb, you'll also start to see other parts of the city on your left, including Mount Davidson, Sutro Tower, and Twin Peaks. The skyline comes into view next, and behind you, you'll see San Bruno Mountain's summit with its bevy of towers. After 0.5 mile on the Saddle Loop Trail you'll pass your first marker counting out half-mile increments along the trail (this one says 1.0 mile). After another 0.25 mile ignore the trail branching off to the right. As the trail enters and exits an area with a few trees, look for a spur trail to your left that leads to a scenic view of the city. From this overlook, you can now see McLaren Park to the north, as well as all the sights you saw before. After exploring the viewpoint, return to the trail and go left to continue your loop.

You're now treated to some new sights. A grassy meadow extends to your left and you can see the bay and East Bay. At 2.2 miles, come to a viewpoint with a bench at the easternmost part of the trail. You can now see Candlestick Point, the Cow Palace, and housing developments in Brisbane—all stretching between you and the bay.

As you reach the 2.0-mile marker, San Bruno Mountain is on your left in the distance. You know you are getting close to the start when you approach an area with eucalyptus off to your left. The trail continues to a picnic area with barbecues and water fountains at 2.7 miles. When you see a trail marker to your left, stay straight to pick up a paved trail and enter an area lined with trees that leads you to a restroom. When you reach the restroom, head left and before you reach the parking lot, turn right on a paved trail to head back to the start of your loop.

GO FARTHER

If you like this hike, check out the Summit Loop Trail (Hike 43) that takes you to the summit of San Bruno Mountain.

42 Eucalyptus Loop Trail

DISTANCE:	1 mile
ELEVATION GAIN:	160 feet
HIGH POINT:	825 feet
DIFFICULTY:	Easy
TIME:	25 minutes
FITNESS:	Walkers, hikers, runners
FAMILY FRIENDLY:	Yes
DOG FRIENDLY:	No
AMENITIES:	Restrooms and picnic sites with benches, barbecue pits, and drinking water near main park entrance
CONTACT:	California Department of Parks and Recreation; San Mateo County Parks Department
GPS:	37° 41' 42.5328" N 122° 26' 3.8328" W
MAP TO:	555 Guadalupe Canyon Pkwy., Brisbane

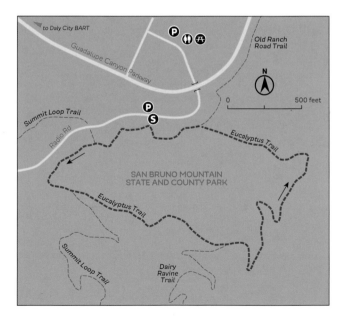

The Eucalyptus Loop Trail is great for beginner hikers and kids.

GETTING THERE

Public Transit: The closest BART stop is Daly City (2.8 miles from trailhead); otherwise, there are no great public transportation options. **Parking:** There is a six-dollar fee for each vehicle entering San Bruno Mountain State and County Park. Pay your fee at the self-registration station in the parking lot at 555 Guadalupe Canyon Pkwy. Then drive through the parking lot to pick up Radio Rd. (unsigned). Radio Rd. continues under Guadalupe Canyon Pkwy. and leads to a small parking lot near the trailhead after 0.15 mile.

The Eucalyptus Loop Trail is a good introduction to San Bruno Mountain. In terms of flora, you'll see eucalyptus, open grasslands, coastal scrub, and blackberry (if the season is right). And in terms of views, you'll see the San Bruno Mountain summit, the San Francisco skyline, and the bay. This hike is not very strenuous—after a gradual climb for the first 0.4 mile, the rest of the trail is gently downhill—so most people use it as part of a larger loop with the Summit Loop Trail, the Dairy Ravine Trail, or both. If you want to do a longer, more difficult hike, I recommend the San Bruno Mountain North Loop (see Hike 41) or the Summit Loop (see Hike 43); however, if you're just getting into hiking or you have young hikers with you, this is a great trail.

GET MOVING

Pick up the trail in the southwest corner of the small Radio Road parking lot. Walk past the information kiosk to locate the trailhead for the Eucalyptus Loop Trail (and many other trails). As this is a loop, you can go either left or right, but this write-up describes the route if you start out heading right. At 0.1 mile, reach a trail marker and the junction with the Summit Loop Trail. Stay left to remain on the Eucalyptus Loop, and at 0.2 mile, enter into one of two eucalyptus groves for which the trail is named. After exiting the grove, come to a second trail marker and a second junction with the Summit Loop Trail at 0.3 mile. Stay left again to stay on the Eucalyptus Loop. Now head into a second grove of eucalyptus; this one is not as tall or as thick as the first one. After you exit the trees, continue on the path, which starts out flat but becomes a gradual incline. You can start to look down on eucalyptus groves and the Saddle Loop Trail on the other side of Guadalupe Canyon Parkway.

At 0.4 mile reach a third trail marker and the junction with the Dairy Ravine Trail as you start to head downhill. Here you'll enjoy the best views of the hike. You'll see the bay, the San Francisco skyline, and eventually the towers atop San Bruno Mountain's summit. At 0.9 mile, you reach a fourth trail marker and the junction with the Old Ranch Road Trail; stay left. Shortly after the junction, the trail splits with no trail marker. Stay left again to continue on the trail and reach the end of your loop.

GO FARTHER

If this hike was easy for you, check out the San Bruno Mountain North Loop (Hike 41) or the Summit Loop (Hike 43). If you want to explore another easy trail, check out the 0.8-mile roundtrip Bog Trail (part of Hike 41).

43 Summit Loop Trail

DISTANCE:	3.3 miles
ELEVATION GAIN:	700 feet
HIGH POINT:	1314 feet
DIFFICULTY:	Moderate
TIME:	1 hour 15 minutes
FITNESS:	Hikers
FAMILY FRIENDLY:	May be too challenging for young children; see Hike 41 for alternatives
DOG FRIENDLY:	No
AMENITIES:	Restrooms, picnic sites with benches, and barbecue pits near main park entrance
CONTACT:	California Department of Parks and Recreation; San Mateo County Parks Department
GPS:	37° 41' 42.5328" N 122° 26' 3.8328" W
MAP TO:	555 Guadalupe Canyon Pkwy., Brisbane

GETTING THERE

Public Transit: The closest BART stop is Daly City (2.8 miles from trailhead); otherwise, there are no great public transportation options. **Parking:** There is a six-dollar fee for each vehicle entering San Bruno Mountain State and County Park. Pay your fee at the self-registration station in the parking lot at 555 Guadalupe Canyon Pkwy. Then drive through the parking lot to pick up Radio Rd. (unsigned). Radio Rd. continues under Guadalupe Canyon Pkwy. and leads to a small parking lot near the trailhead after 0.15 mile.

The radio towers on 1314-foot San Bruno Mountain are a common sight for Bay Area residents both during the day and at night. While you can drive to the top of the mountain, I think it's much more satisfying to get to the summit on your own two feet. There is significant elevation gain on this hike, but the route is pretty short, so it should be achievable for most. This is a straightforward uphill climb to the top, and it's packed with fantastic views. Looking north, you'll be able to see the ocean, the bay, and the city in between. To the south, the peninsula unfolds beneath you. Around you in the far distance, you'll be

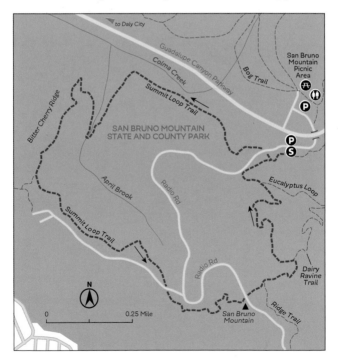

Hikers get far-ranging views from the Summit Trail.

able to see Mount Diablo, Mount Hamilton, Montara Mountain, and, on especially clear days, the Farallon Islands. As views are a big part of this hike's appeal, hike on a sunny day. It can be windy close to the summit, so be sure to pack an extra layer.

GET MOVING

Pick up the trail in the southwest corner of the small Radio Road parking lot. Walk past the information kiosk to locate the trailhead for the Summit Loop Trail (and many other trails). At 0.1 mile, reach the first trail marker and a junction with the Eucalyptus Loop Trail. Stay right to stay on the Summit Loop. While this is a loop, and you could turn either way here, I like starting in this direction as you get great views of the San Francisco skyline as you climb to the summit. Each time you need to catch your breath, you can turn around to take in the views. Cross Radio Road, and look for a trail marker across the street. Though this is the Summit Loop, you will actually be heading downhill for the next 0.5 mile. Your descent is along Colma Creek and April Brook, which you can hear but won't likely see (unless it's recently rained). Start your 1.8-mile ascent with a climb on a narrow trail along Bitter Cherry Ridge. The trail is flanked by thick plant life like blackberry bushes, coastal scrub, and, unfortunately, poison oak. You will start to get views of San Bruno Mountain's summit above and San Francisco below.

At 2 miles (1.3 miles into the climb), cross a paved road and pick up the trail on the other side next to the trail marker. You will cross Radio Road and reach the summit at 2.4 miles. On the summit, you can see what remains of a former Nike missile early warning radar site as well as large TV and radio towers. In 1949 KRON was the first television station to construct a tower on the summit, and KQED and KTVU soon followed. While most stations now transmit from Sutro Tower, many stations, including KNTV, still broadcast from here.

From the summit, it's a descent of just under a mile to return to the start. Cross Radio Road and look for the trail marker to the left of the building with large towers on top of it. Follow the Summit Loop Trail about 400 feet to a junction, where you will see a trail marker pointing out the Ridge Trail to the right and the continuation of the Summit Trail ahead. Stay straight here and at the next spur trail to the left. After 0.2 mile, pass a turnoff for the Dairy Ravine Trail to your right. After another 0.5 mile, you reach a trail marker where you turn left to follow the Summit Loop Trail (while not labeled as such, this is also part of the Eucalyptus Loop, Hike 42). Walk through a small eucalyptus grove, and when you reach a trail marker for the Summit Loop, turn right to finish your loop (though the arrow on the marker points left).

GO FARTHER
Check out the San Bruno Mountain North Loop (Hike 41) or nearby Sign Hill (Hike 44) for a short but challenging 1.1-mile hike.

44 **Sign Hill**

DISTANCE:	1.1 miles
ELEVATION GAIN:	360 feet
HIGH POINT:	580 feet
DIFFICULTY:	Challenging
TIME:	45 minutes
FITNESS:	Hikers
FAMILY FRIENDLY:	May be too steep for young children
DOG FRIENDLY:	On leash
AMENITIES:	Benches
CONTACT:	South San Francisco Parks and Recreation Department
GPS:	37° 39' 59.2416" N 122° 25' 23.0124" W
MAP TO:	Ridgeview Ct. and Carnelian Rd., South San Francisco

GETTING THERE

Public Transit: From South San Francisco BART, take the South City Shuttle (SCS, Bay 6) on its clockwise route to Hillside Blvd. and Chestnut Ave., which drops you 0.3 mile from the trailhead. SCS runs on weekdays only. You can also walk from the South San Francisco BART Station, which is 1.7 miles away. **Parking:** There is a small parking lot at the trailhead at

A unique perspective of the South San Francisco: The Industrial City sign

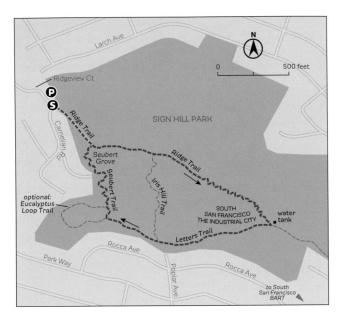

the intersection of Ridgeview Ct. and Carnelian Rd. in South San Francisco.

Perched on the southern slope of aptly named Sign Hill, the Bay Area's version of the Hollywood sign: "South San Francisco: The Industrial City" looms high in the air, a beacon for those traveling toward the city on US 101 north. After years of San Francisco living, I was thrilled to finally get to see the sign up close. This hike takes you above and below the sign, so you can see it from various angles.

Two aspects of this short hike surprised me: The letters are much bigger than you think (sixty feet tall!). They are so big that as I walked by them, at times it was hard to make out which letter I was near. I was also surprised that this 1.1-mile hike could be so challenging. Not only are the ascents at the beginning and end of the hike difficult, but the descent to the

A BEACON ON THE HILLSIDE

In 1923, the South San Francisco Chamber of Commerce used powdered lime to paint "South San Francisco: The Industrial City" on the south slope of Sign Hill. This temporary publicity stunt was designed to draw attention to the community and its businesses. Five years later, a bond measure was passed to make the sign a permanent fixture. In April 1929, South San Francisco–based Cement Gun Construction Company created the current sixty-foot-tall concrete letters. The sign was added to the National Register of Historic Places and the California Office of Historic Preservation in 1996.

bottom of the letters was also challenging, involving a number of tight switchbacks along a steep downhill section.

If you can deal with the steep ascents and descent, you'll love this route. The panoramic peninsula views are spectacular, and airplane buffs will love spotting the frequent San Francisco International Airport departures and arrivals. While the south side of the hill is publicly owned, the north side is privately owned and is being considered for a housing development. The Friends of Sign Hill and San Bruno Mountain Watch have joined forces to preserve the untouched native habitat.

GET MOVING

Pick up the Ridge Trail at the parking lot trailhead on Ridgeview Court. Follow the wide, paved trail a steep 0.1 mile to the top, which has several towers, including one that is strung with lights and serves as the hill's electrically powered Christmas tree. From here, the path slopes gently and then steeply downhill.

At 0.3 mile take a series of twenty or so switchbacks to the bottom of the hill to avoid slipping and to protect the hill from erosion. You'll start to see the letters below you. At

The Letters Trail leads you along the bottom of Sign Hill's famous sign.

the bottom of the switchbacks, walk toward a large creamy-yellow structure (perhaps an old water tank) and turn right to pick up the 0.2-mile-long Letters Trail that takes you below the sign and gives you a better vantage point from which to appreciate the letters.

At the end of the Letters Trail, the difficult ascent back to the Ridge Trail begins. Here, you can choose between the Iris Hill Trail to your right (0.25 mile) or the Seubert Trail to your left (0.35 mile). The Iris Hill Trail is steep, stair-filled, and direct. I like the Seubert Trail as it has fewer stairs and more switchbacks, and it allows you to take a detour to explore the Eucalyptus Loop Trail. If you take the Seubert Trail, you'll reach a grove of trees called Seubert Grove just before arriving back at the Ridge Trail. When you reach the Ridge Trail, turn left to walk back down the hill and to the parking lot.

MR. SIGN HILL

The Seubert Trail and Seubert Grove are named after Alphonse Seubert, a South San Francisco resident and member of the city's beautification committee. It is estimated that he single-handedly planted 5000 trees, which he frequently tended over the years. Mr. Sign Hill, as he was called, was also involved in the creation of the hill's trail system. In 1991 he received the National Arbor Day Foundation's Lawrence Enersen Award for his dedication to tree planting and conservation and for his eye toward community improvement. Seubert passed away in 2006.

GO FARTHER

Sign Hill includes thirty acres of open space and nearly 2 miles of hiking trails. If you didn't take the Iris Hill Trail on your first ascent, you may want to go up and down it. Or, for a slight change of scenery, head to nearby San Bruno Mountain State and County Park for a number of other trails and views (see Hikes 41–43).

Next page: A hiker walks high above the fog on the Matt Davis Trail, Trail 49. (photo by Jon Cosner)

MOUNTAINS
OF MARIN

With so many outdoor opportunities in Marin County, it was difficult to limit my selection to just six hikes. I ended up with three hikes in the Marin Headlands and three on Mount Tamalpais—all within an hour's drive from San Francisco.

The Marin Headlands is a part of the Golden Gate National Recreation Area situated just north of the Golden Gate Bridge. Once occupied by the Miwok tribe, the headlands offer impressive Golden Gate Bridge views, coastal trails, and military history.

Mount Tamalpais is 2571 feet at its peak and covers 6300 acres. Upon discovering the mountain in 1770, Spanish explorers named it La Sierra de Nuestro Padre de San Francisco. It was then changed to Tamalpais, a Miwok word (*tamal* means "bay" or "coast" and *pais* means "mountain"). Most locals, however, just call it Mount Tam. On the mountain, you'll wander through grasslands and redwoods, enjoy Stinson Beach and Bolinas Bay views, and reach the tallest point on the mountain.

Note: You will have to pay a toll (at this writing up to $7.25 or $6.25 with FasTrak) going southbound on the Golden Gate Bridge into San Francisco. Going northbound across the Golden Gate Bridge is free.

45 Slacker Hill

DISTANCE:	3.3 miles
ELEVATION GAIN:	900 feet
HIGH POINT:	930 feet
DIFFICULTY:	Challenging
TIME:	1 hour 20 minutes
FITNESS:	Hikers
FAMILY FRIENDLY:	May be too steep for some children
DOG FRIENDLY:	No
AMENITIES:	Restrooms at Vista Point; porta potties in Conzelman Lot
CONTACT:	Golden Gate National Recreation Area; California Coastal Trail
GPS:	37° 49' 56.4744" N 122° 28' 56.0568" W
MAP TO:	North Tower Golden Gate Parking, Mill Valley

GETTING THERE

Public Transit: Golden Gate Transit bus 10 to the US 101 off-ramp (Sausalito Lateral stop). Make sure to press the stop button on the bridge to request this stop or the driver will keep going. *Weekends only:* MUNI bus 76X to US 101 to Conzelman Rd. (GGNRA entrance sign). **Parking:** Park at the lot at the end of Conzelman Rd., where the hike starts, or park at the Vista Point parking lot (first exit over the Golden Gate Bridge) and add 0.15 mile to your hike.

This quick and straightforward Marin Headlands hike provides one of the best possible views of the Golden Gate Bridge, San Francisco, and the bay. While you can drive along Conzelman Road in the Marin Headlands and stop for views, those lookout points can be packed with tourists. The uphill trek to Slacker Hill will get your heart pumping and you may even have the trail to yourself. This is a great place to take in a sunrise or a sunset. Go on a sunny day to make the most of the views, but make sure to bring sunscreen as this is a very exposed route.

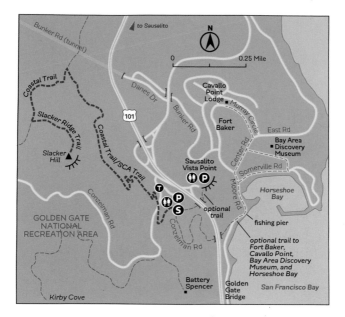

GET MOVING

If you are starting your hike at the Sausalito Vista Point, make sure you are on the side of the lot closest to the highway. With the visitor center at your back, walk toward US 101. Look for a metal gate and descend the stairway to walk through a tunnel under the Golden Gate Bridge. Take a stairway and then a sidewalk to reach the North Tower Golden Gate parking lot. Continue on a sidewalk on the south side of the lot. When you reach a road on your left with a crosswalk, look ahead for a trail marker for the Coastal Trail at the start of your hike.

Head up a few stairs and enter a small grove of trees— your only shade on this route. At 0.1 mile, reach Conzelman Road. Look back for views of the Golden Gate Bridge, the San Francisco skyline, the Bay Bridge, Alcatraz, and Angel Island. Cross at the crosswalk, and pick up the SCA Trail (Coastal Trail) on the other side of the road. For 0.3 mile, you'll walk

WHAT'S IN A NAME?

The origin of the name Slacker Ridge, or Slacker Hill, is unknown. Some believe the name is ironic—that only the enthusiastic hiker will take this spur trail. Others believe it comes from army deserters (formerly known as "slackers") from Fort Baker and other nearby military posts.

along a few long uphill switchbacks lined with coastal scrub as you climb high above busy US 101. Across the highway, you can see Fort Baker, the bay, and Angel Island. When the switchbacks end, your route heads north in the direction of the Robin Williams Tunnel. Whenever you need a rest, look south to take in better and better views.

When you reach a junction with the Coastal Trail at 1.1 miles, stay left to follow it toward McCullough Road. The din of car traffic will finally die down. After 0.3 mile, reach a sign for McCullough Road. Just after this, look for a trail marker to your left for Slacker Ridge, now just 0.2 mile away. This turnoff is the short but steep climb to the top of 930-foot Slacker Hill. For most of your ascent, the grade will be in the double digits, so pace yourself. At the top of the hill, you reach a wide clearing where you take in sweeping views of the Golden Gate Bridge, the bay, and San Francisco. When you've soaked in the scenery, return the way you came.

GO FARTHER

For an extra 1.9 miles roundtrip with 200 feet of climbing, visit Fort Baker with options such as Horseshoe Bay, the Bay Area Discovery Museum, and Cavallo Point Lodge at Fort Baker. From the North Tower Golden Gate parking lot, descend Conzelman Road using the bike lane to enter the road (here, the rest of the road is blocked off with a gate). Continue downhill, watching out for bicycles. After 0.6 mile, pass

Stunning city and bridge views are the highlight of the Slacker Hill hike.

under the Golden Gate Bridge and reach a gate. Continue on Moore Road (unsigned) and pass a fishing pier and parking area. Take your first right onto Somerville Road after 0.1 mile to walk around the water and explore Horseshoe Bay. To visit the rest of Fort Baker, continue on Moore Road and head right on Center Road at the fork. Make sure you're walking on the sidewalk on the left side of the road. Take your second right to visit the Bay Area Discovery Museum in another 0.1 mile, or go left onto Murray Circle to visit Cavallo Point Lodge in about 0.3 mile. Here, you'll find a restaurant and bar—and a spa if you really need it! Return the way you came.

FORT BAKER

Sitting on approximately 335 acres, Fort Baker was completed in 1910 as permanent housing for soldiers working on the nearby batteries—Yates, Spencer, Kirby, Duncan, and Orlando Wagner. In 1995 the military transferred the land to the Golden Gate National Recreation Area, and the last soldiers left the base in 2000. Fort Baker officially became a park in 2002.

46 Hill 88

DISTANCE:	5.2 miles
ELEVATION GAIN:	1130 feet
HIGH POINT:	830 feet
DIFFICULTY:	Challenging
TIME:	2 hours 10 minutes
FITNESS:	Hikers
FAMILY FRIENDLY:	May be too challenging for some children; the 1.5-mile Lagoon Trail is an easier option
DOG FRIENDLY:	Yes
AMENITIES:	Restroom and picnic area with barbecues in the Fort Cronkhite parking lot
CONTACT:	Golden Gate National Recreation Area
GPS:	37° 49' 56.1360" N 122° 32' 22.4376" W
MAP TO:	Fort Cronkhite parking lot, Sausalito

GETTING THERE

Public Transit: *Weekends only:* MUNI bus 76X stops at Fort Cronkhite Parking Lot at the intersection of Kirkpatrick St. and Mitchell Rd. in Sausalito. **Parking:** There is ample parking in the Fort Cronkhite parking lot.

Hill 88 is part of Fort Cronkhite, a World War II military post situated next to Rodeo Beach and the Pacific Ocean. The well-preserved fort includes barracks, a mess hall, and supply buildings, which today house nonprofits such as the Marine Mammal Center, NatureBridge, and more. The fort's military history isn't just on the ground—it's also high in the hills. On this route, you'll pass by World War II–era Battery Townsley (open the first Sunday of the month from noon to 4:00 PM), and you'll summit 833-foot Hill 88, a former Nike missile radar station. Finished in 1955, the officially named Site SF88-C was the control center for Nike Missile Site SF88-L located down the hill at Fort Barry.

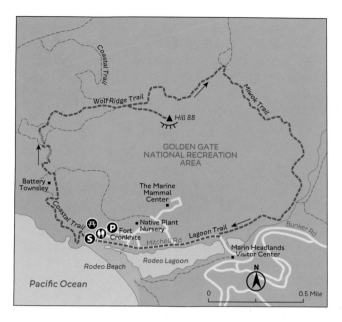

The landscape is covered in chaparral and grasslands with few trees, so wear sunscreen and a hat on sunny days, when you'll be treated to great views of Rodeo Beach, Mount Tam, downtown San Francisco, Sutro Tower, and the Golden Gate Bridge. You'll also want to keep an eye on the sky to spot the nineteen species of birds that circle the area, including hawks, eagles, falcons, and more.

GET MOVING

Pick up the paved trail next to the restrooms at the Fort Cronkhite parking lot, where you'll see a Coastal Trail marker for Battery Townsley and Hill 88. After 0.1 mile, turn left and go up stairs to a dirt trail, the Coastal Trail. Continue on the trail and follow it as it curves to the right. If you look back toward Rodeo Beach, you can see San Francisco's Sutro Tower in the distance. At 0.3 mile when you come to a T intersection with a paved section of the Coastal Trail, turn left to follow signs for the Wolf Ridge Trail and Hill 88. Stay on this paved trail for 0.2 mile until you reach Battery Townsley at 0.7 mile. As you climb up the hill, you can see a green structure, the back of the battery.

BATTERY TOWNSLEY

During World War II, Battery Townsley and Battery Davis (located in San Francisco's Fort Funston) protected both sides of the Golden Gate. Battery Townsley's two 16-inch guns were 68 feet long and could shoot a one-ton projectile almost 25 miles into the ocean. The guns were only fired for target practice, and when fired, they were so powerful that they knocked anyone in the vicinity off their feet. To see what these guns looked like, check out the gun outside the battery that was originally mounted on the battleship USS *Missouri*.

When you run into another paved road just after Battery Townsley, turn left and continue following the markers for the Coastal Trail, climbing an impressive stone and wooden stairway on your way. At 0.9 mile, turn right at a paved section of the Coastal Trail (don't follow the arrow that points back the way you came) and climb another long wooden stairway. At 1.1 miles, the trail splits at a small hill. Follow the trail left toward some military ruins, then climb to the top of the hill, which is covered in other wood, concrete, and metal ruins. Look straight ahead to see a mint-green building. This is the summit of Hill 88. Climb and descend two more small hills in short succession. At the bottom of the second hill, look left to see a junction with a number of trail markers. For now you'll continue on the paved path to climb to the top of your third hill, Hill 88, at 1.6 miles. Once on the summit, walk around the ruins and visit the lookout point to your right.

Looking south toward Rodeo Beach and beyond from Hill 88

After exploring Hill 88, return the way you came to the junction with all the trail markers. Turn right to pick up the Wolf Ridge Trail and take in views of Mount Tam and Tennessee Valley. When you reach a junction with the Miwok Trail at 2.9 miles, turn right to follow it toward the Rodeo Valley Trail. Stay on the Miwok Trail for 1.1 miles. This section of the hike overlooking the Gerbode Valley is mostly downhill with some flat stretches. Watch your step on the steep downhill sections.

The trail flattens out at 4 miles, and at 4.5 miles, the trail ends at a white gate next to a parking area. Look for a crosswalk to cross Bunker Road (unsigned), and then turn right to walk on the Lagoon Trail for 0.7 mile back to your start.

GO FARTHER

Have a picnic in the area near the Fort Cronkhite parking lot, explore Rodeo Beach, or visit the Marin Headlands Visitor Center.

47 From Pirates to Zen

DISTANCE:	9.0 miles
ELEVATION GAIN:	2100 feet
HIGH POINT:	1030 feet
DIFFICULTY:	Challenging
TIME:	4 hours
FITNESS:	Hikers
FAMILY FRIENDLY:	May be too difficult for young children; families wanting a shorter route can hike to Tennessee Beach for a 3.4-mile roundtrip alternative
DOG FRIENDLY:	No
AMENITIES:	Restrooms and picnic benches in Tennessee Valley parking area; restrooms, picnic tables, and benches in Muir Beach parking area; restrooms and seating at Pelican Inn
CONTACT:	Golden Gate National Recreation Area
GPS:	37° 51' 36.4328 N 122° 32' 10.6728 W
MAP TO:	Tennessee Valley trailhead

GETTING THERE

Public Transit: None. **Parking:** There is a parking lot at the Tennessee Valley trailhead toward the end of Tennessee Valley Rd.

There are so many aspects of this hike to like. There are few more breathtaking sights than walking along the Pacific Ocean on the Coastal Trail, and this route starts with almost 4.5 miles of coastal views. Muir Beach is a beautiful halfway point and a great place to stop and have a picnic. Others can stop for a bite at the Pelican Inn, a sixteenth-century-style inn and restaurant near the beach. The return trip meanders through the Green Gulch Farm Zen Center, an organic farm and Zen retreat that has you feeling like you've been temporarily swept away to Japan. And the Green Gulch, Coyote Ridge, and Miwok trails give you expansive valley views. This

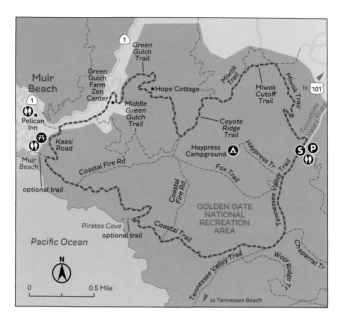

hike is a challenge due to its length and elevation, but the scenery makes it worth every step. This trail is best done on a sunny day; bring sunscreen as there is almost no tree cover.

GET MOVING

Locate the Tennessee Valley trailhead and follow the sign toward Tennessee Beach and the Coastal Fire Road. Walk along the paved Tennessee Valley Trail, passing the Haypress Camp and Fox trails at 0.2 and 0.3 mile. At 0.6 mile, bear right on the trail (now dirt) toward the Coastal Trail. At 0.8 mile, stay right again to continue toward the Coastal Trail. At 1.2 miles, bear right and uphill onto the Coastal Trail toward Muir Beach. Start a steep 0.6-mile climb that gains almost 500 feet. While this climb can be tough, you'll start to take in increasingly beautiful views of the ocean. At the summit of this hill, the Coastal Fire Road branches off to the right, but

Muir Beach from the Coastal Trail

you will bear left to continue toward Pirates Cove. The trail begins a sometimes-steep descent with ocean views to your left. After 0.4 mile, a spur trail heads left for Pirates Cove. This 0.1-mile roundtrip option is a scramble down to the beach and back. There is little to no beach to explore at high tide.

After Pirates Cove, the trail goes inland and uphill before heading back along the ocean. After 1 mile, pass the other end of the Coastal Fire Road you passed before and bear right on a wide trail rather than the more narrow and steep uphill trail to your left. You are now heading downhill as Muir Beach comes into view. When you're almost down to the beach, reach a marker for Kaasi Road (*kaasi* means "salmon" in the Miwok language). Turn right on Kaasi Road toward the Middle Green Gulch Trail, or turn left to take a detour to Muir Beach that adds about 0.1 mile to your hike. There are restrooms and a picnic area in the beach parking lot.

At the next bend in the trail, go left to continue on Kaasi Road toward the Middle Green Gulch Trail. Then at the next intersection you can either turn right on Middle Green Gulch Trail or continue on Kaasi Road to the Pelican Inn, located at 10 Pacific Way. The trail leads you to the inn's parking lot (which adds 0.4 mile roundtrip).

THE PELICAN INN

The Pelican Inn was built in 1978 to look like a sixteenth-century Tudor inn. The inn boasts 500-year-old redwood support beams, a wood floor from a San Francisco warehouse demolished in the early 1900s, and black paneling at the bar from Laker's Hotel, a seventeenth-century inn. This is a popular stop on weekends, so if the bar area and dining room are full, you can rest your legs and eat on the lawn.

Once on Middle Green Gulch Trail, follow the trail marker for the Green Gulch Farm Zen Center. You'll reach a gate for the farm in 0.15 mile. Go through it and close it behind you. Walk by three fields and bear left when you see a turnoff on your right for the Middle Green Gulch Trail. (If you're tired, you can also take the Middle Green Gulch Trail back to the start for a shorter hike.) Continue through the farm, passing greenhouses and Green Dragon Organic Nursery. Exit the farm area through another gate and follow a sign for the Welcome Center. When you reach the first Zen Center buildings, bear left when you can, and pick up a gravel road bordered by tall eucalyptus trees. As you walk around the center, be respectful of the visitors. Turn right when you reach a paved

GREEN DRAGON TEMPLE

The Green Gulch Farm Zen Center, also called Green Dragon Temple, was established in 1972, not long after the death of Shunryu Suzuki Roshi in 1971. Roshi was a Japanese Zen priest and author of *Zen Mind, Beginner's Mind*. The center has two sister sites: the Zen Center in San Francisco and Tassajara Zen Mountain Center in Carmel Valley, California. Combined, the three comprise one of the largest Buddhist centers outside Asia. The Green Gulch Farm Zen Center offers a public program on Sundays.

road opposite a dirt parking lot. Turn right again at a second parking lot.

Continue through a gate and bear left onto the Green Gulch Trail when your trail splits. Stay left at the second fork in the trail as you approach the biggest climb of the hike, almost 900 feet in less than 2 miles. As you climb, enjoy valley views and glimpses of Muir Beach and the Pacific Ocean. When you are 0.8 mile into your climb, reach Hope Cottage, a former personal retreat space owned by the Zen Center. When you reach a T at the end of Green Gulch Trail, turn left to pick up the Coyote Ridge Trail (unsigned). On sunny days, you'll have views of Sutro Tower and the top of the San Francisco skyline. You'll head uphill for the first 0.3 mile of this trail and then downhill for another 0.2 mile. Turn right at an intersection with the Miwok Trail to head back to Tennessee Valley. After 0.3 mile, take a singletrack on the right, the Miwok Cutoff Trail for 0.2 mile and then reconnect with the main Miwok Trail. Continue another mile to the Tennessee Valley parking lot.

GO FARTHER

To explore more of this special landscape, head to Tennessee Beach.

48 Muir Woods from Mountain Home Inn

DISTANCE:	4.3 miles
ELEVATION GAIN:	870 feet
HIGH POINT:	970 feet
DIFFICULTY:	Moderate
TIME:	2 hours
FITNESS:	Hikers
FAMILY FRIENDLY:	Families may want to drive directly to the Muir Woods main entrance for an easier hike
DOG FRIENDLY:	No

AMENITIES:	Restroom in parking lot across from the Mountain Home Inn; bench at junction of Lost Trail and Canopy View Trail; benches in Muir Woods
CONTACT:	California Department of Parks and Recreation; Friends of Mount Tam; National Park Service; Golden Gate National Recreation Area
GPS:	37° 54' 36.1656" N 122° 34' 37.7544" W
MAP TO:	Mountain Home Inn, Mill Valley

GETTING THERE

Public Transit: None. **Parking:** There is a small parking lot across the street from the Mountain Home Inn on Panoramic Hwy. and another small lot that's across the street from 760 Panoramic Hwy.

Muir Woods is famous for its redwoods. More than a million people visit each year, which can make the monument feel like a tourist trap and can also make parking difficult. For these reasons, I like taking the back entrance to Muir Woods. A combination of the Trestle Trail, Alice Eastwood Road, the Panoramic Trail, Canopy View Trail, Lost Trail, and Fern Creek Trail takes you on the downhill journey from Panoramic Highway to Muir Woods. As you descend, the redwoods get larger and more frequent. Your route should remain relatively quiet until you reach the Redwood Creek Trail in Muir Woods.

When you reach Muir Woods, spend as much time as you like taking in the trees and the environment. Then muster your energy for the 800-plus-foot climb looping back toward your start on the Canopy View Trail. As most of the hike takes place in tree cover, this hike is fine to do on both sunny and cloudy days.

GET MOVING

With the Mountain Home Inn on your right and the parking lot on your left, walk to the end of the lot and look for a small trail marker for the Trestle Trail. Take a stairway and dirt trail down to paved Alice Eastwood Road and take a left. At 0.1

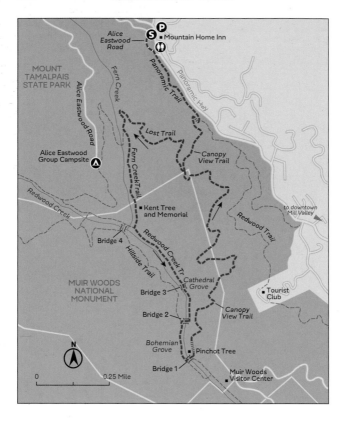

mile, you'll reach a marker for the Panoramic Trail. Follow the Panoramic Trail and after another 0.2 mile, take a right down a stairway to pick up the Canopy View Trail (formerly the Ocean View Trail). Pass some large boulders and start heading downhill. The trail is soon lined with trees and ferns. At 0.6 mile, take a right at the marker for the Lost Trail. On this trail, you'll start to see redwoods.

After 0.5 mile on the Lost Trail, arrive at a junction with the Fern Creek Trail and a bridge over a fallen tree. Turn left here toward the Redwood Creek Trail (formerly the Main Trail), and

The Redwood Creek Trail leads hikers into Muir Woods.

walk along a wooden fence. At 1.5 miles, you reach the sign welcoming you into Muir Woods National Monument, and in another 200 feet, you reach the fallen Kent Tree and Kent Memorial.

Your trail soon splits around Cathedral Grove. Just after the grove, you'll pass a bridge labeled Bridge 3. Continue to

A CALIFORNIA COASTAL TREASURE

California coastal redwoods are the tallest trees in the world—growing to a height of more than 320 feet and a width of 27 feet at their base. Depending on climate, they can grow from one inch to two to three feet a year. For their size, they have a surprisingly shallow root system. Their roots grow outward—as much as 100 feet from the base—instead of downward, and they intertwine with the roots of other redwoods to increase their stability.

Redwoods are named for their red bark. Over time, this bark has evolved for survival. Its thickness (up to a foot) helps protect against fire damage, and its tannins prevent insect damage. Repeated fires can burn through the bark and expose the center of the tree to dry rot. Later, fires can hollow out the rotted portions (you will see some hollowed-out trees along the trail).

THE COUPLE WHO SAVED THE REDWOODS

In the nineteenth century, redwoods were plentiful and covered an estimated 2 million acres between Big Sur and southern Oregon. Logging started in the 1850s as a consequence of the explosive population growth during the gold rush. In 1905, Congressman William Kent and his wife, Elizabeth Thacher Kent, bought 611 acres of redwood forest for $45,000, and in 1907, the couple donated 295 acres to the federal government. One year later, in 1908, President Theodore Roosevelt took advantage of the Antiquities Act that had been passed in 1906 to make the woods a national monument. Roosevelt wanted to name the new monument after Kent, but Kent insisted it be named Muir Woods after conservationist John Muir.

A Douglas fir was named for William Kent, and the Kent Memorial (a small plaque) was placed there in December 1928. The Kent Tree was once the tallest tree in the woods. A crack was discovered in the tree in January 2003, and it fell in March 2003.

Bridge 2, cross to the other side, and turn left to visit Bohemian Grove. Stay on this side of the trail (the Bohemian Grove Trail) for 0.2 mile until you reach Bridge 1. At Bridge 1, cross back over the bridge and turn left. (Do not exit the park; otherwise, you'll need to pay an entrance fee to reenter.) Pass the Pinchot Tree, one of the largest and oldest trees in the forest and then look for the Canopy View Trail on your right. Take the stairs to start on this trail, and after 1.3 miles, reach the intersection with the Lost Trail—continue straight and head uphill on the well-trodden Canopy View Trail.

You soon emerge from the trees and when you reach the large boulders you saw at the start of the hike, follow the trail to the right. Climb the stairway and make a left at the Panoramic Trail. Stay on the Panoramic Trail, making sure not to head right up to Panoramic Highway. Then continue on Alice Eastwood Road to the Trestle Trail, which takes you back to the parking lot where you started.

GO FARTHER

If you're hungry, grab a bite at the Mountain Home Inn. Or, if you still have hiking energy, do Hike 50, Mount Tam East Peak.

49 Matt Davis and Steep Ravine Loop

DISTANCE:	6.5 miles
ELEVATION GAIN:	1830 feet
HIGH POINT:	1585 feet
DIFFICULTY:	Challenging
TIME:	3 hours 10 minutes
FITNESS:	Hikers
FAMILY FRIENDLY:	May be too challenging for some children
DOG FRIENDLY:	No
AMENITIES:	Restroom in Pantoll parking lot
CONTACT:	California Department of Parks and Recreation; Friends of Mount Tam
GPS:	37° 53' 57.7392" N 122° 38' 14.3448" W
MAP TO:	Stinson Beach Fire Station

GETTING THERE

Public Transit: None. **Parking:** Free parking is available at three beach parking lots off Shoreline Hwy. (Highway 1), a quarter mile from the start.

Matt Davis was known by some as the dean of trail workers, and the trail that bears his name was created in 1931 as a more level alternative to the Dipsea Trail. This is a classic Mount Tam loop hike with a great mix of scenery: woods, open grasslands, coastal scrub, and Bolinas Bay and Stinson Beach views. While you can start this hike at Pantoll station—short for Panoramic Toll and named for the toll booth that was near this location on Panoramic Highway—I like starting near the Stinson Beach Fire Station. By starting in Stinson Beach, you'll complete the uphill portion of the hike first, then descend for much of the rest of the hike, starting at the Pantoll parking lot. This is a popular loop, so trails can be crowded, especially on weekends.

GET MOVING

These directions start from the central beach parking lot, which is open year-round. Head to the northwest corner of the lot and cross a small footbridge to Calle del Mar. Walk one block to Shoreline Highway (Highway 1), turn right, and turn left onto Belvedere Avenue. Continue north past the Stinson Beach Fire Station and Community Center, and look for the Matt Davis trailhead on your right.

The route starts with a wooded ascent lined with ferns. At 0.1 mile, bear left where a trail breaks off to the right. At 0.2 mile, turn right at a trail marker to stay on the Matt Davis Trail. This is the start of a series of switchbacks and stairs. At 0.7

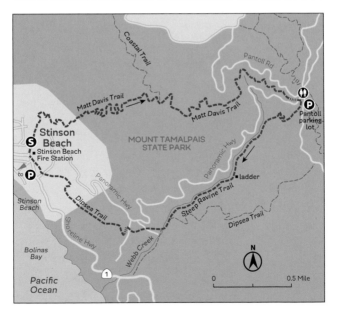

California poppies dot the Matt Davis Trail in spring. (photo by Jon Cosner)

mile, look for Table Rock, a large boulder. Look for a small spur trail to your left that leads to the top of the rock with views of the forest and Stinson Beach (you'll have to navigate around some trees to get here). After this detour, you still have about a mile of switchbacks.

After the switchbacks, leave the woods and enter wide open grasslands with a few patches of woods. You are still heading uphill, but you're already done with more than 80 percent of the climbing on this route. Here you have views of the ocean or the fog, depending on the weather. Pass a junction with the Coastal Trail at 2.1 miles, and stay left at a junction with a Matt Davis trail marker at 2.3 miles. Continue on the Matt Davis Trail until it ends at the Pantoll parking lot at 3.6 miles. Cross Pantoll Road, which you can reach by descending some stairs, and enter the parking lot for water fountains and restrooms.

The descent starts here. Pick up the Steep Ravine Trail from the southeastern end of the Pantoll parking lot. If you're facing the restrooms, this should be on your right. Stay on the trail for 1.5 miles, enjoying ferns, a creek, and redwoods. At one point, you'll even descend a ladder to stay on the trail. Reach a junction with the Dipsea Trail at 5.1 miles but stay right rather than crossing the creek. Here the Dipsea and Steep Ravine trails overlap for a short, 0.1-mile stretch. When you reach the next junction, stay right to follow the Dipsea Trail. This trail climbs for 0.1 mile, leaving tree cover and crossing a fire road. The trail soon heads downhill, giving you views of Stinson Beach and Bolinas Bay. Arrive at a junction with another fire road after 0.1 mile, cross the road, and descend a stairway. The next 0.6 mile of your trail is exposed and has more views of the beach and bay. Continue 0.3 mile to reach Panoramic Highway. Cross the road through a parking area and continue on the Dipsea Trail for 0.1 mile to reach Shoreline Highway (Highway 1). Turn right on Shoreline Highway, go left on Calle del Mar for one block, and cross the footbridge to return to the parking lot. Or turn right to return to the trailhead.

GO FARTHER

If you've worked up an appetite, head to Shoreline Highway to the center of Stinson Beach, where you'll find a selection of restaurants and snack bars. There are also picnic areas by the parking lots.

50 Mount Tam East Peak

DISTANCE:	6.1 miles
ELEVATION GAIN:	1600 feet
HIGH POINT:	2571 feet
DIFFICULTY:	Challenging
TIME:	2 hours 45 minutes
FITNESS:	Hikers
FAMILY FRIENDLY:	May be too challenging for young children; head to the East Peak parking lot (Map to: Friends of Mount Tam) to go on shorter hikes with less elevation gain
DOG FRIENDLY:	No
AMENITIES:	Restroom in parking lot across from Mountain Home Inn; picnic area by Throckmorton Ridge Fire

	Station; restrooms and picnic benches next to visitor center in the East Peak parking lot; picnic areas, restrooms, snacks, and drinks at West Point Inn
CONTACT:	California Department of Parks and Recreation; Marin Municipal Water District; Friends of Mount Tam
GPS:	37° 54' 36.1656" N 122° 34' 37.7544" W
MAP TO:	Mountain Home Inn

GETTING THERE

Public Transit: None. **Parking:** There is a small parking lot across the street from the Mountain Home Inn on Panoramic Hwy. and another small lot that's across the street from 760 Panoramic Hwy.

At 2571 feet, Mount Tam's East Peak provides one of the best panoramic views in the Bay Area. The mountain was once home to the Mount Tamalpais and Muir Woods Scenic Railway. Built in 1896, it was called the "Crookedest Railroad in the World" for its 281 curves in just 8.25 miles. To get to Mount Tam from the city, San Franciscans would board a ferry to Sausalito and then a train to Mill Valley, where they would start their forty-five-minute trip to the summit. Once there, they would take in the views and dine at the now defunct Tavern of Tamalpais. Starting in 1902, riders could take the gravity car down to Mill Valley or Muir Woods. The "gravity man" would be asked to "turn on" the gravity to start the car on its 7 percent grade, and would be responsible for maintaining a speed of 12 miles per hour for the entire descent. The railroad's popularity waned as more people bought cars, and a 1929 fire destroyed many of the tracks. The tracks were never rebuilt, and the line shut down permanently in 1930. Although the railroad is gone, you can still trace its former route on Old Railroad Grade.

My favorite time to do this hike is a sunny day during the rainy season. With the sun, you get the panoramic views, and with the rainy season, you get streams and waterfalls along some of the trails.

GET MOVING

From the Mountain Home Inn, walk north alongside Panoramic Highway. After about 300 feet, pick up a road to your right signed for Fire Station Exit. Head uphill and take a left onto Hogback Road, a wide dirt trail just after the Marin County Fire Department sign. Pass the Marin County Fire Department building and then a large green water tank. Pass the Matt Davis Trail junction at 0.4 mile and the Hoo-Koo-E-Koo Trail junction at 0.5 mile. Continue on a steep climb until you reach a junction with Old Railroad Grade at 0.7 mile. Turn left,

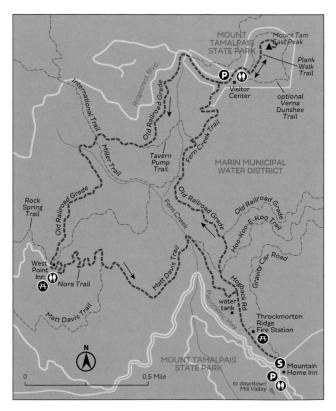

and continue for 0.4 mile. At 1.1 miles, look for the Fern Creek trailhead on the right. Follow this tree-covered singletrack with stairs uphill. Stay on the Fern Creek Trail for 0.7 mile, passing a water tank and a junction with the Tavern Pump Trail, and eventually reaching a paved road (no traffic) where a sign points right toward East Peak. You'll want to remember this road, as you'll want to come back here later.

Cross the road and climb a few steps to pick up a trail that soon brings you to East Ridgecrest Boulevard, another paved road (this one has vehicle traffic). Take a right, watching for cars and bicycles as you walk through the parking lot. From here, there are many options. The visitor center, a small green building, is on the left and is open from 11:00 AM to 4:00 PM on weekends. You can also visit the Gravity Car Barn to learn more about the Mount Tam and Muir Woods Scenic Railway. Or follow the Verna Dunshee Trail, a 0.7-mile loop around East Peak.

To reach East Peak, take the Plank Walk Trail to the left of the restroom. As the trail climbs, you'll begin to see panoramic views of Marin below. At 2.1 miles, reach the summit, marked by a fire watch tower, Mount Tam Lookout, that is still in use today by the Marin County Fire Department (lookout is not open to the public). Soak in the views of Marin, the East Bay, and San Francisco. When you're ready, retrace your steps to the parking lot. Walk to the paved road where the Fern Creek Trail let out on before. Turn right (away from the parking lot) and be careful as the road leads to East Ridgecrest Boulevard. Just after you reach East Ridgecrest and as it begins to curve left, turn left onto Old Railroad Grade. Stay right on the trail as there are many cyclists doing their descent from the summit here. You'll be on this trail for 1.4 miles. Pass the Tavern Pump Trail and the International Trail on your way, and the Rock Spring Trail right before you reach the West Point Inn. After the junction with Rock Spring Trail, Old Railroad Grade circles the inn and a picnic area at 4.1 miles.

The view from Mount Tam's East Peak

With the front of the inn at your back, look for a trailhead for the Nora Trail, which you follow for 0.5 mile as it heads downhill, passing through redwoods. When you reach the Matt Davis Trail marker, stay left (instead of right over a bridge) to follow it for 1.1 miles. At the Hoo-Koo-E-Koo Trail junction, continue straight on the Matt Davis Trail. At the junction with Hogback Road at 5.7 miles, turn right and pass the fire station to return to your start.

GO FARTHER

If you're hungry, grab a bite at the Mountain Home Inn. Or, if you still have hiking energy, you can hike from the Mountain Home Inn to Muir Woods (see Hike 48).

WEST POINT INN

Built in 1904, and 1781 feet up the southern slope of Mount Tam, the West Point Inn was once a stop on the Mount Tam Railway. The trip to the summit from here was just eight short minutes. Today, a reserve of roughly 600 volunteers runs and maintains the inn. You can stay overnight, but bring your own bedding. If you're just stopping by, pick a Sunday when the inn holds their pancake breakfasts (see the inn's website for dates).

APPENDIX: TRAILS BY TYPE

EASY

1. Fort Funston to the Cliff House
4. Fort Funston Loop
5. Lake Merced
7. Candlestick Point State Recreation Area
8. India Basin to AT&T Park
9. AT&T Park to Pier 39
10. Pier 39 to the Golden Gate Bridge
11. Stow Lake and Strawberry Hill
18. Visitacion Valley Greenway
19. Bayview Park
22. Lobos Creek Valley Trail
23. Presidio Promenade
29. Wine Tasting on Treasure Island
30. Alcatraz Agave Trail
32. Barbary Coast Trail
41. San Bruno Mountain North Loop
42. Eucalyptus Loop Trail

MODERATE

2. Lands End Trail
6. A Stroll with Sutro
12. Land of Lakes
16. Pine Lake to the Panhandle
17. The Philosopher's Way
20. Park Trail
21. Mountain Lake Trail
24. Goldsworthy Gallery Tour
25. Presidio Coastal Trail
26. Presidio Bay Area Ridge Trail

27. Presidio Anza Trail

28. Angel Island

31. Old Mission Road

33. Bay to Breakers

35. The 500 Club

39. Peaks of Potrero

43. Summit Loop Trail

48. Muir Woods from Mountain Home Inn

CHALLENGING

3. Batteries to Bluffs

13. Interior Greenbelt and Mount Sutro

14. Creeks to Peaks

15. Mount Davidson and Edgehill Mountain

34. Castro to Twin Peaks Loop

36. Stairways to Heaven

37. Walk on the Wild Side

38. Beauty of Bernal

40. Sunset Stairway Stroll

44. Sign Hill

45. Slacker Hill

46. Hill 88

47. From Pirates to Zen

49. Matt Davis and Steep Ravine Loop

50. Mount Tam East Peak

UP TO 1 MILE

18. Visitacion Valley Greenway

22. Lobos Creek Valley Trail

30. Alcatraz Agave Trail

42. Eucalyptus Loop Trail

1 TO 3 MILES

3. Batteries to Bluffs

4. Fort Funston Loop

6. A Stroll with Sutro

7. Candlestick Point State Recreation Area

9. AT&T Park to Pier 39

11. Stow Lake and Strawberry Hill

13. Interior Greenbelt and Mount Sutro
17. The Philosopher's Way
19. Bayview Park
38. Beauty of Bernal
39. Peaks of Potrero
40. Sunset Stairway Stroll
41. San Bruno Mountain North Loop
44. Sign Hill

3-PLUS TO 6 MILES

1. Fort Funston to the Cliff House
2. Lands End Trail
5. Lake Merced
8. India Basin to AT&T Park
10. Pier 39 to the Golden Gate Bridge
12. Land of Lakes
14. Creeks to Peaks
15. Mount Davidson and Edgehill Mountain
16. Pine Lake to the Panhandle
20. Park Trail
21. Mountain Lake Trail
23. Presidio Promenade
24. Goldsworthy Gallery Tour
25. Presidio Coastal Trail
26. Presidio Bay Area Ridge Trail
27. Presidio Anza Trail
28. Angel Island
29. Wine Tasting on Treasure Island
31. Old Mission Road
32. Barbary Coast Trail
34. Castro to Twin Peaks Loop
35. The 500 Club
36. Stairways to Heaven
37. Walk on the Wild Side
43. Summit Loop Trail
45. Slacker Hill
46. Hill 88
48. Muir Woods from Mountain Home Inn

MORE THAN 6 MILES

33. Bay to Breakers
47. From Pirates to Zen
49. Matt Davis and Steep Ravine Loop
50. Mount Tam East Peak

WITH LOTS OF ELEVATION GAINS (700-PLUS FEET)

14. Creeks to Peaks
15. Mount Davidson and Edgehill Mountain
16. Pine Lake to the Panhandle
28. Angel Island
34. Castro to Twin Peaks Loop
35. The 500 Club
36. Stairways to Heaven
37. Walk on the Wild Side
38. Beauty of Bernal
40. Sunset Stairway Stroll
43. Summit Loop Trail
45. Slacker Hill
46. Hill 88
47. From Pirates to Zen
48. Muir Woods from Mountain Home Inn
49. Matt Davis and Steep Ravine Loop
50. Mount Tam East Peak

WITH FOREST SECTIONS

13. Interior Greenbelt and Mount Sutro
15. Mount Davidson and Edgehill Mountain
(Mount Davidson only)
17. The Philosopher's Way
26. Presidio Bay Area Ridge Trail
48. Muir Woods from Mountain Home Inn
49. Matt Davis and Steep Ravine Loop

GOOD FOR OCEAN VIEWS

1. Fort Funston to the Cliff House
2. Lands End Trail
3. Batteries to Bluffs
4. Fort Funston Loop

5. Lake Merced
6. A Stroll with Sutro
20. Park Trail (end of hike only)
21. Mountain Lake Trail (end of hike only)
23. Presidio Promenade (end of hike only)
25. Presidio Coastal Trail
26. Presidio Bay Area Ridge Trail (end of hike only)
27. Presidio Anza Trail (end of hike only)
40. Sunset Stairway Stroll (Grand View Park only)
43. Summit Loop Trail
45. Slacker Hill (end of hike only)
46. Hill 88
47. From Pirates to Zen

GOOD FOR BAY VIEWS

7. Candlestick Point State Recreation Area
8. India Basin to AT&T Park
9. AT&T Park to Pier 39
10. Pier 39 to the Golden Gate Bridge
19. Bayview Park
28. Angel Island
29. Wine Tasting on Treasure Island
30. Alcatraz Agave Trail

GOOD FOR GOLDEN GATE BRIDGE VIEWS

2. Lands End Trail
3. Batteries to Bluffs
10. Pier 39 to the Golden Gate Bridge
    (end of hike only)
20. Park Trail (end of hike only)
23. Presidio Promenade (second half of hike only)
25. Presidio Coastal Trail
27. Presidio Anza Trail (end of hike only)
28. Angel Island
29. Wine Tasting on Treasure Island
30. Alcatraz Agave Trail
45. Slacker Hill (end of hike only)
46. Hill 88

APPENDIX: LAND MANAGERS

Alcatraz Island: Golden Gate National Recreation Area, Fort Mason, B201, San Francisco, CA 94123, (415) 561-4900, www.nps.gov/alca/index.htm

Bay Area Ridge Trail: 1007 General Kennedy Avenue, #3, San Francisco, CA 94129, (415) 561-2595, www.ridgetrail.org, info@ridgetrail.org

California Coastal Trail: Coastwalk California, 555 S. Main Street, Suite 1, Sebastopol, CA 95472, (707) 829-6689, info@coastwalk.org

California Department of Parks and Recreation: P.O. Box 942896, Sacramento, CA 94296, (800) 777-0369, www.parks.ca.gov, info@parks.ca.gov

Golden Gate National Recreation Area: National Park Service, Building 201, Fort Mason, San Francisco, CA 94123, (415) 561-4700, www.nps.gov/goga/index.htm

Juan Bautista de Anza National Historic Trail: National Park Service, 333 Bush Street, Suite 500, San Francisco, CA 94104, (415) 623-2344, www.nps.gov/juba

Marin Municipal Water District: 220 Nellen Avenue, Corte Madera, CA 94925, (415) 945-1455, www.marinwater.org

Muir Woods National Monument: National Park Service, 1 Muir Woods Road, Mill Valley, CA 94941, (415) 388-2595, www.nps.gov/muwo/contacts.htm

Port of San Francisco: Pier 1, The Embarcadero, San Francisco, CA 94111, (415) 274-0400, www.sfport.org, webmaster@sfport.com

Presidio Trust: 103 Montgomery Street, P.O. Box 29052, San Francisco, CA 94129, (415) 561-5300, www.presidio.gov/, presidio@presidiotrust.gov

San Francisco Bay Trail: Association of Bay Area Governments, 375 Beale Street, Suite 700, San Francisco, CA 94105, (415) 820-7900, http://baytrail.org

San Francisco Museum and Historical Society: P.O. Box 420470, San Francisco, CA 94142, (415) 537-1105, www.sfhistory.org, info@sfhistory.org

San Francisco Recreation and Park Department: McLaren Lodge-Golden Gate Park, 501 Stanyan Street, San Francisco, CA 94117, (415) 831-2700, http://sfrecpark.org/, rpdinfo@sfgov.org

San Mateo County Parks Department: 455 County Center, 4th Floor, Redwood City, CA 94063, (650) 363-4020, parks.smcgov.org/, ParksandRecreation@smcgov.org

South San Francisco Parks and Recreation Department: 33 Arroyo Drive, South San Francisco, CA 94080, (650) 829-3800, web-rec@ssf.net, www.ssf.net/377/Parks-Recreation

Starr King Open Space: http://starrkingopenspace.org, starrkingboard@gmail.com

Treasure Island Development Authority: One Avenue of Palms, Suite 241, San Francisco, CA 94130, (415) 274-0660, http://sftreasureisland.org/

University of California San Francisco Public and Community Relations: 3333 California Street, Suite 103, San Francisco, CA 94143, (415) 476-6296

Visitacion Valley Greenway Project: 186 Arleta Avenue, San Francisco, CA 94134, (415) 468-0639, http://visvalleygreenway.org, info@visvalleygreenway.org

Zappos.com Bay to Breakers: (415) 231-3130, www.zapposbaytobreakers.com

INDEX

Adams, Ansel 128, 129
Agave Trail 159, 170–173
Agua Vista Park 58
Alcatraz 170–173
Alfred E. "Nobby" Clarke
    Mansion 194
Alta California 152
Angel Island 160–165
AT&T Park 61

Baker Beach 126–27, 142, 144
Barbary Coast Trail 181–87
Batteries to Bluffs 33–37, 145
Battery Boutelle 36, 115
Battery Chamberlin 144
Battery Cranston 146
Battery Crosby 35–36
Battery Davis 39, 256
Battery Davis Trail 39–40
Battery East Trail 68, 122, 136
Battery Godfrey 36, 145
Battery Marcus Miller 36, 145–46
Battery Townsley 254, 256
Bay Area Ridge Trail 44, 71, 97, 140,
    147–51
Bay Front Park 58
Bay to Breakers 175, 188–92
Bayview Park 71, 112–15
Bog Trail 232–34
Broderick-Terry Duel Landmark
    Park 43–44
Buena Vista Park 101–02, 199, 202
Burning Man arts festival 126–27,
    144

California Coastal Trail 23,142–47,
    251–52, 255–56, 258–59

Candlestick Point State Recreation
    Area 50–54
Canopy View Trail 263–64, 266
cavalry stables 118, 120, 135
Chain of Lakes 77–78
China Basin Park 56, 59
Chinese Pavilion 74
Cliff House, The 26, 28–29, 46, 50
coastal gun batteries 36
Coit Tower 187, 205, 207
Coit, Lillian Hitchcock 207, 209
Corona Heights Park 199, 202
Creeks to Peaks 71, 86–91
Crissy Field 64, 68, 118, 121–22, 136
Crissy Field Overlook 132, 135–36
Crocker, Charles 28, 115, 231

de Anza, Juan Bautista 124, 152, 157
disc golf course 80–81

Earth Wall 138–40
Ecology Trail 140
Edgehill Mountain 95–96, 99
El Camino Del Mar Trail 32
Elk Glen Lake 78
El Polín Spring 141
Esmeralda Slides 219
Eucalyptus Loop Trail (San Bruno
    Mountain) 236–39
Eucalyptus Loop Trail
    (Sign Hill) 246

Fern Creek Trail 264, 273
Filbert Street Steps 204–05
Font, Father Pedro 154, 157
Fort Baker 252–53
Fort Funston 24, 26–27, 37–40, 256

Fort Mason 66
Fort Point 36, 68, 69, 122, 157
Funston Beach Trail 26, 39

Glen Canyon Park 19, 71, 87–90, 211
Golden Gate Bridge 34, 36–38, 64,
    68–69, 74, 85, 118, 122, 132, 136,
    140, 142, 144, 145–46, 148, 151,
    156, 163, 169, 171, 196, 201, 227,
    250–53, 255
Golden Gate Park 15, 28, 71, 72–73,
    76–78, 103, 190, 227
Golden Gate Heights Park 229
Grand View Park 227–28
Golden Gate National Recreation
    Area 64, 66, 68
Goldsworthy, Andy 117, 123, 136–39,
    148, 180
Great Highway Seawall and
    Promenade 27
Green Gulch Farm Zen Center,
    The 258, 261
Green Gulch Trail 262
Greenwich Street Steps 204, 210

Hayes Street Hill 189–190
Hearst, George 115
Hearst, William Randolph 113, 115
Heron's Head Park 56–57
Hidden Garden Steps 227
Hill 88 254–57
Hogback Trail 272, 274
Horse Trail 39–40
Huntington Falls 72–74

Immigrant Point Connector
    Trail 157
Immigrant Point Overlook 154–55
Ina Coolbrith Park 209
India Basin Shoreline Park 54, 56
Interior Greenbelt 71, 82–86
Iris Hill Trail 246–47

Jack Early Park 187, 206

John Muir Sand Ladder 40
John McLaren Park 71, 103
Juan Bautista de Anza Trail 152–57
Julius Kahn Playground 124, 141

Kaasi Road 260
Kent Tree and Memorial 265–66
Kent, William and Elizabeth
    Thacher 266
Kite Hill Open Space 195

Lagoon Trail 257
Lake Merced 40–45
Lands End labyrinth 31, 32
Lands End Trail 29–33, 47–48
Letterman District 134
Letters Trail 246
Lincoln Park Steps 32
Lloyd Lake 81, 190
Lobos Creek Valley Trail 128–31
Lobos Valley Overlook 131, 155
Lombard Street (crooked section)
    208–09, 222
Lost Trail 264, 266
Lovers' Lane 123, 138

Mallard Lake 78
Marin Headlands 249
Marine Cemetery Vista 126
Marshall's Beach 36
Matt Davis Trail 267–69
McLaren, John 71, 73, 103
Metson Lake 79
Middle Green Gulch Trail 260–61
Middle Lake 80
Misión San Francisco de Asís
    (Mission Dolores) 138, 176, 178
Miwok people (Coast Miwok) 164,
    249
Miwok Trail 257, 262
Morgan, Julia 113–14, 225
mosaic steps. See 16th Avenue Tiled
    Steps and Hidden Garden Steps
Mountain Home Inn 263, 272

Mountain Lake 123–24, 154
Mountain Lake Trail 122–27
Mount Davidson 71, 91, 93–95
Mount Livermore 161–62
Mount Olympus 97, 101, 199, 200–01
Mount Sutro Open Space Reserve 19, 71, 82–86, 131, 227
Mount Tamalpais (Mount Tam) 249, 255, 257, 267, 270–74
Mount Tamalpais and Muir Woods Scenic Railway 271, 273
Muir Beach 258–60, 262
Muir, John 73, 266

Nobby" Clarke Mansion, Nobby's Folly. See Alfred E. "Nobby" Clarke
North Lake 80

Ocean View Trail. See Canopy View Trail
Old Guadalupe Trail 232–34
Old Mission Road 138, 175–81
Old Railroad Grade 271–73
O'Shaughnessy Seawall 28–29

Pacific Overlook 145, 150, 154, 156
Panoramic Trail 263, 264, 266
Park Archives and Records Center 118, 121, 135
Park Trail 118–22, 155
Pelican Inn, The 258, 260–61
Philosopher's Way 71, 102–07
Pier 39 61, 63, 66, 187
Pine Lake 71, 97-8
Pink Triangle Park 199
Pirates Cove 260
Plank Walk Trail 273
Playland at the Beach 28, 49
Portsmouth Square 182, 184
Powder Magazine 139
Presidio, The 118–57
Presidio Golf Club 120, 124

Presidio Landmark Apartments 126, 129
Presidio Officers' Club 135, 138–39, 177
Presidio Pet Cemetery 118, 121–22
Presidio Promenade 121, 131–36
Public Health Service District 118, 119, 155

redwood trees 263–66, 269, 274
Rob Hill Campground 148, 150–51, 155
Rodeo Beach 254–55

Saddle Loop Trail 232–35, 238
San Bruno Mountain State and County Park 231–42
San Francisco Maritime National Historical Park 64, 66, 183, 187
Saints Peter and Paul Church 187, 207, 209–10
Sand Ladder (Baker Beach) 35, 38, 145
Sand Ladder (John Muir). See John Muir Sand Ladder
San Francisco Bay Trail 23, 51, 56, 48, 61, 64, 67, 122, 136
San Francisco National Cemetery 118, 120, 132, 135, 140, 148
San Francisco National Cemetery Overlook 120, 140, 147–48
Seubert, Alphonse 247
Seubert Trail 246–47
Seward Street Slides 193–95
Sign Hill 231, 243–47
16th Avenue Tiled Steps 227, 228
Slacker Hill 250–53
South Lake (Golden Gate Park) 78–80
South Lake (Lake Merced) 43
Spire 138, 140, 148
Spreckels Lake 80, 190
Starr King Open Space 223–24

Steep Ravine Trail 269–70
Strauss, Levi 205
Strawberry Hill 72–74
Stow Lake 72–75, 81
Summit Loop Trail 238–42
Sunset Trail (Angel Island) 161–63
Sunset Trail (Fort Funston) 38–40
Sutro, Adolph 19, 28, 30, 46, 48, 49,
    82, 85, 90, 95–96, 201
Sutro Baths 46–48
Sutro Dunes 46, 49
Sutro Heights Park 46, 48
Sutro Tower 38, 74, 94, 105, 113, 131,
    193, 196, 227, 235, 242, 255, 262

Tales of the City (book) 204, 209
Tank Hill 97, 100, 197
Transamerica Pyramid 186
Treasure Island 165–69
Tree Fall 138, 139

Trestle Trail 263, 266
Twin Peaks 71, 87–88, 91, 100, 193,
    196

US Marine Hospital 126, 129, 155

Vermont Street 209, 222
Verna Dunshee Trail 273
Visitacion Valley Greenway 71,
    107–11

Warm Water Cove Park 58
Washington Square Park 182, 187,
    207, 209
Wave Organ 67
West Point Inn 273–74
Wolf Ridge Trail 257
Wood Line 123, 138, 180
Works Progress Administration
    (WPA) 49, 113–14

ABOUT THE AUTHOR

ALEXANDRA KENIN GREW UP IN Wyckoff, New Jersey, and is proud to be a Jersey girl. She studied French and business at Georgetown University and then spent a few years working and playing in New York City. While living in New York, she took a fateful vacation to San Francisco, which influenced her to move to the City by the Bay. But before making it out west, she had some more work to do. She earned an MBA from the Wharton School and an MA from the Lauder Institute—both at the University of Pennsylvania.

After graduation, she moved to San Francisco and worked as a product marketing manager at Google for nearly five years. After leaving Google, she began exploring the city, eventually coming up with the idea for her urban hiking tour company, Urban Hiker SF. Urban Hiker SF was founded in 2012 and explores the stairways, hills, and hiking trails of the city.

Alexandra is passionate about travel and tries to visit a new country every year (she's up to forty-six so far). When she's not traveling or out on the trails, she lives with her partner, Brett, in San Francisco.

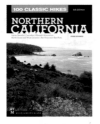